THE Eminence IN Shadow

4

Art **Anri Sakano**
Original Story **Daisuke Aizawa**
Character Design **Touzai**

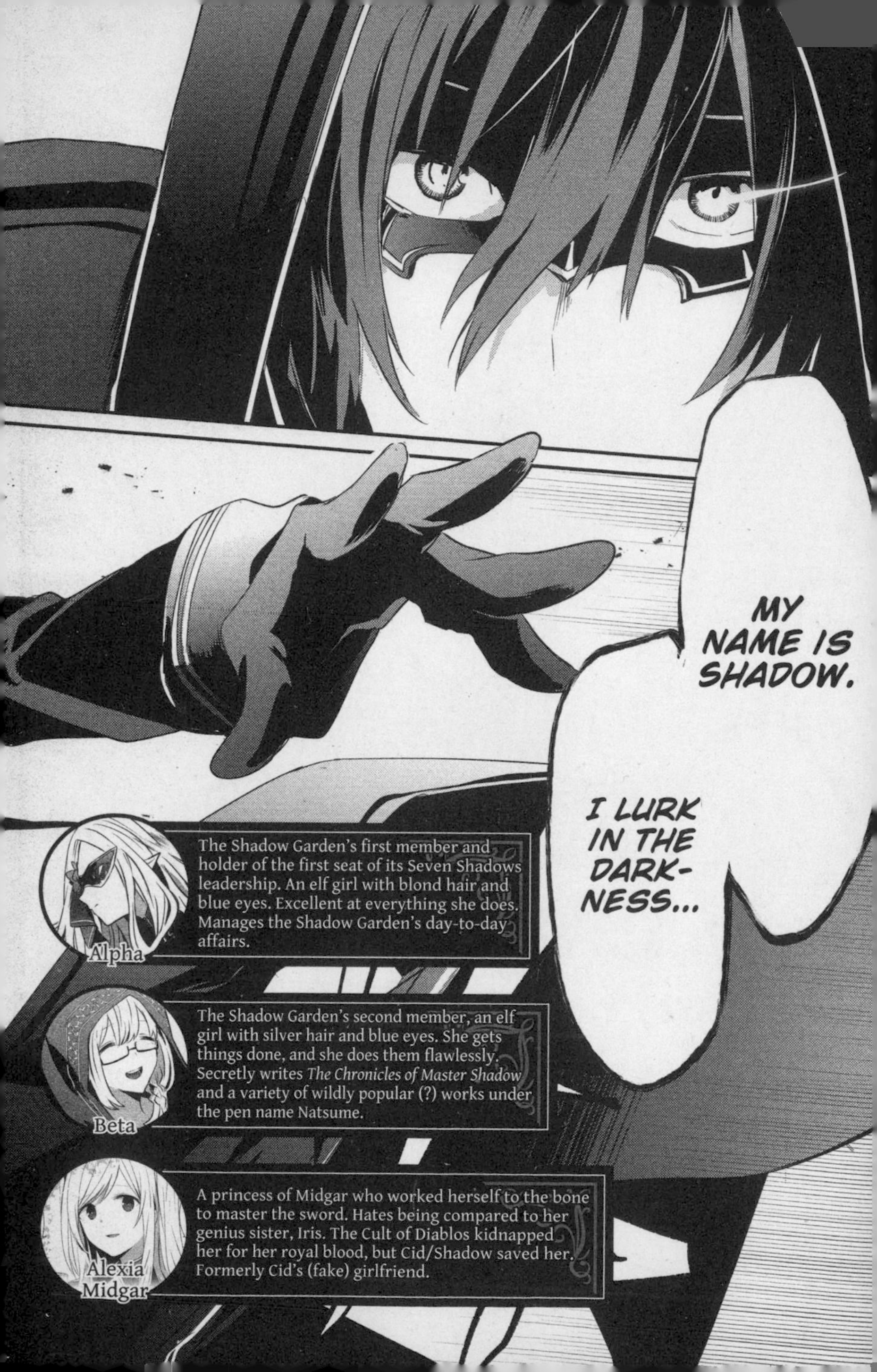
MY NAME IS SHADOW.
I LURK IN THE DARK-NESS...
The Shadow Garden's first member and holder of the first seat of its Seven Shadows leadership. An elf girl with blond hair and blue eyes. Excellent at everything she does. Manages the Shadow Garden's day-to-day affairs.
Alpha
The Shadow Garden's second member, an elf girl with silver hair and blue eyes. She gets things done, and she does them flawlessly. Secretly writes *The Chronicles of Master Shadow* and a variety of wildly popular (?) works under the pen name Natsume.
Beta
A princess of Midgar who worked herself to the bone to master the sword. Hates being compared to her genius sister, Iris. The Cult of Diablos kidnapped her for her royal blood, but Cid/Shadow saved her. Formerly Cid's (fake) girlfriend.
Alexia Midgar

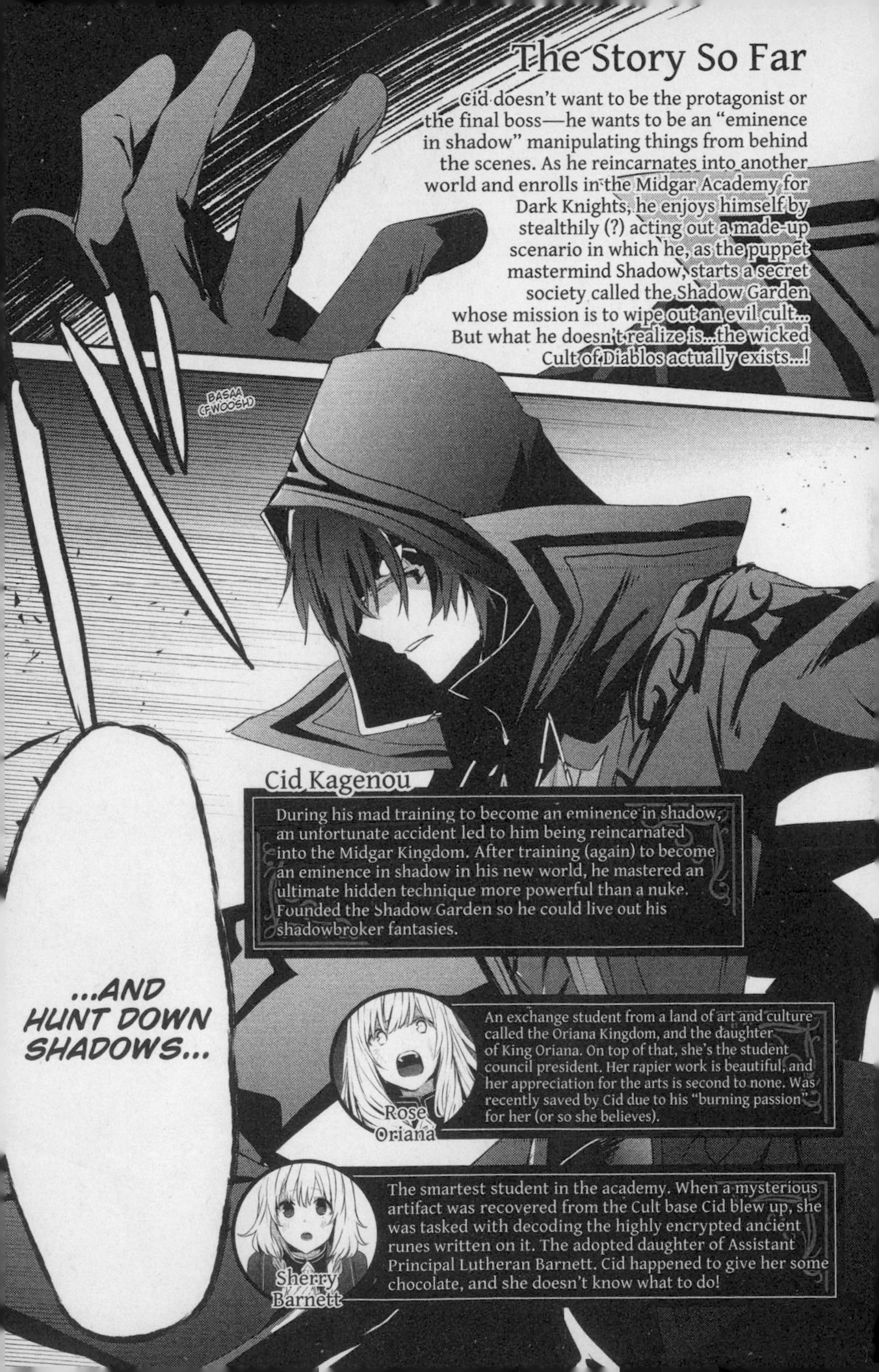
BASAA (FWOOSH)
...AND HUNT DOWN SHADOWS...

The Story So Far

Cid doesn't want to be the protagonist or the final boss—he wants to be an "eminence in shadow" manipulating things from behind the scenes. As he reincarnates into another world and enrolls in the Midgar Academy for Dark Knights, he enjoys himself by stealthily (?) acting out a made-up scenario in which he, as the puppet mastermind Shadow, starts a secret society called the Shadow Garden whose mission is to wipe out an evil cult... But what he doesn't realize is...the wicked Cult of Diablos actually exists...!

Cid Kagenou

During his mad training to become an eminence in shadow, an unfortunate accident led to him being reincarnated into the Midgar Kingdom. After training (again) to become an eminence in shadow in his new world, he mastered an ultimate hidden technique more powerful than a nuke. Founded the Shadow Garden so he could live out his shadowbroker fantasies.

Rose Oriana

An exchange student from a land of art and culture called the Oriana Kingdom, and the daughter of King Oriana. On top of that, she's the student council president. Her rapier work is beautiful, and her appreciation for the arts is second to none. Was recently saved by Cid due to his "burning passion" for her (or so she believes).

Sherry Barnett

The smartest student in the academy. When a mysterious artifact was recovered from the Cult base Cid blew up, she was tasked with decoding the highly encrypted ancient runes written on it. The adopted daughter of Assistant Principal Lutheran Barnett. Cid happened to give her some chocolate, and she doesn't know what to do!

[CONTENTS]

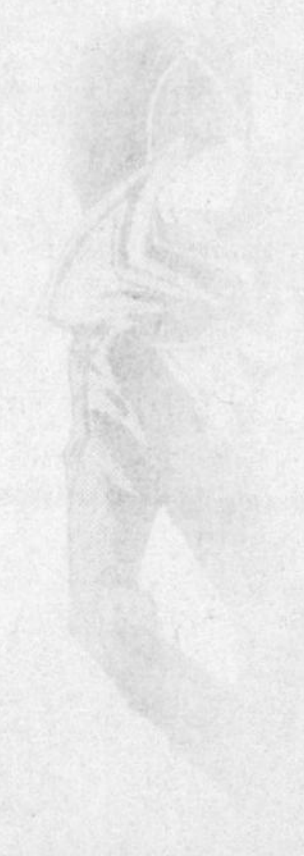

Episode.13

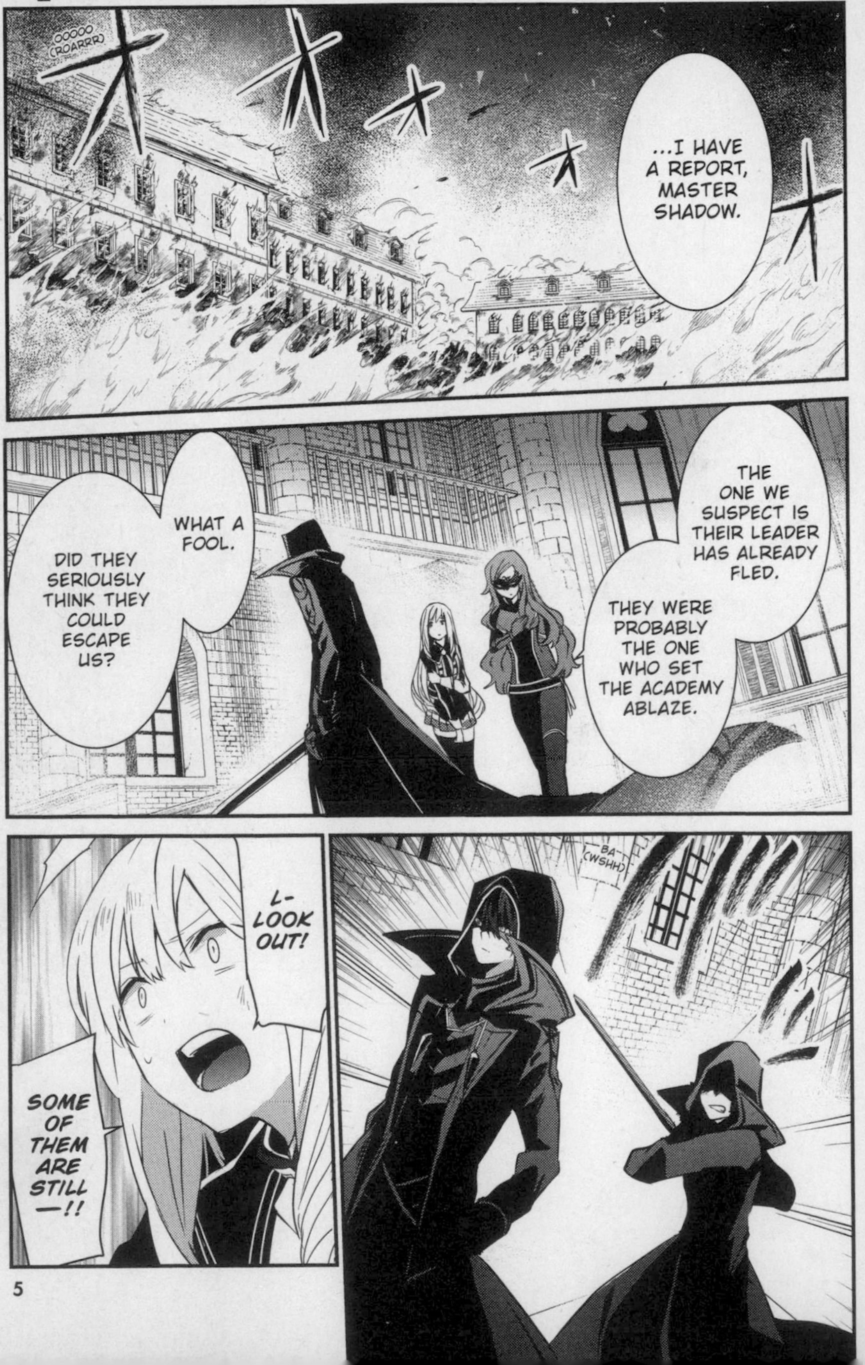
OOOOO (ROARRR)
...I HAVE A REPORT, MASTER SHADOW.
THE ONE WE SUSPECT IS THEIR LEADER HAS ALREADY FLED.
THEY WERE PROBABLY THE ONE WHO SET THE ACADEMY ABLAZE.
WHAT A FOOL.
DID THEY SERIOUSLY THINK THEY COULD ESCAPE US?
BA (WSHH)
L-LOOK OUT!
SOME OF THEM ARE STILL —!!

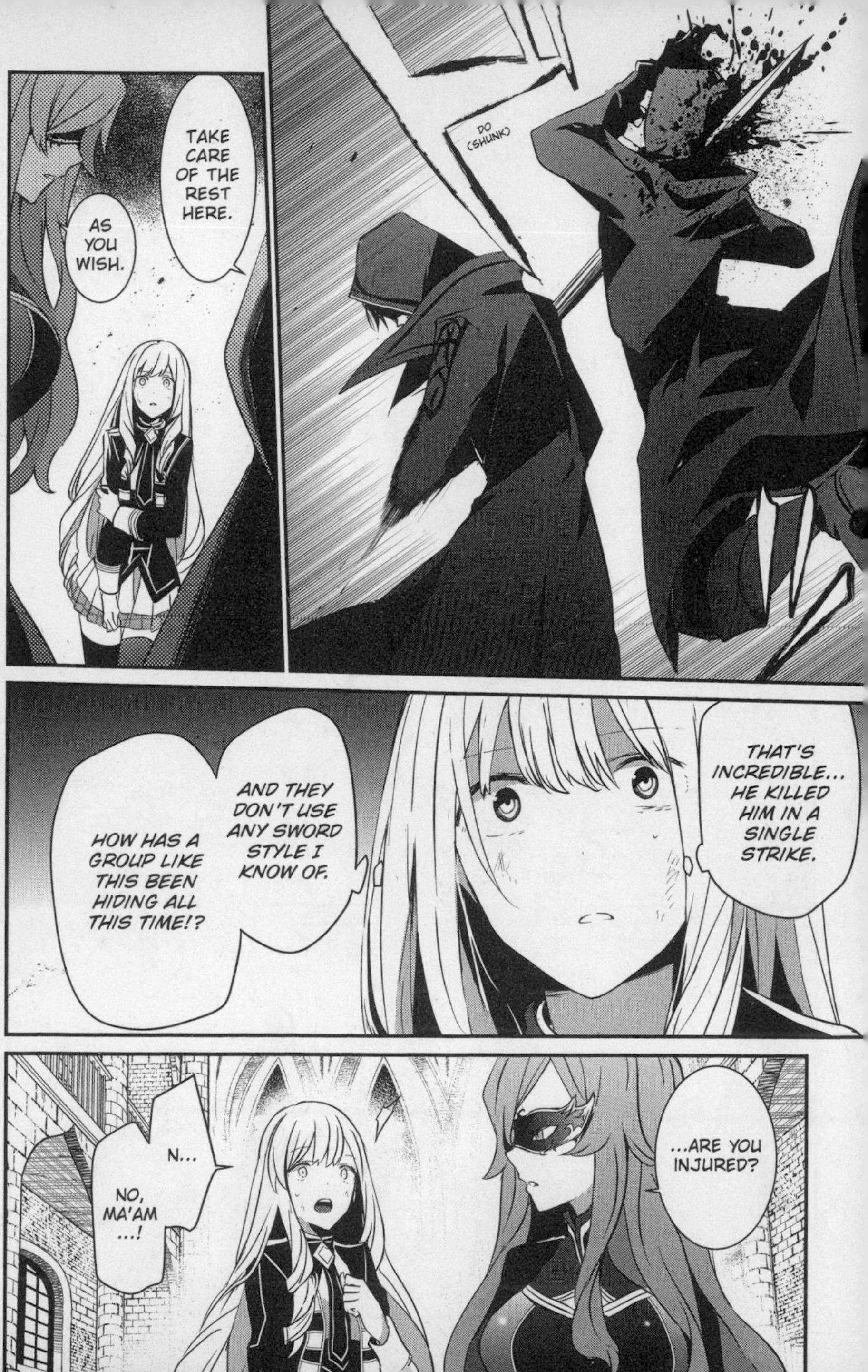
DO (SHUNK)
TAKE CARE OF THE REST HERE.
AS YOU WISH.
THAT'S INCREDIBLE... HE KILLED HIM IN A SINGLE STRIKE.
AND THEY DON'T USE ANY SWORD STYLE I KNOW OF.
HOW HAS A GROUP LIKE THIS BEEN HIDING ALL THIS TIME!?
...ARE YOU INJURED?
N...
NO, MA'AM ...!

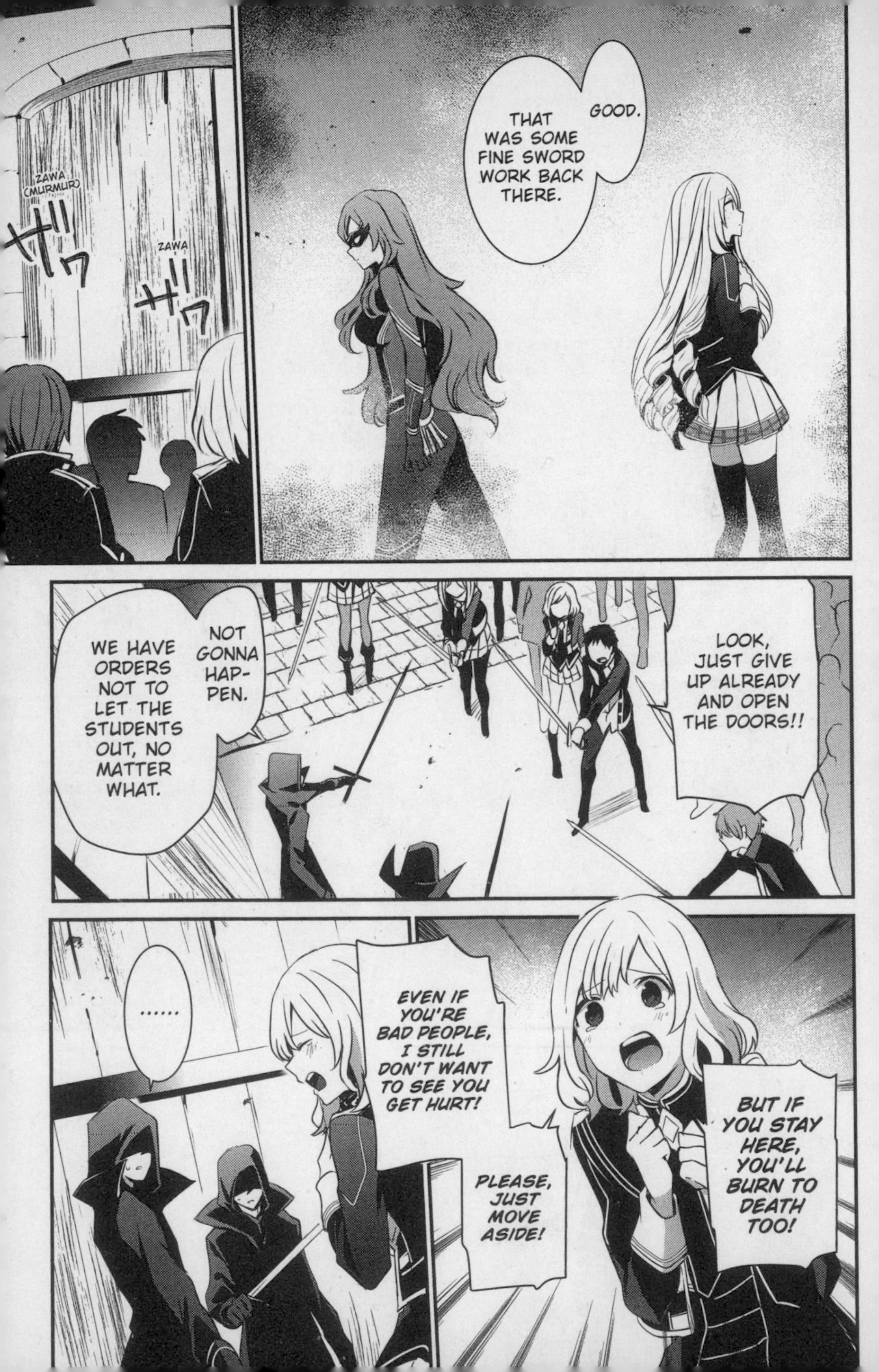
GOOD.
THAT WAS SOME FINE SWORD WORK BACK THERE.
ZAWA (MURMUR)
ザワ
ZAWA
ザワ
LOOK, JUST GIVE UP ALREADY AND OPEN THE DOORS!!
NOT GONNA HAP-PEN.
WE HAVE ORDERS NOT TO LET THE STUDENTS OUT, NO MATTER WHAT.
EVEN IF YOU'RE BAD PEOPLE, I STILL DON'T WANT TO SEE YOU GET HURT!
BUT IF YOU STAY HERE, YOU'LL BURN TO DEATH TOO!
PLEASE, JUST MOVE ASIDE!
......

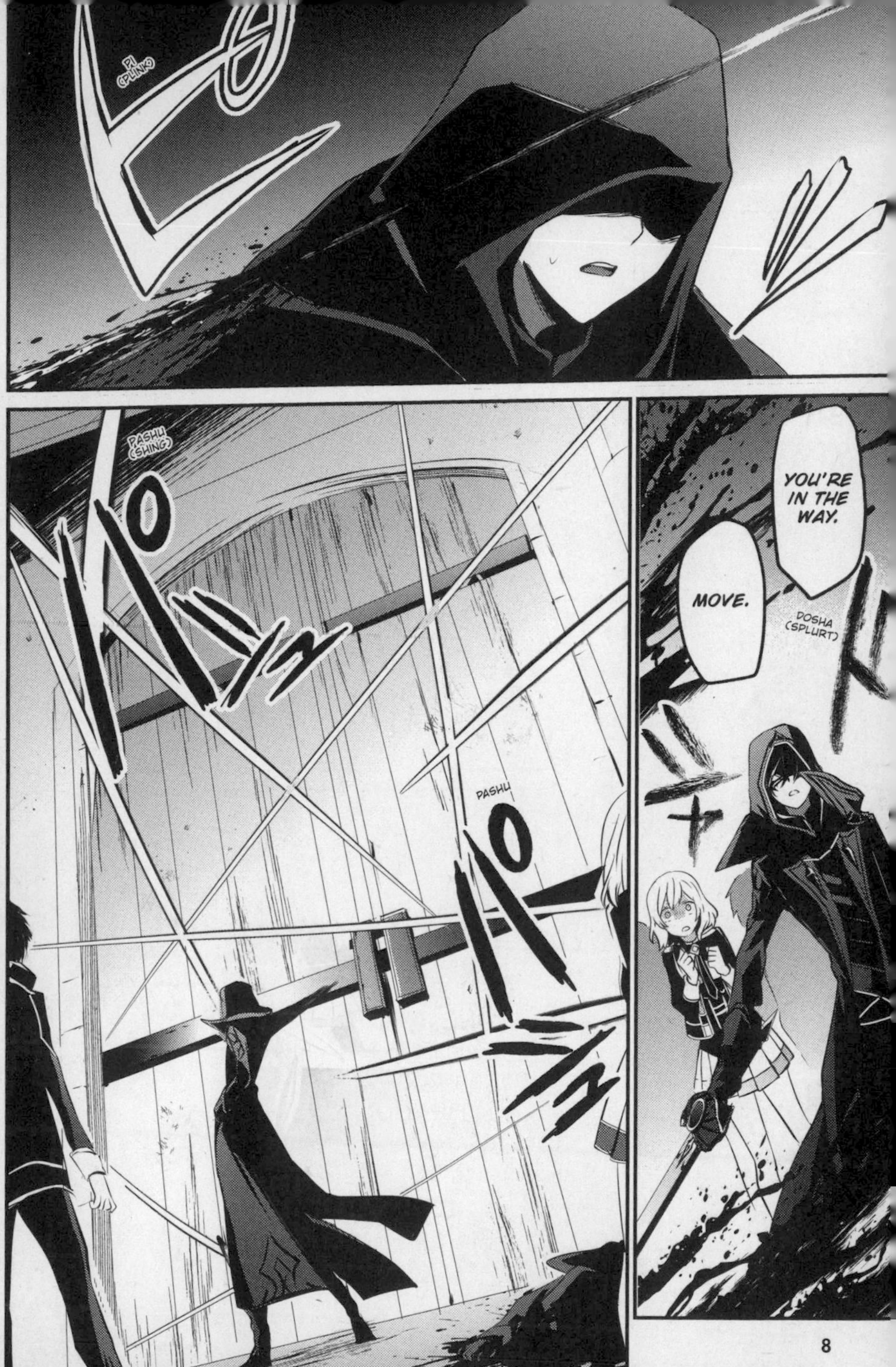
PI (PLINK)
YOU'RE IN THE WAY.
MOVE.
DOSHA (SPLURT)
PASHU (SHING)
PASHU

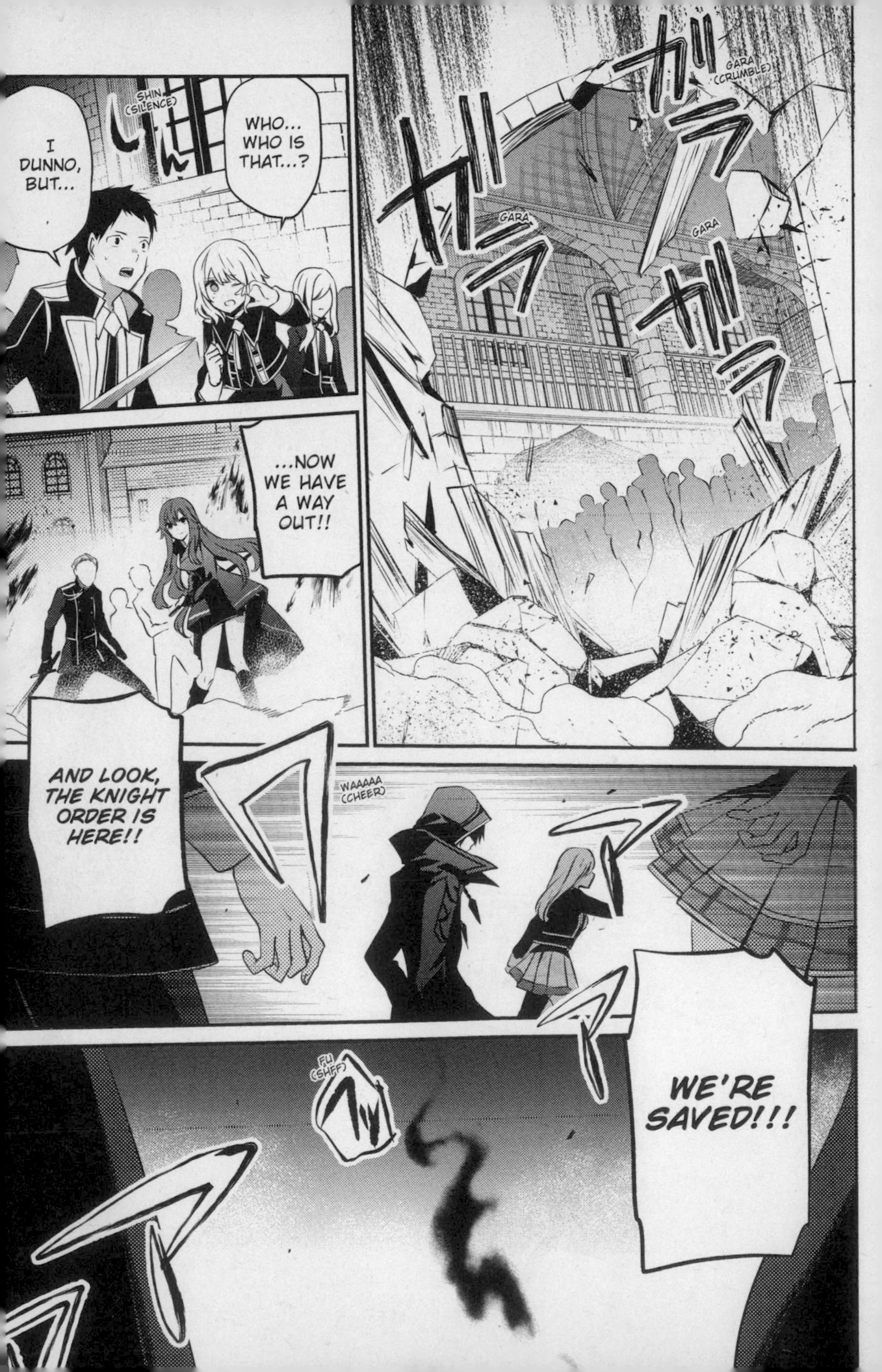
GARA (CRUMBLE)
GARA
GARA
WHO... WHO IS THAT...?
SHIN (SILENCE)
I DUNNO, BUT...
...NOW WE HAVE A WAY OUT!!
WAAAAA (CHEER)
AND LOOK, THE KNIGHT ORDER IS HERE!!
WE'RE SAVED!!!
FU (SHFF)

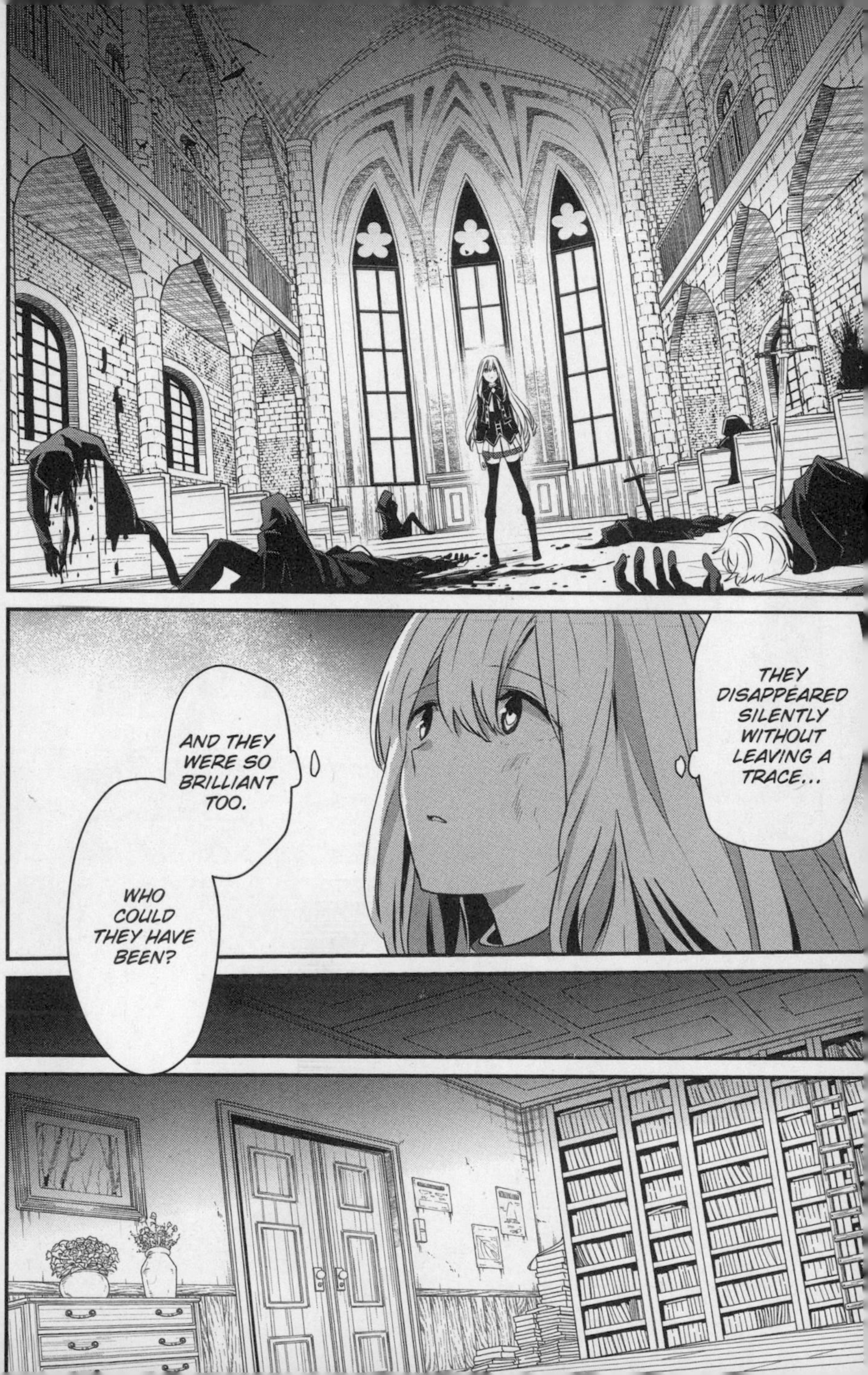
THEY DISAPPEARED SILENTLY WITHOUT LEAVING A TRACE...
AND THEY WERE SO BRILLIANT TOO.
WHO COULD THEY HAVE BEEN?

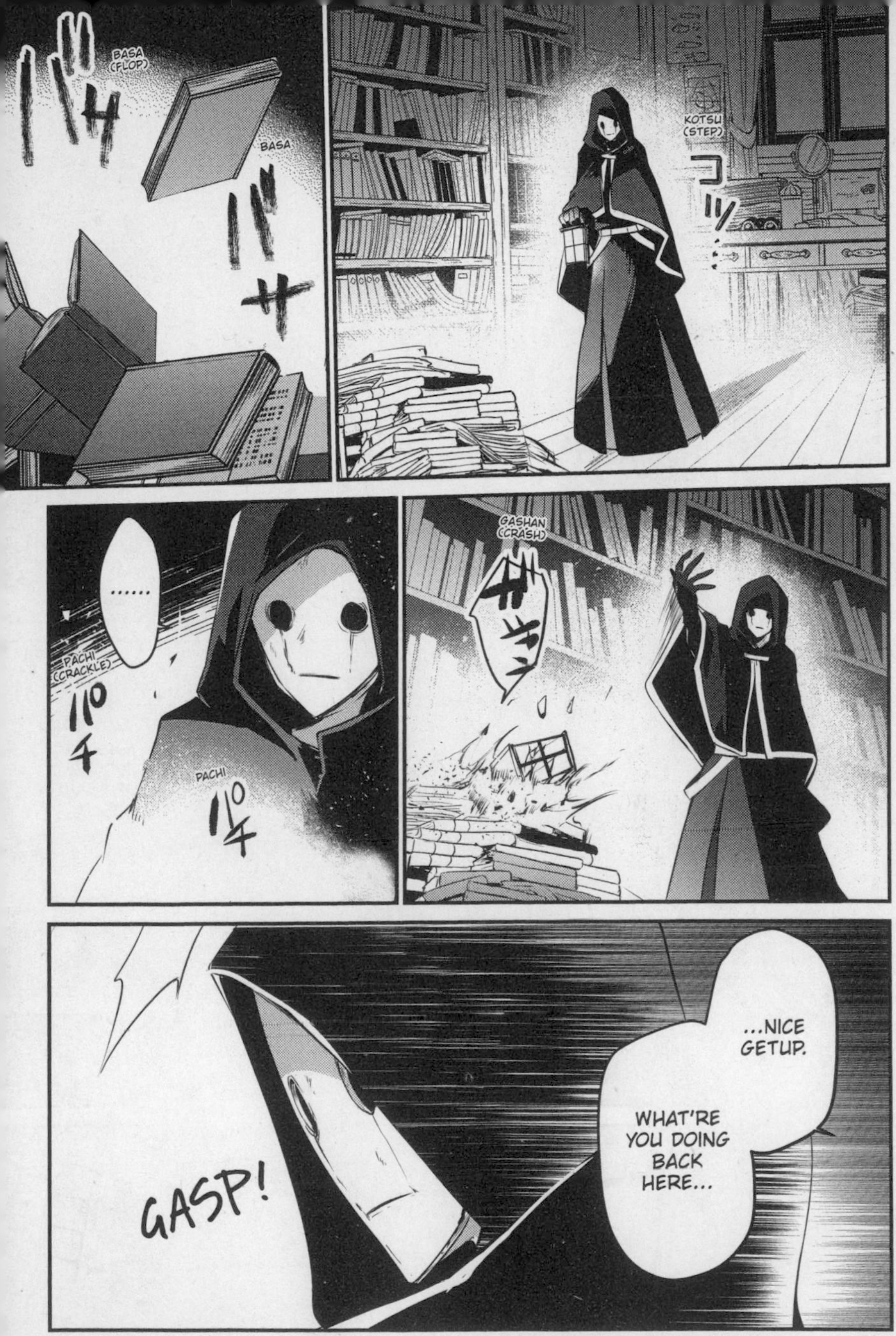
KOTSU (STEP)
BASA (FLOP)
BASA
GASHAN (CRASH)
......
PACHI (CRACKLE)
PACHI
...NICE GETUP.
WHAT'RE YOU DOING BACK HERE...
GASP!

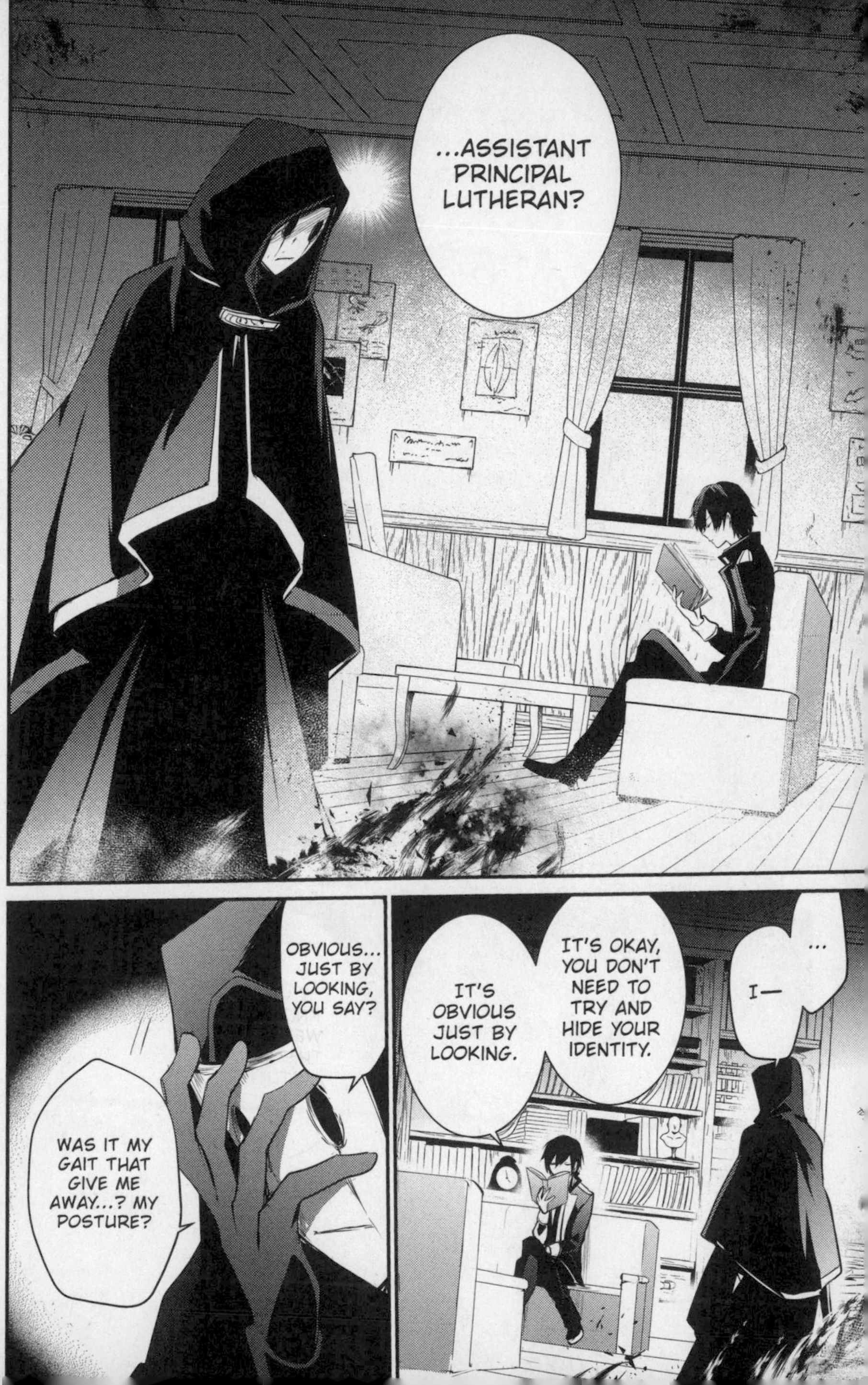
...ASSISTANT PRINCIPAL LUTHERAN?
...
I—
IT'S OKAY, YOU DON'T NEED TO TRY AND HIDE YOUR IDENTITY.
IT'S OBVIOUS JUST BY LOOKING.
OBVIOUS... JUST BY LOOKING, YOU SAY?
WAS IT MY GAIT THAT GIVE ME AWAY...? MY POSTURE?

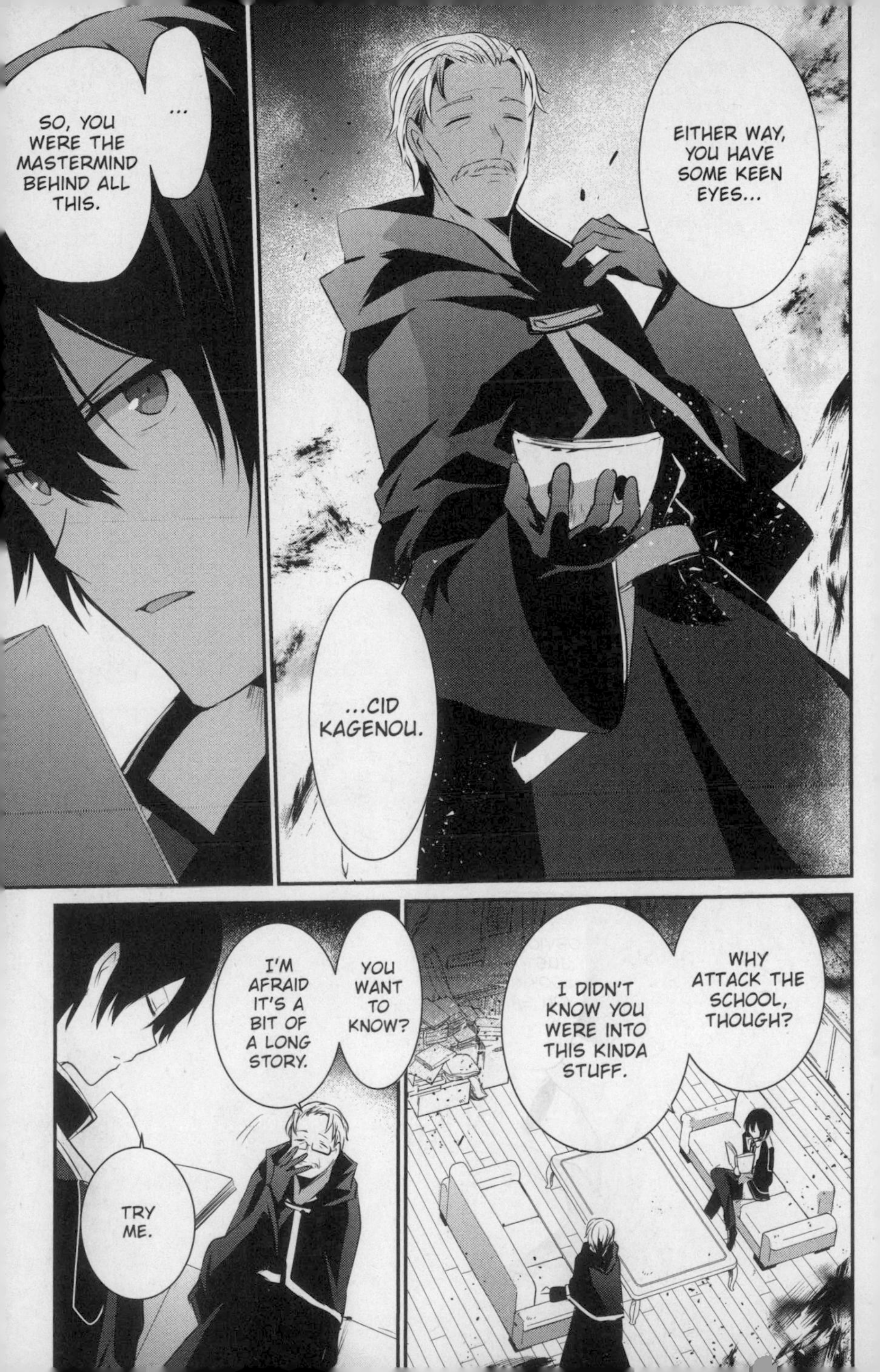
EITHER WAY, YOU HAVE SOME KEEN EYES...
...CID KAGENOU.
...
SO, YOU WERE THE MASTERMIND BEHIND ALL THIS.
WHY ATTACK THE SCHOOL, THOUGH?
I DIDN'T KNOW YOU WERE INTO THIS KINDA STUFF.
YOU WANT TO KNOW?
I'M AFRAID IT'S A BIT OF A LONG STORY.
TRY ME.

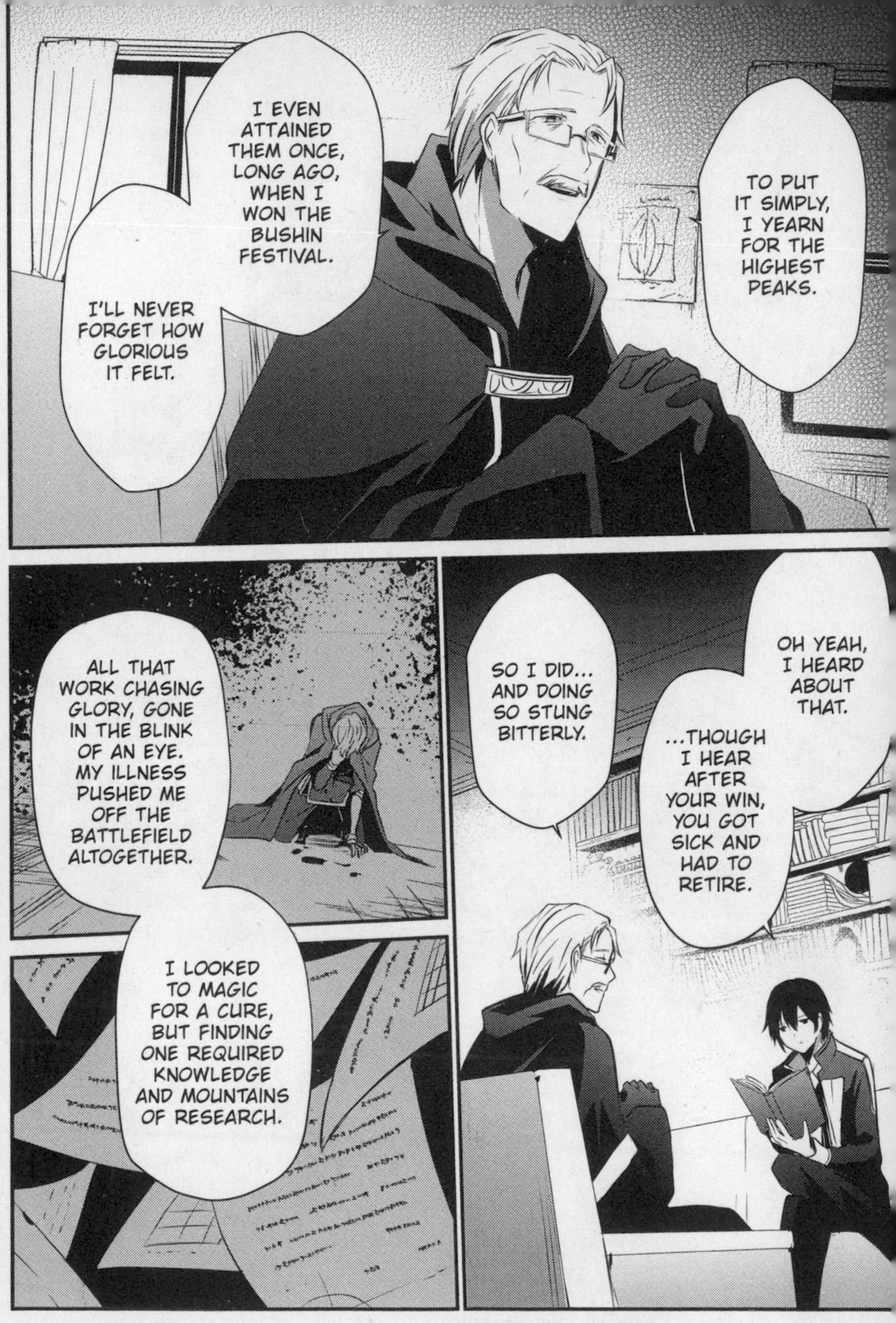
TO PUT IT SIMPLY, I YEARN FOR THE HIGHEST PEAKS.
I EVEN ATTAINED THEM ONCE, LONG AGO, WHEN I WON THE BUSHIN FESTIVAL.
I'LL NEVER FORGET HOW GLORIOUS IT FELT.
OH YEAH, I HEARD ABOUT THAT.
...THOUGH I HEAR AFTER YOUR WIN, YOU GOT SICK AND HAD TO RETIRE.
SO I DID... AND DOING SO STUNG BITTERLY.
ALL THAT WORK CHASING GLORY, GONE IN THE BLINK OF AN EYE. MY ILLNESS PUSHED ME OFF THE BATTLEFIELD ALTOGETHER.
I LOOKED TO MAGIC FOR A CURE, BUT FINDING ONE REQUIRED KNOWLEDGE AND MOUNTAINS OF RESEARCH.

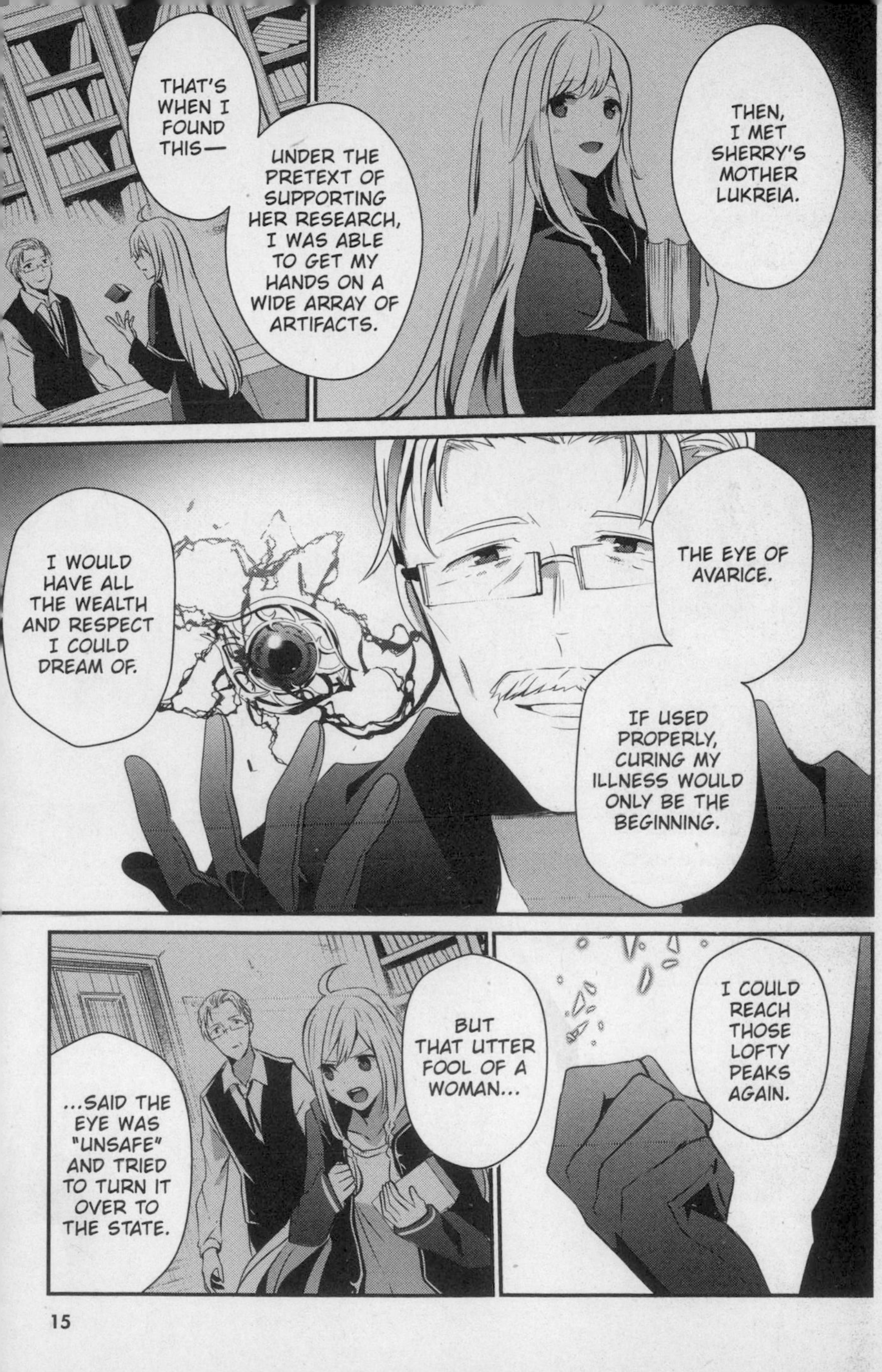
THEN, I MET SHERRY'S MOTHER LUKREIA.
UNDER THE PRETEXT OF SUPPORTING HER RESEARCH, I WAS ABLE TO GET MY HANDS ON A WIDE ARRAY OF ARTIFACTS.
THAT'S WHEN I FOUND THIS—
THE EYE OF AVARICE.
IF USED PROPERLY, CURING MY ILLNESS WOULD ONLY BE THE BEGINNING.
I WOULD HAVE ALL THE WEALTH AND RESPECT I COULD DREAM OF.
I COULD REACH THOSE LOFTY PEAKS AGAIN.
BUT THAT UTTER FOOL OF A WOMAN...
...SAID THE EYE WAS "UNSAFE" AND TRIED TO TURN IT OVER TO THE STATE.

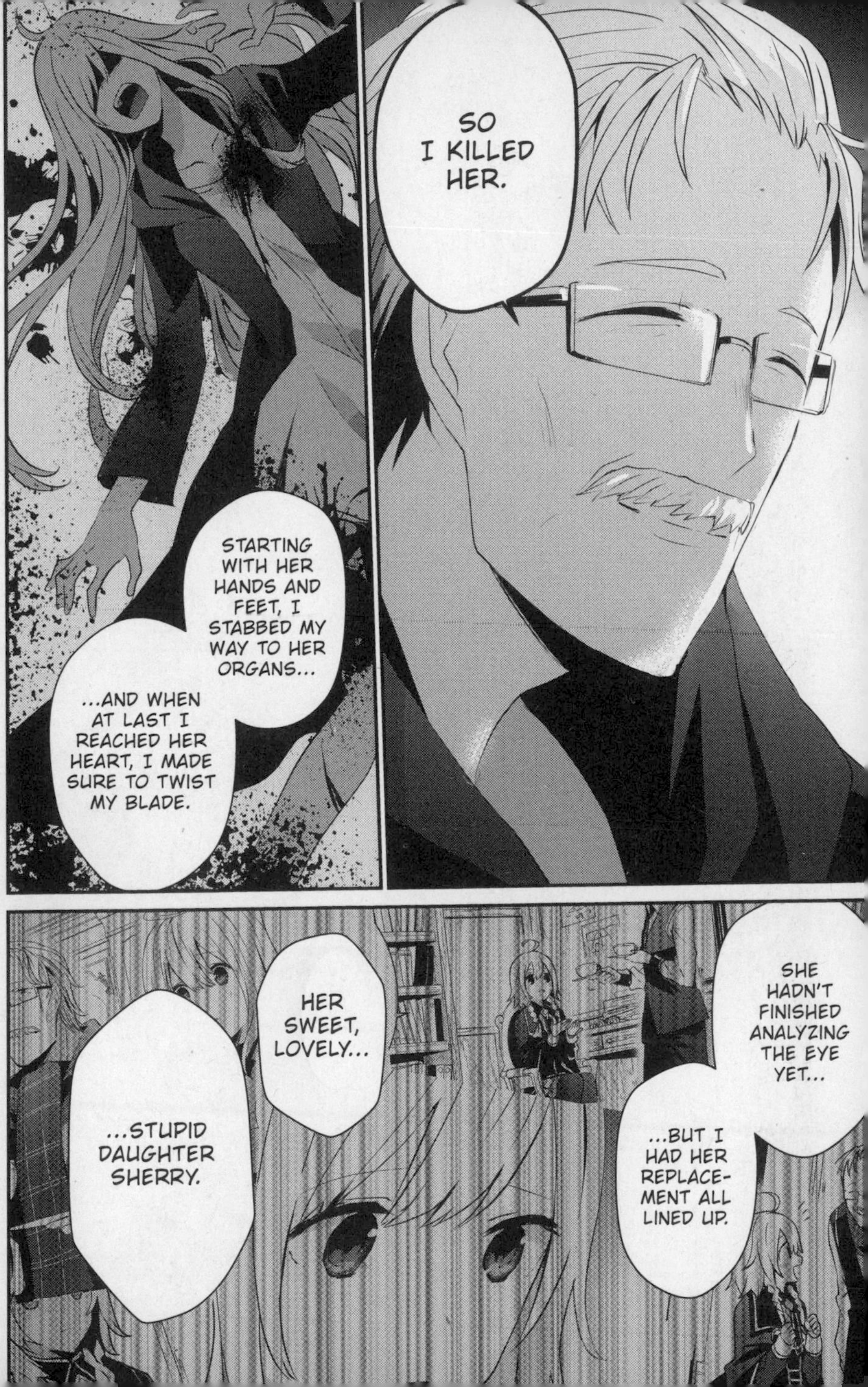
SO I KILLED HER.
STARTING WITH HER HANDS AND FEET, I STABBED MY WAY TO HER ORGANS...
...AND WHEN AT LAST I REACHED HER HEART, I MADE SURE TO TWIST MY BLADE.
SHE HADN'T FINISHED ANALYZING THE EYE YET...
...BUT I HAD HER REPLACE-MENT ALL LINED UP.
HER SWEET, LOVELY...
...STUPID DAUGHTER SHERRY.

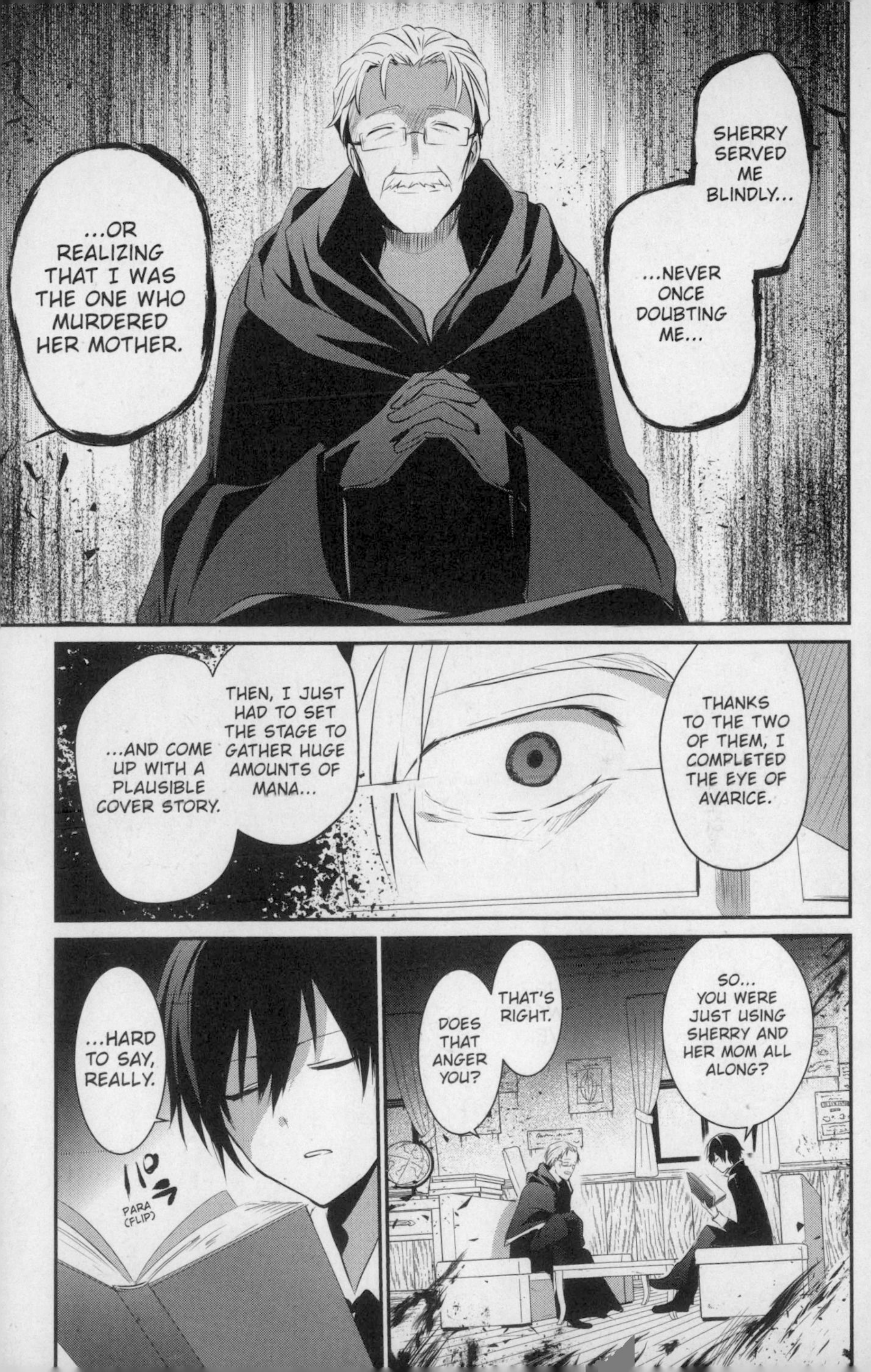
SHERRY SERVED ME BLINDLY...
...NEVER ONCE DOUBTING ME...
...OR REALIZING THAT I WAS THE ONE WHO MURDERED HER MOTHER.
THANKS TO THE TWO OF THEM, I COMPLETED THE EYE OF AVARICE.
THEN, I JUST HAD TO SET THE STAGE TO GATHER HUGE AMOUNTS OF MANA...
...AND COME UP WITH A PLAUSIBLE COVER STORY.
SO... YOU WERE JUST USING SHERRY AND HER MOM ALL ALONG?
THAT'S RIGHT.
DOES THAT ANGER YOU?
...HARD TO SAY, REALLY.
PARA (FLIP)

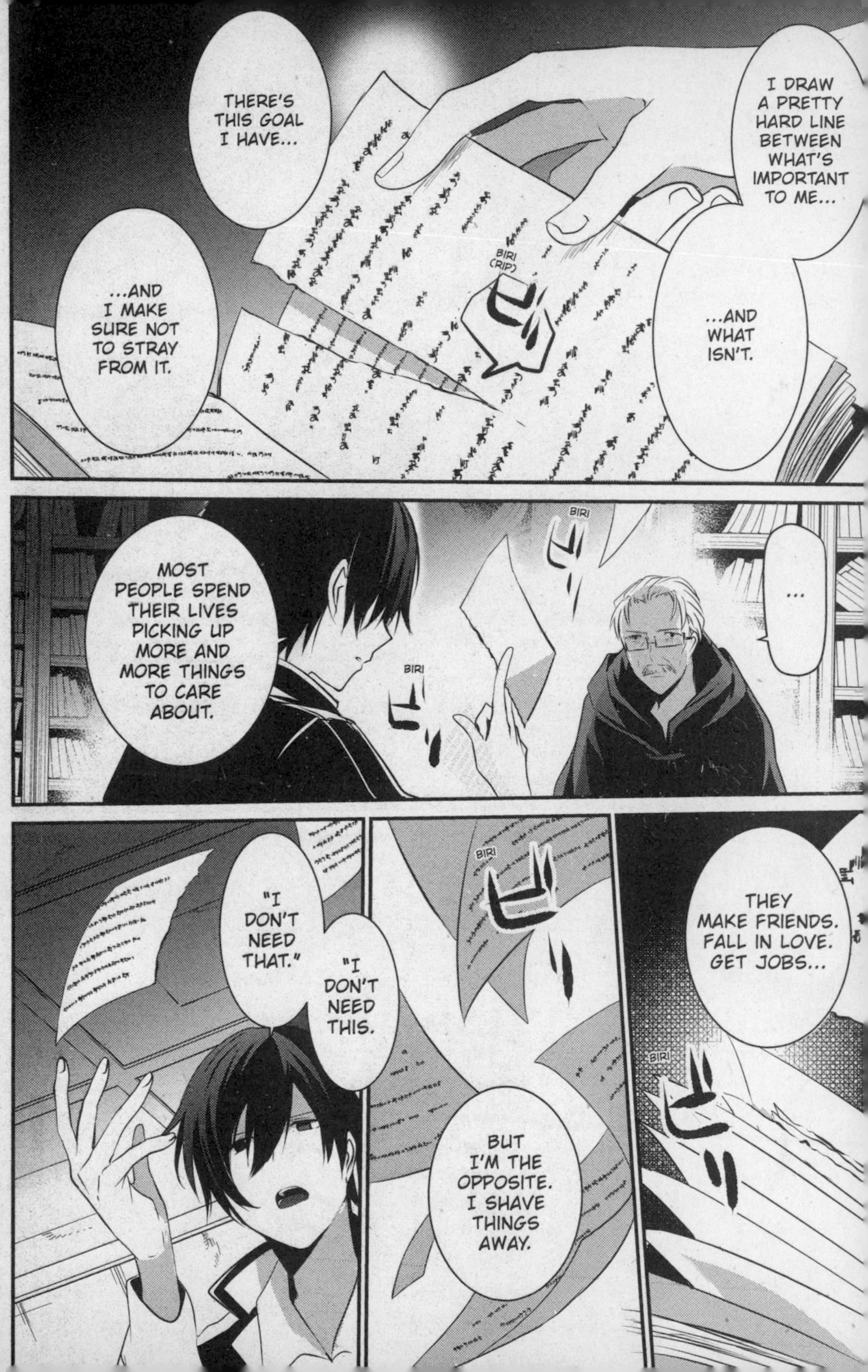
I DRAW A PRETTY HARD LINE BETWEEN WHAT'S IMPORTANT TO ME...
...AND WHAT ISN'T.
BIRI (RIP)
THERE'S THIS GOAL I HAVE...
...AND I MAKE SURE NOT TO STRAY FROM IT.
...
BIRI
BIRI
MOST PEOPLE SPEND THEIR LIVES PICKING UP MORE AND MORE THINGS TO CARE ABOUT.
THEY MAKE FRIENDS. FALL IN LOVE. GET JOBS...
BIRI
BIRI
BUT I'M THE OPPOSITE. I SHAVE THINGS AWAY.
"I DON'T NEED THIS.
"I DON'T NEED THAT."

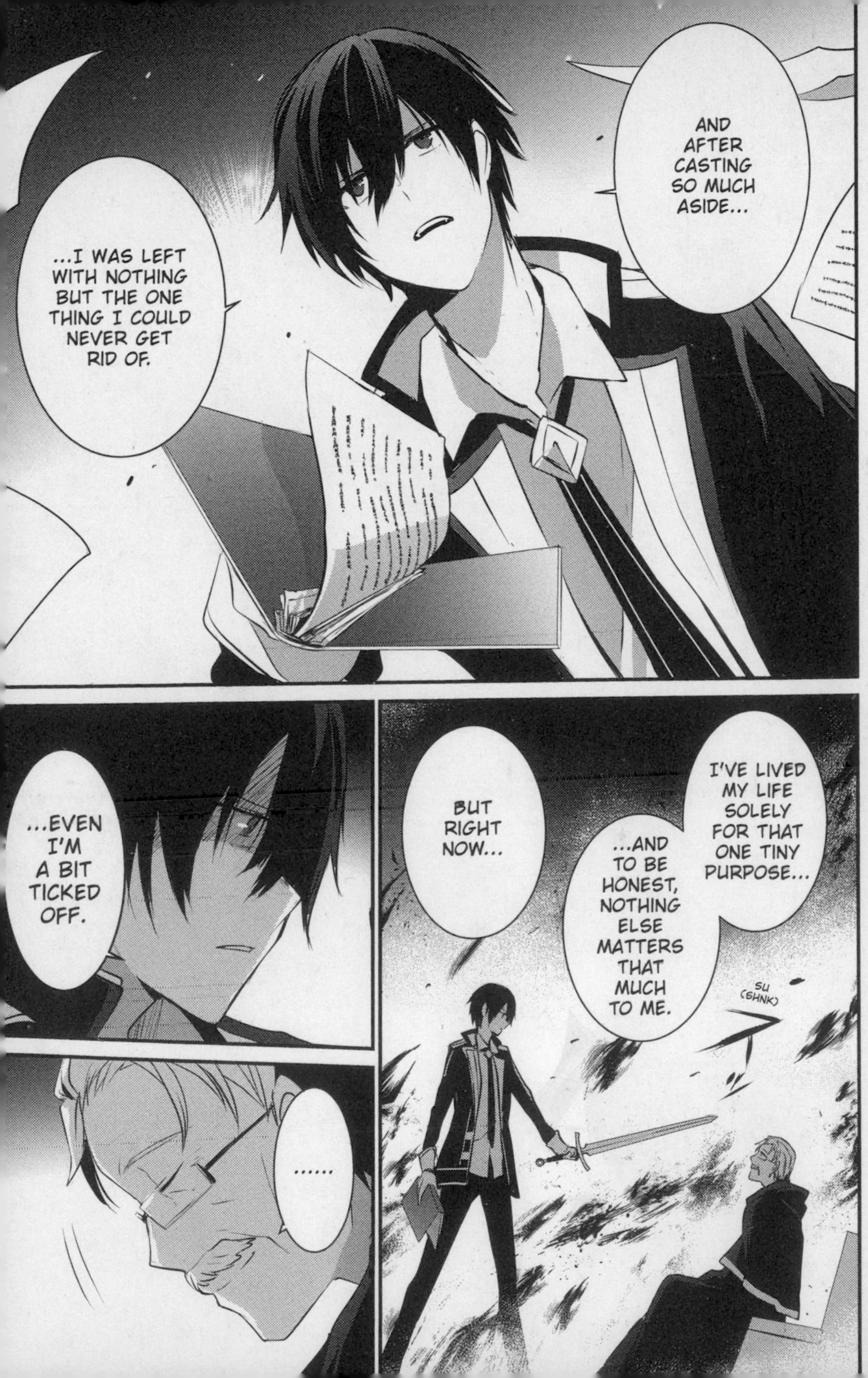
AND AFTER CASTING SO MUCH ASIDE...
...I WAS LEFT WITH NOTHING BUT THE ONE THING I COULD NEVER GET RID OF.
I'VE LIVED MY LIFE SOLELY FOR THAT ONE TINY PURPOSE...
...AND TO BE HONEST, NOTHING ELSE MATTERS THAT MUCH TO ME.
BUT RIGHT NOW...
SU (SHNK)
...EVEN I'M A BIT TICKED OFF.
......

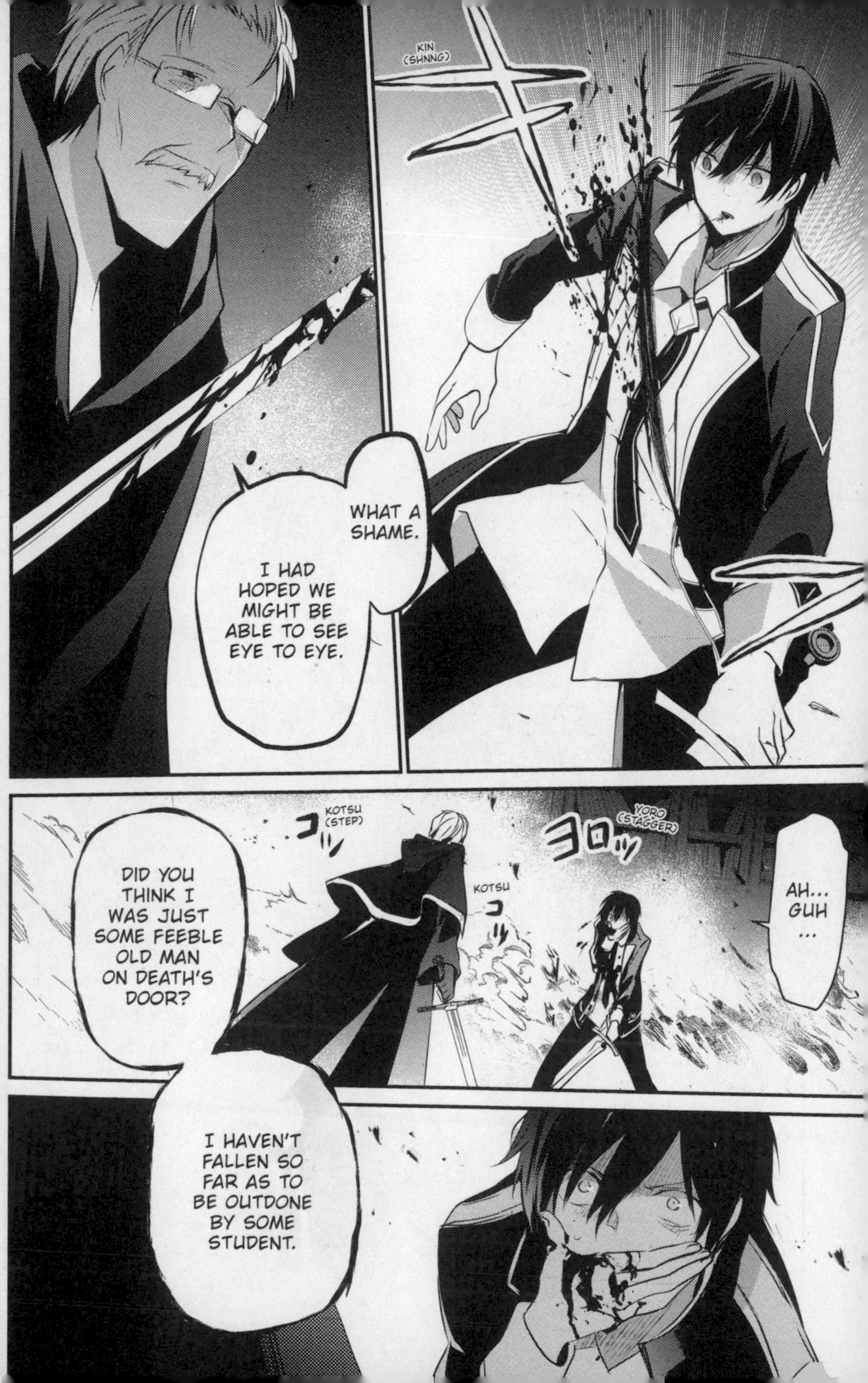
KIN (SHNNG)
WHAT A SHAME.
I HAD HOPED WE MIGHT BE ABLE TO SEE EYE TO EYE.
AH... GUH...
YORO (STAGGER)
KOTSU
KOTSU (STEP)
DID YOU THINK I WAS JUST SOME FEEBLE OLD MAN ON DEATH'S DOOR?
I HAVEN'T FALLEN SO FAR AS TO BE OUTDONE BY SOME STUDENT.

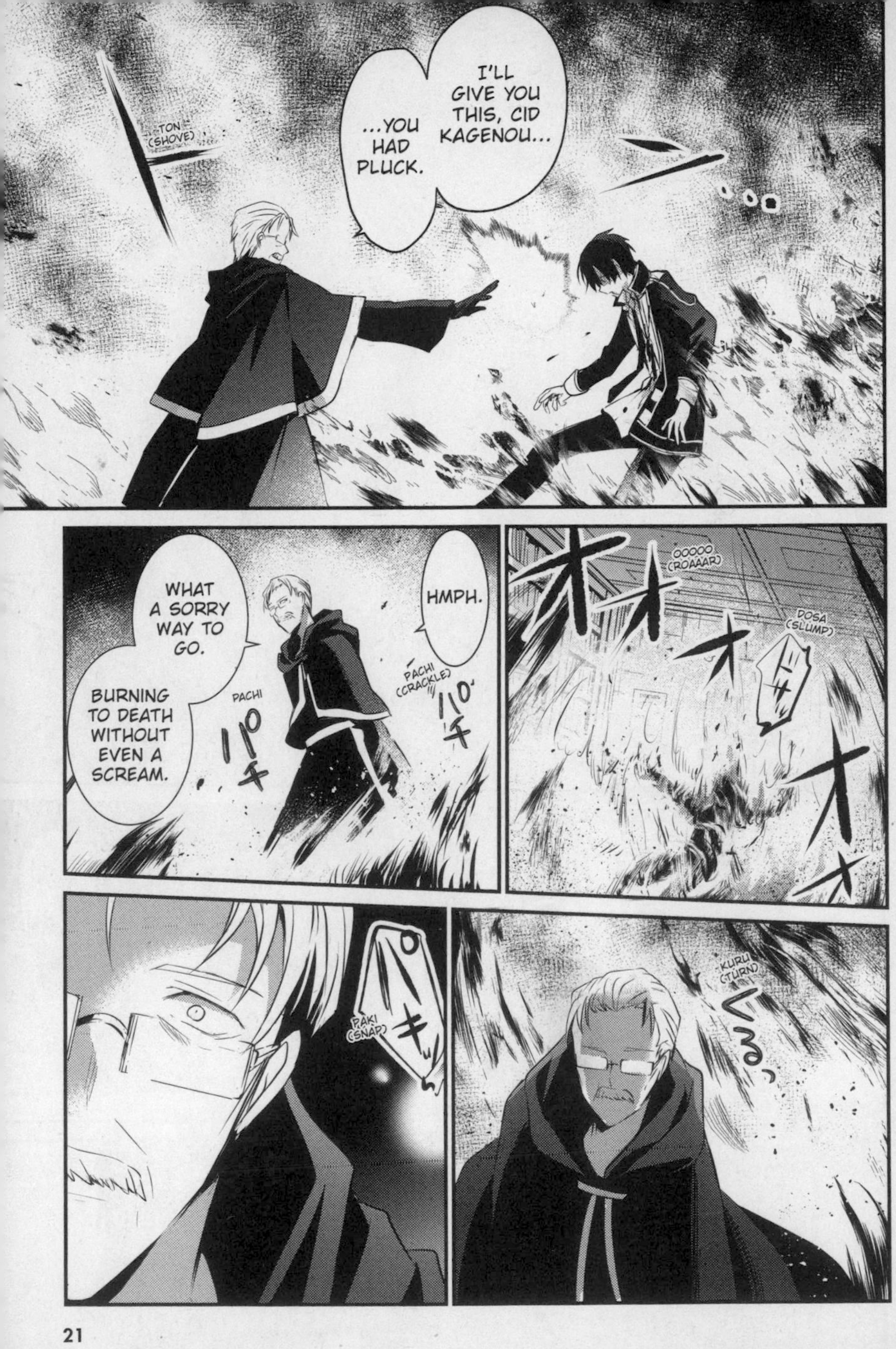
TON (SHOVE)
I'LL GIVE YOU THIS, CID KAGENOU...
...YOU HAD PLUCK.
...
OOOOO (ROAAAR)
DOSA (SLUMP)
HMPH.
PACHI (CRACKLE)
WHAT A SORRY WAY TO GO.
BURNING TO DEATH WITHOUT EVEN A SCREAM.
PACHI
KURU (TURN)
PAKI (SNAP)

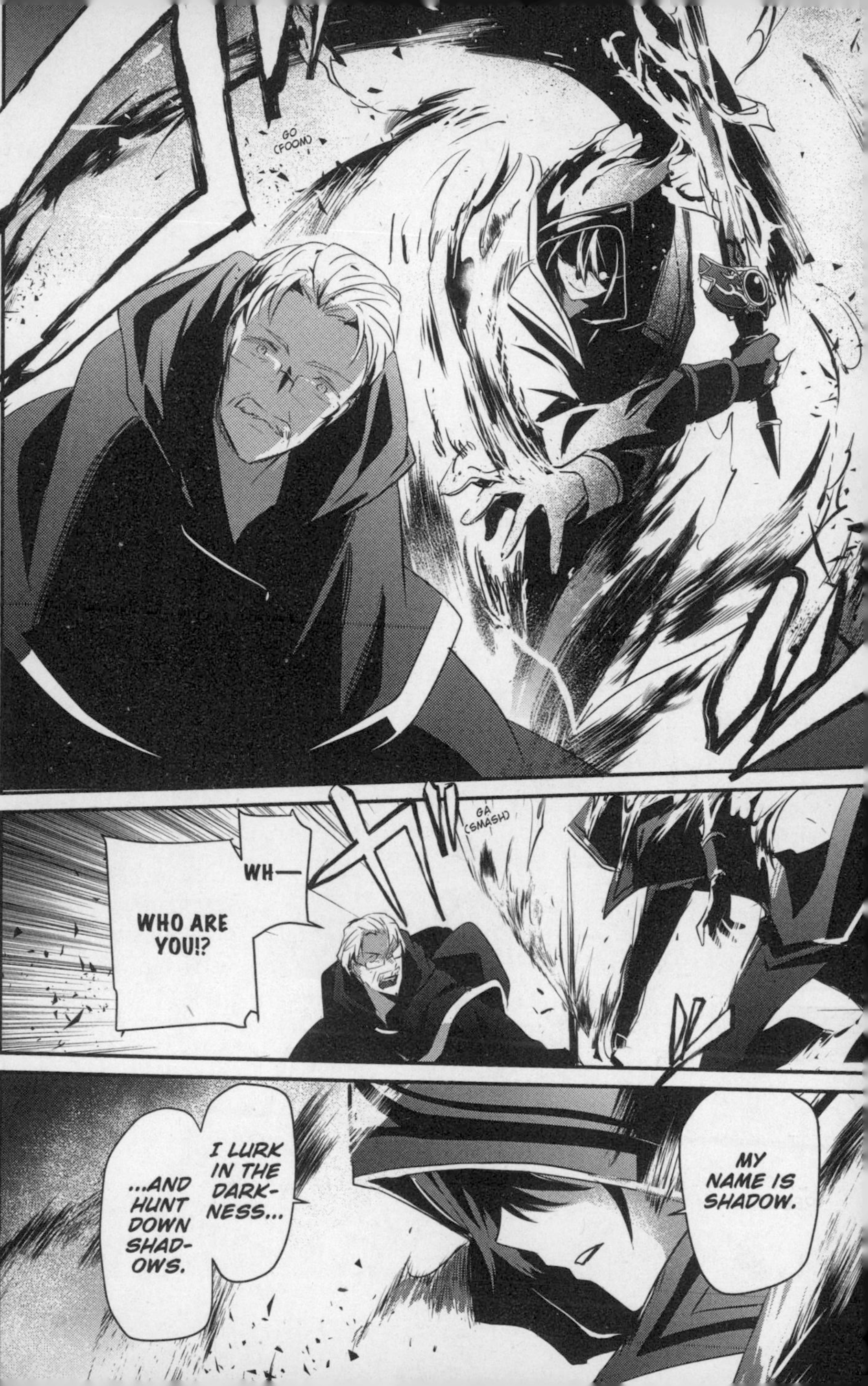
GO (FOOM)
GA (SMASH)
WH—
WHO ARE YOU!?
MY NAME IS SHADOW.
I LURK IN THE DARKNESS...
...AND HUNT DOWN SHADOWS.

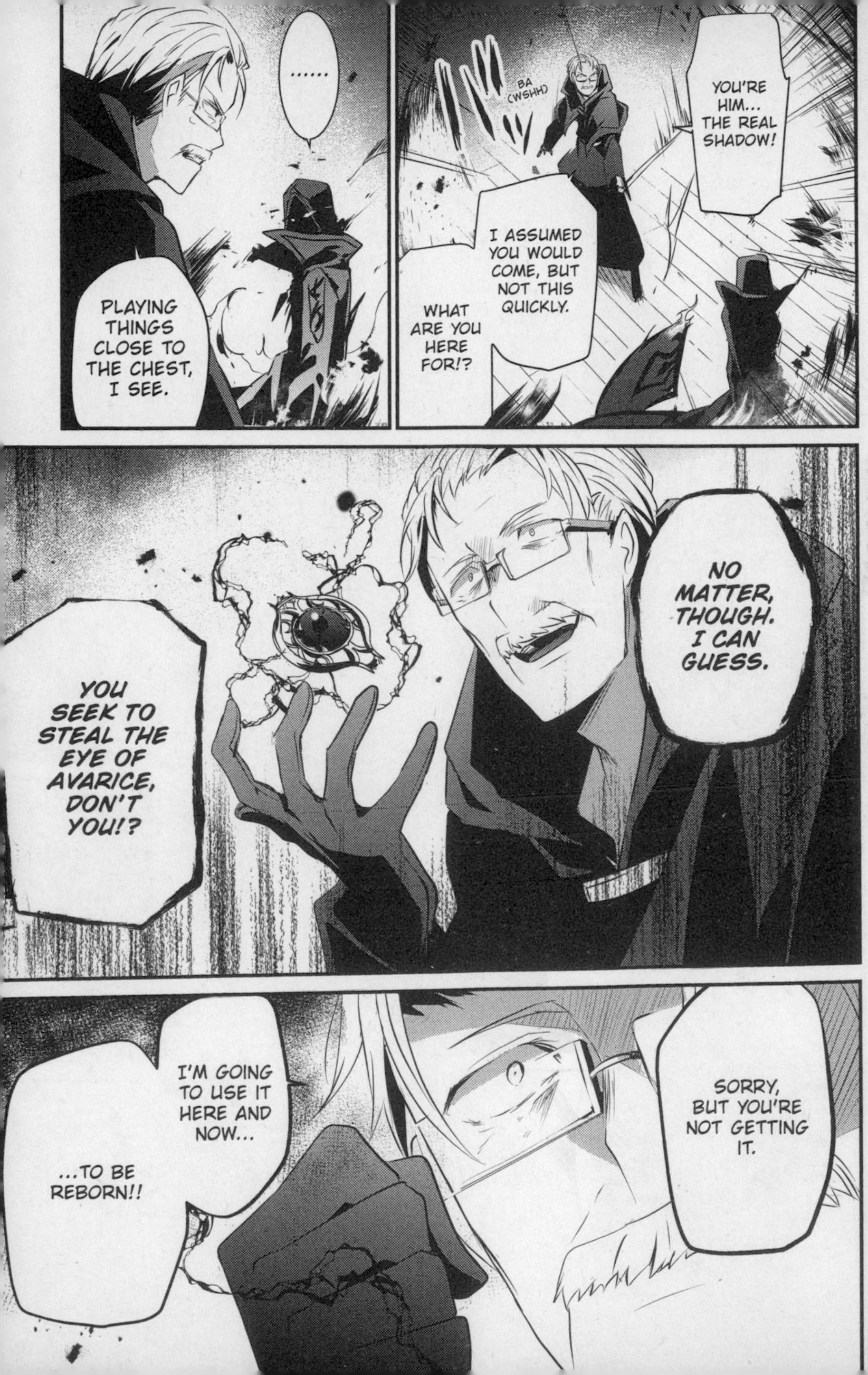
YOU'RE HIM... THE REAL SHADOW!
BA (WSHH)
I ASSUMED YOU WOULD COME, BUT NOT THIS QUICKLY.
WHAT ARE YOU HERE FOR!?
......
PLAYING THINGS CLOSE TO THE CHEST, I SEE.
NO MATTER, THOUGH. I CAN GUESS.
YOU SEEK TO STEAL THE EYE OF AVARICE, DON'T YOU!?
SORRY, BUT YOU'RE NOT GETTING IT.
I'M GOING TO USE IT HERE AND NOW...
...TO BE REBORN!!

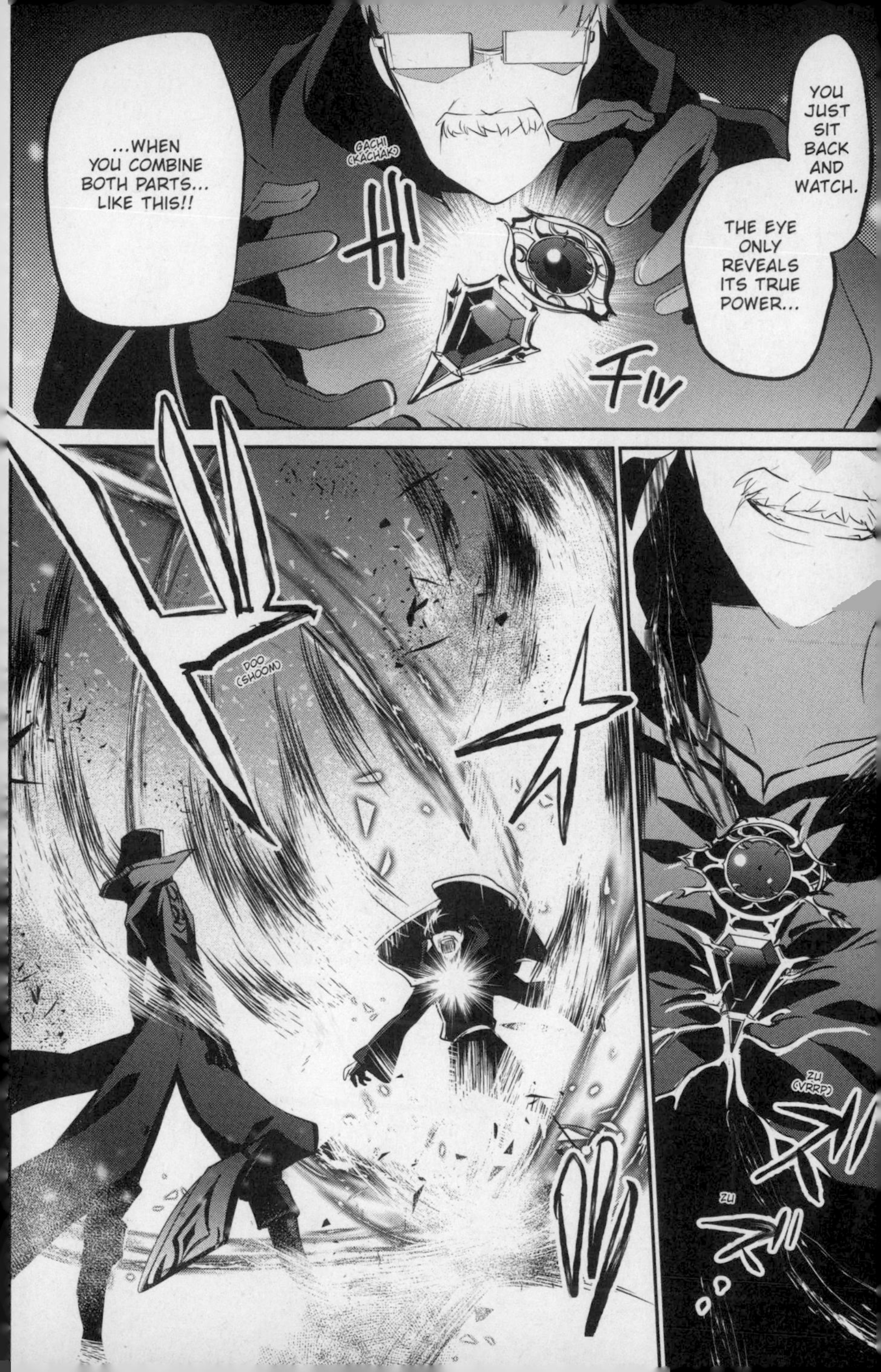
YOU JUST SIT BACK AND WATCH.
THE EYE ONLY REVEALS ITS TRUE POWER...
GACHI (KACHAK)
...WHEN YOU COMBINE BOTH PARTS... LIKE THIS!!
ZU (VRRP)
ZU
DOO (SHOOM)

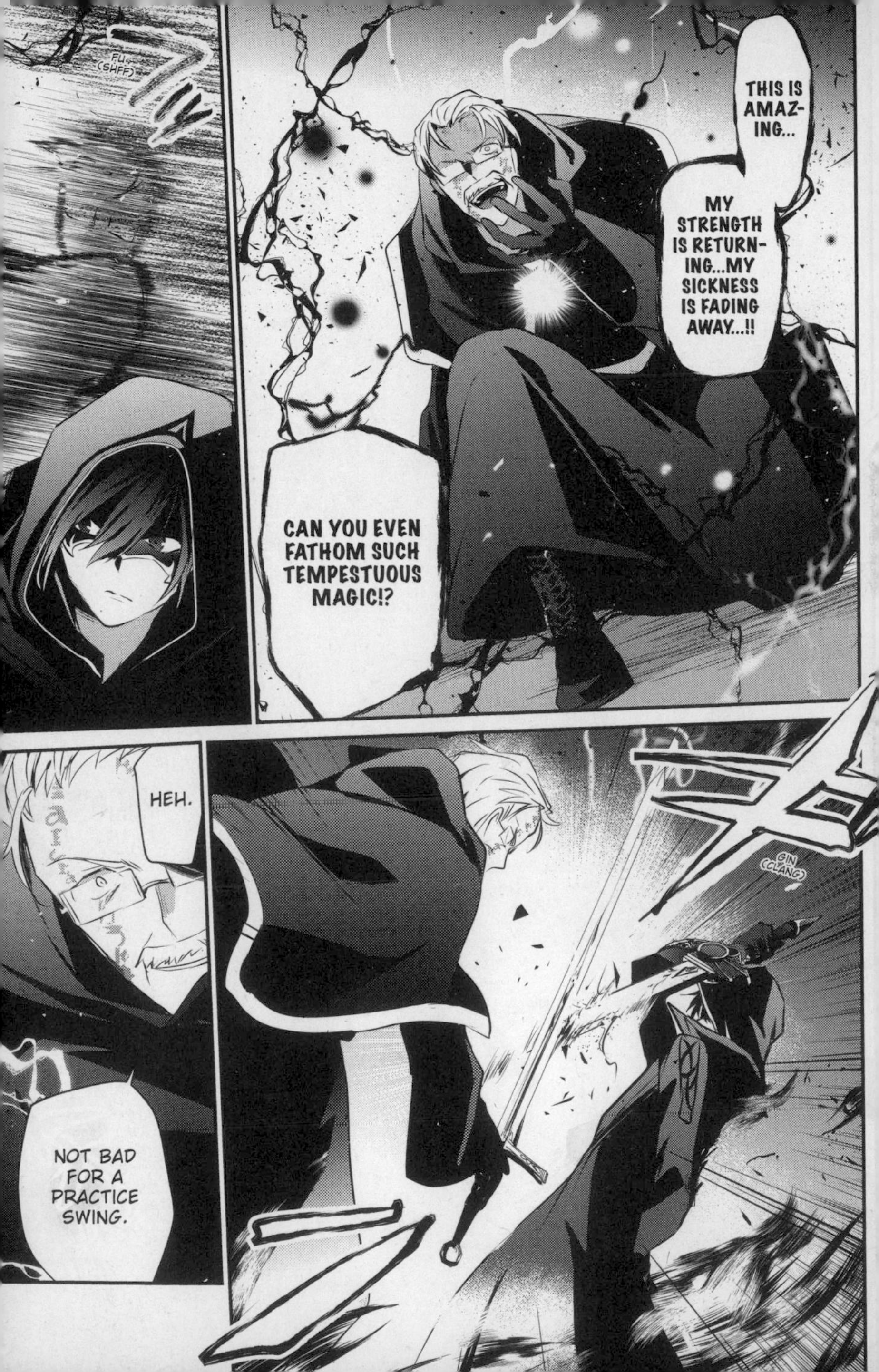
THIS IS AMAZ-ING...
MY STRENGTH IS RETURN-ING...MY SICKNESS IS FADING AWAY...!!
CAN YOU EVEN FATHOM SUCH TEMPESTUOUS MAGIC!?
FU (SHFF)
GIN (CLANG)
HEH.
NOT BAD FOR A PRACTICE SWING.

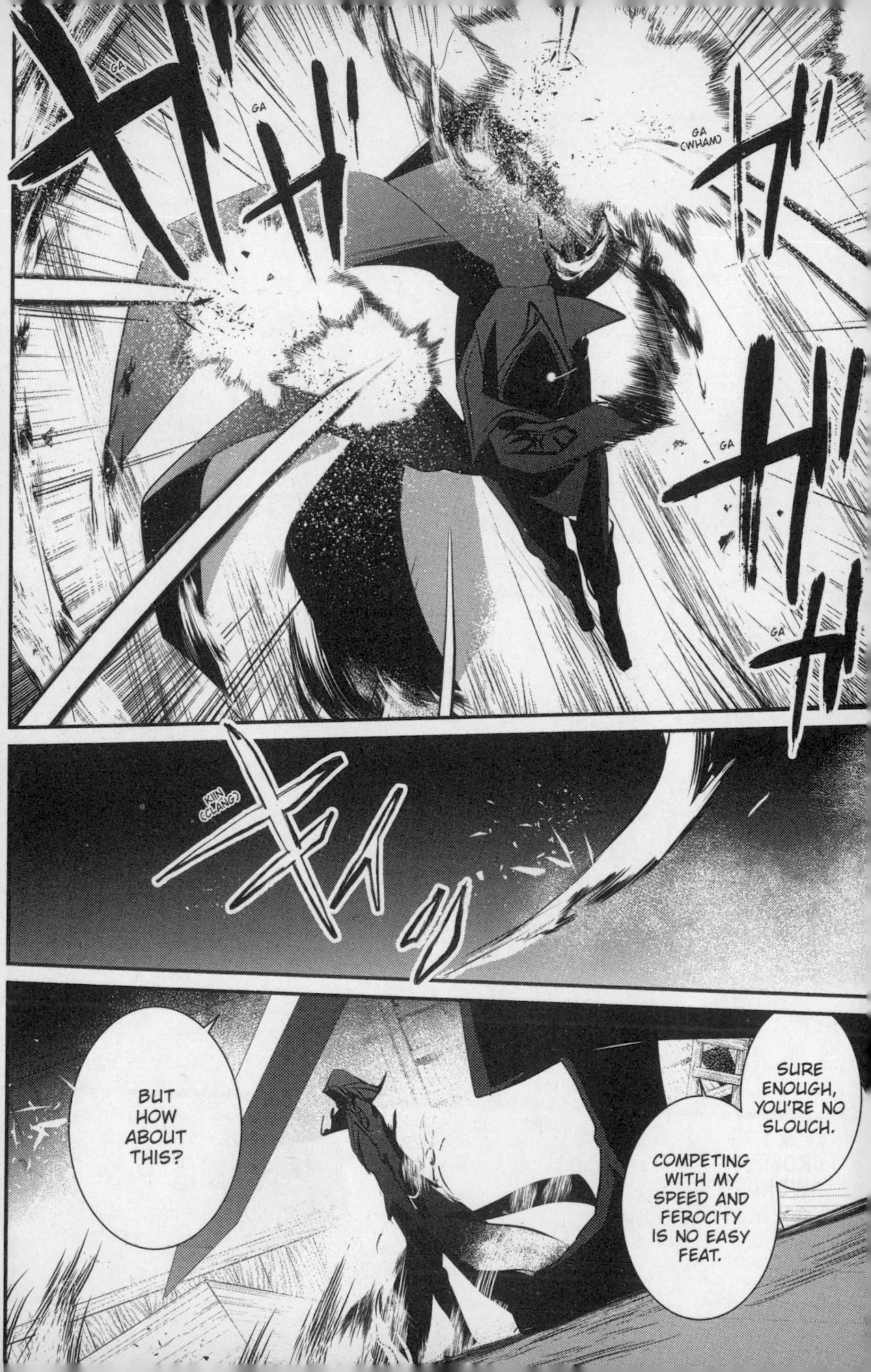
GA (WHAM)
GA
GA
GA
GA
KIIN (CLANG)
SURE ENOUGH, YOU'RE NO SLOUCH.
COMPETING WITH MY SPEED AND FEROCITY IS NO EASY FEAT.
BUT HOW ABOUT THIS?

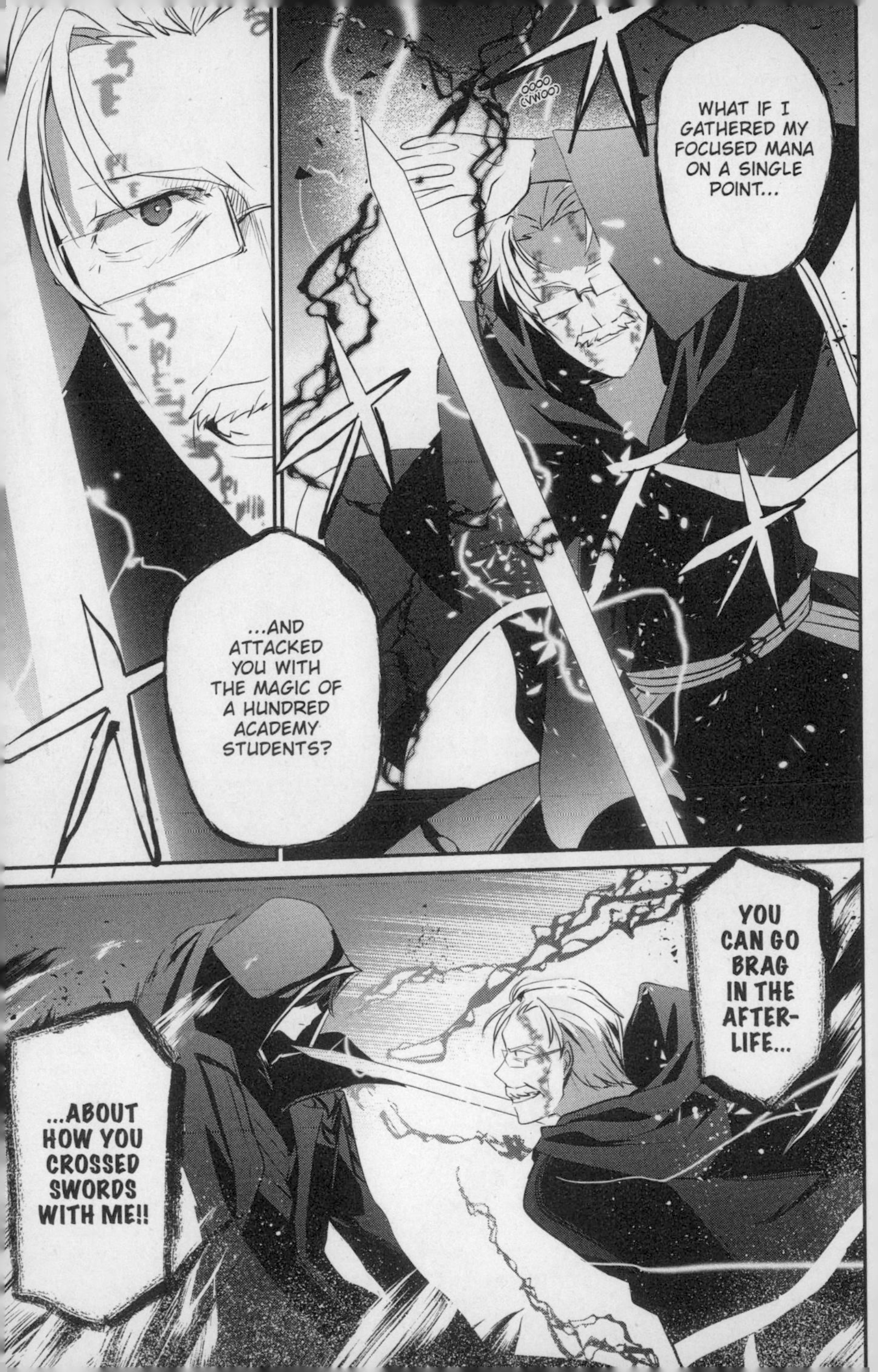
WHAT IF I GATHERED MY FOCUSED MANA ON A SINGLE POINT...
...AND ATTACKED YOU WITH THE MAGIC OF A HUNDRED ACADEMY STUDENTS?
YOU CAN GO BRAG IN THE AFTER-LIFE...
...ABOUT HOW YOU CROSSED SWORDS WITH ME!!

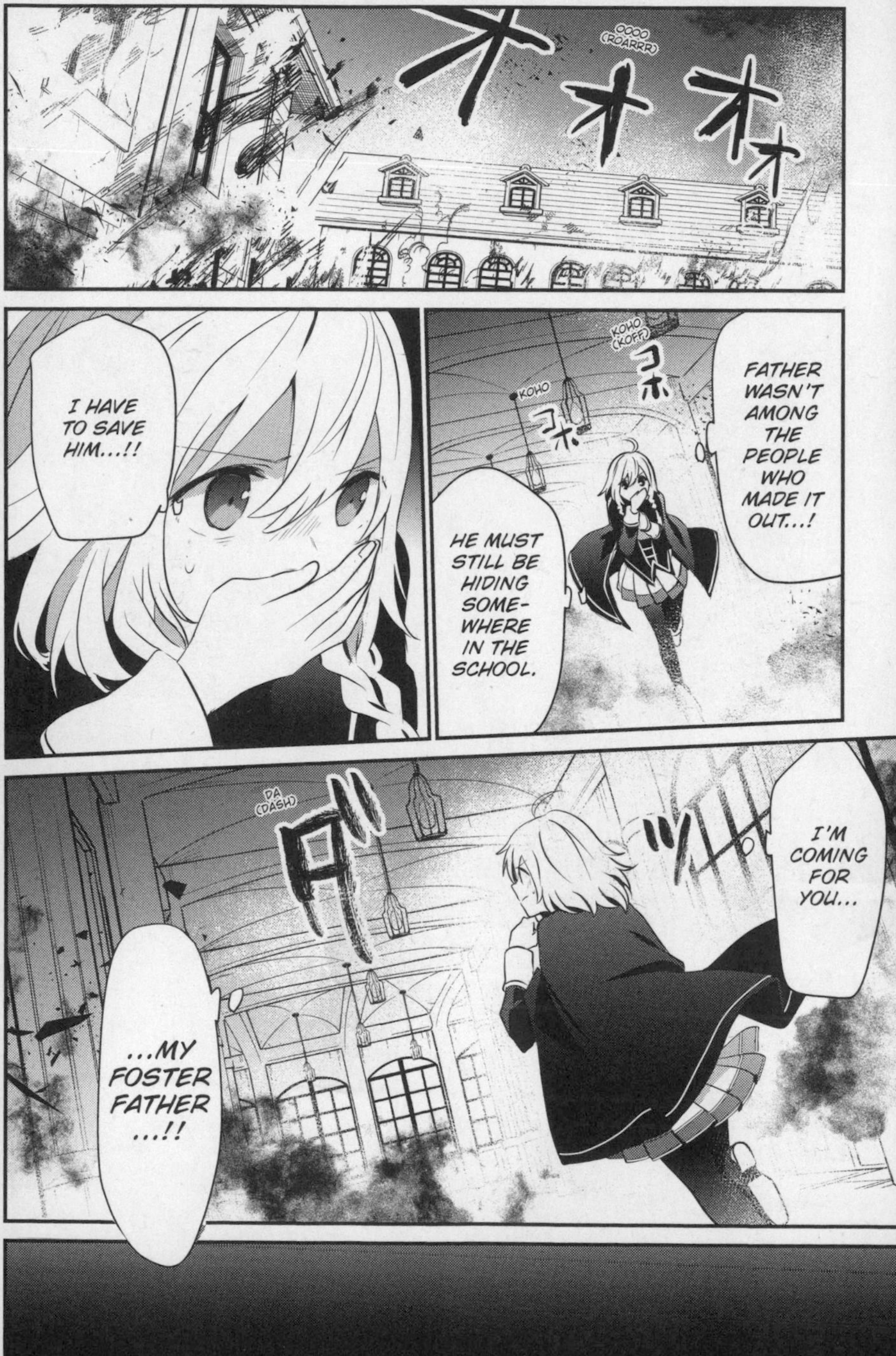

OOOO (ROARRR)
KOHO (KOFF)
KOHO
FATHER WASN'T AMONG THE PEOPLE WHO MADE IT OUT...!
HE MUST STILL BE HIDING SOME-WHERE IN THE SCHOOL.
I HAVE TO SAVE HIM...!!
DA (DASH)
I'M COMING FOR YOU...
...MY FOSTER FATHER ...!!

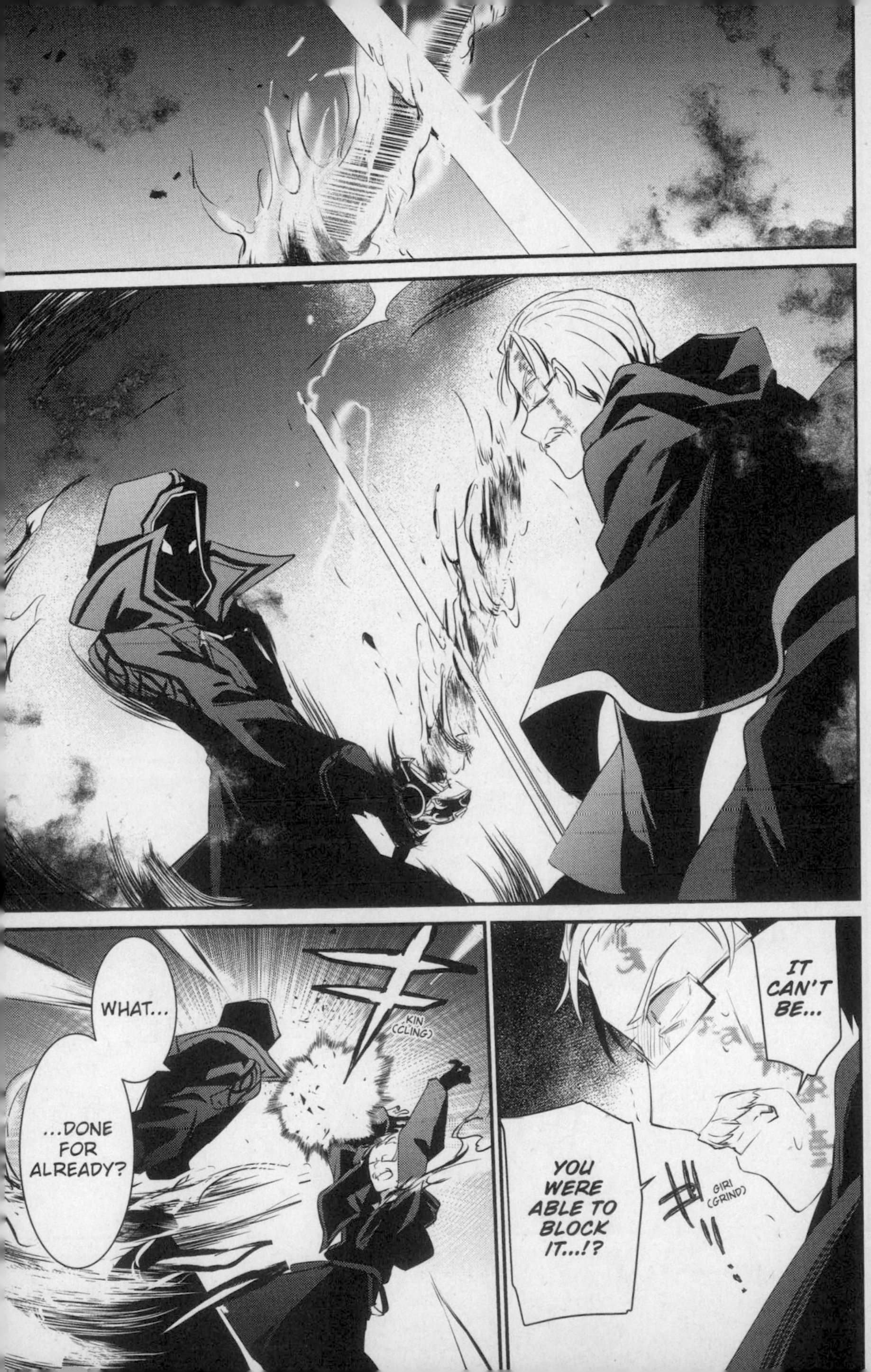
IT CAN'T BE...
GIRI (GRIND)
YOU WERE ABLE TO BLOCK IT...!?
KIN (CLING)
WHAT...
...DONE FOR ALREADY?

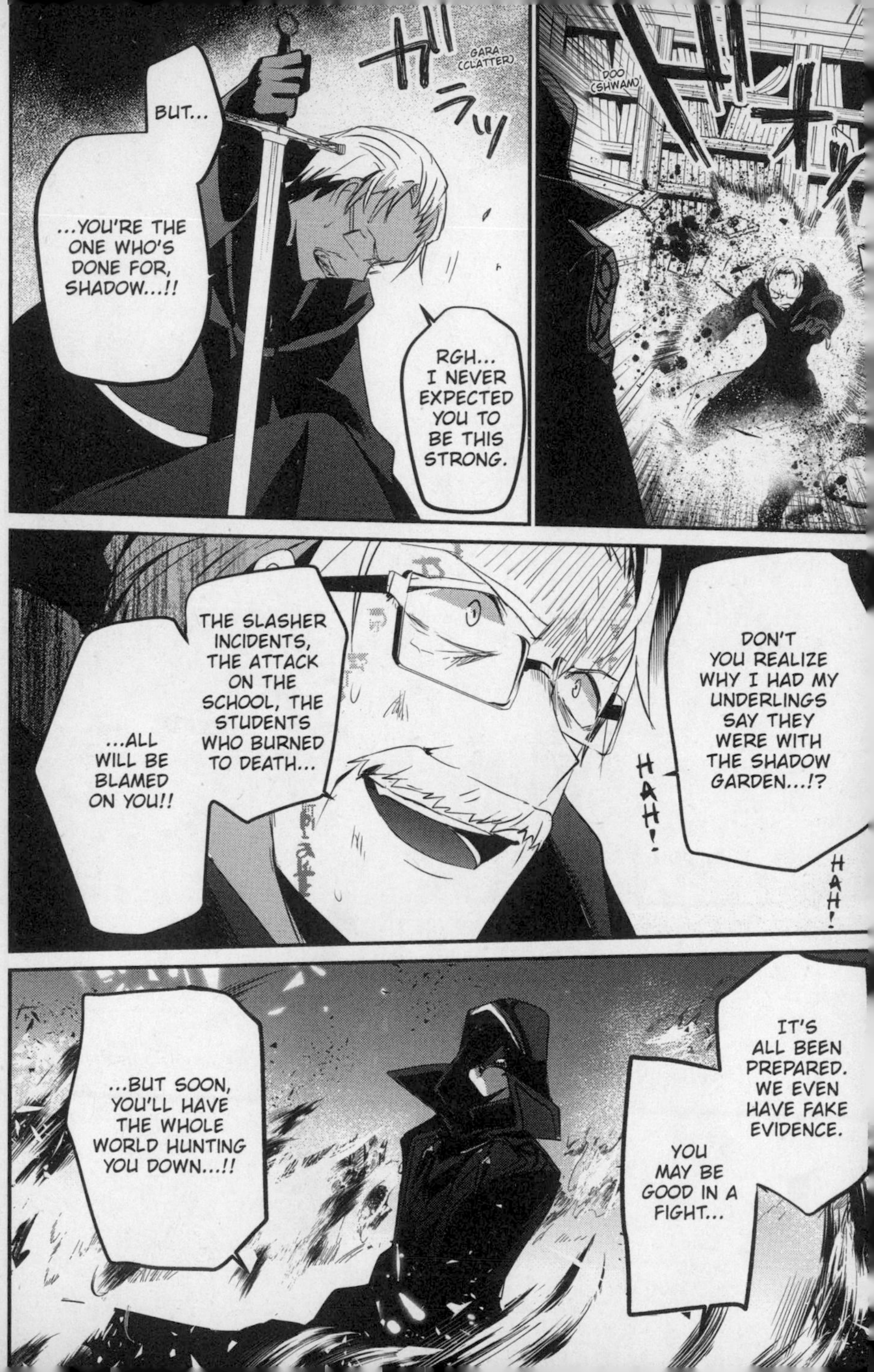
DOO (SHWAM)
GARA (CLATTER)
RGH... I NEVER EXPECTED YOU TO BE THIS STRONG.
BUT...
...YOU'RE THE ONE WHO'S DONE FOR, SHADOW...!!
DON'T YOU REALIZE WHY I HAD MY UNDERLINGS SAY THEY WERE WITH THE SHADOW GARDEN...!?
HAH! HAH!
THE SLASHER INCIDENTS, THE ATTACK ON THE SCHOOL, THE STUDENTS WHO BURNED TO DEATH...
...ALL WILL BE BLAMED ON YOU!!
IT'S ALL BEEN PREPARED. WE EVEN HAVE FAKE EVIDENCE.
YOU MAY BE GOOD IN A FIGHT...
...BUT SOON, YOU'LL HAVE THE WHOLE WORLD HUNTING YOU DOWN...!!

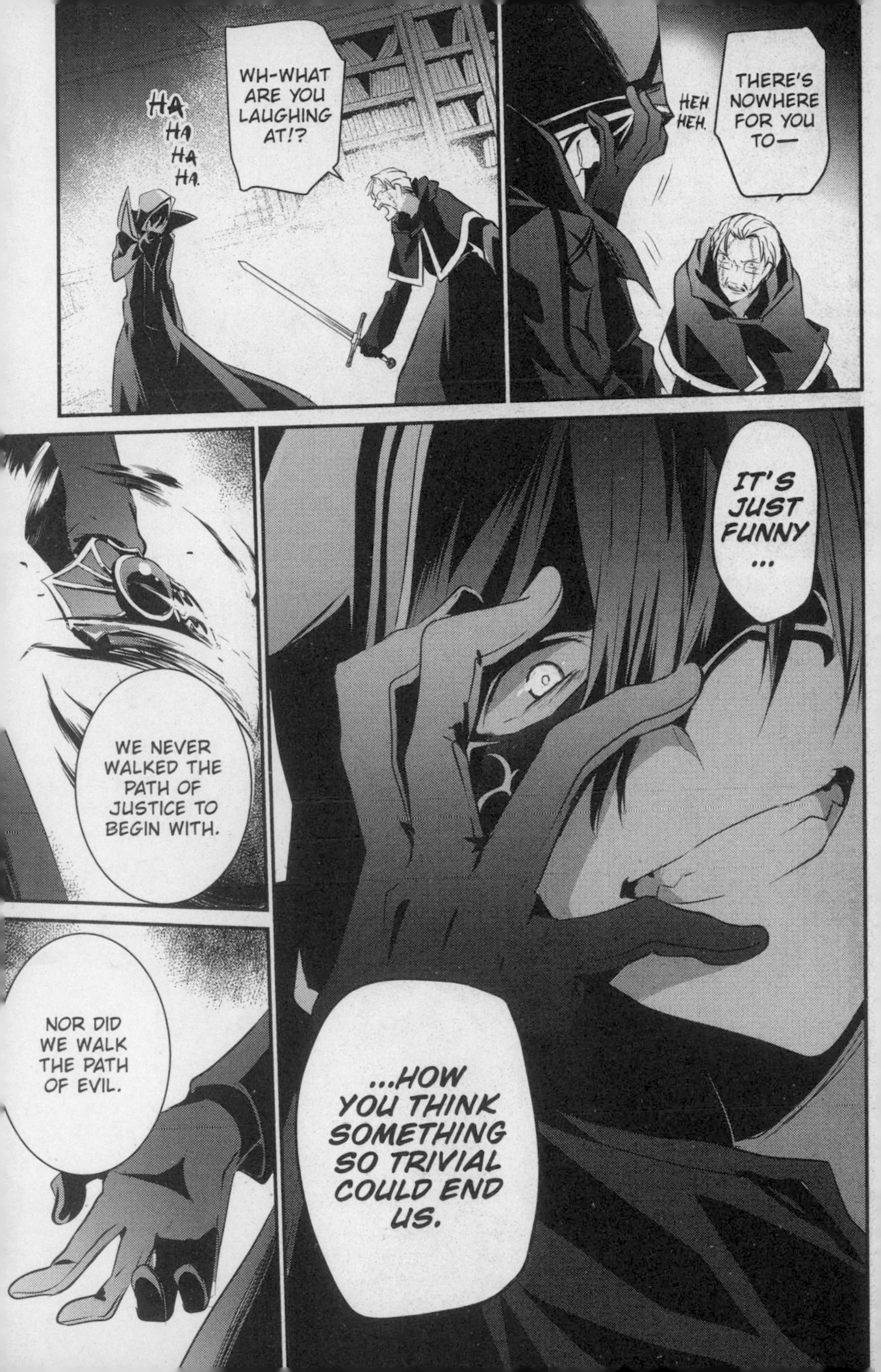
THERE'S NOWHERE FOR YOU TO—
HEH HEH.
WH-WHAT ARE YOU LAUGHING AT!?
HA HA HA HA.
IT'S JUST FUNNY...
...HOW YOU THINK SOMETHING SO TRIVIAL COULD END US.
WE NEVER WALKED THE PATH OF JUSTICE TO BEGIN WITH.
NOR DID WE WALK THE PATH OF EVIL.

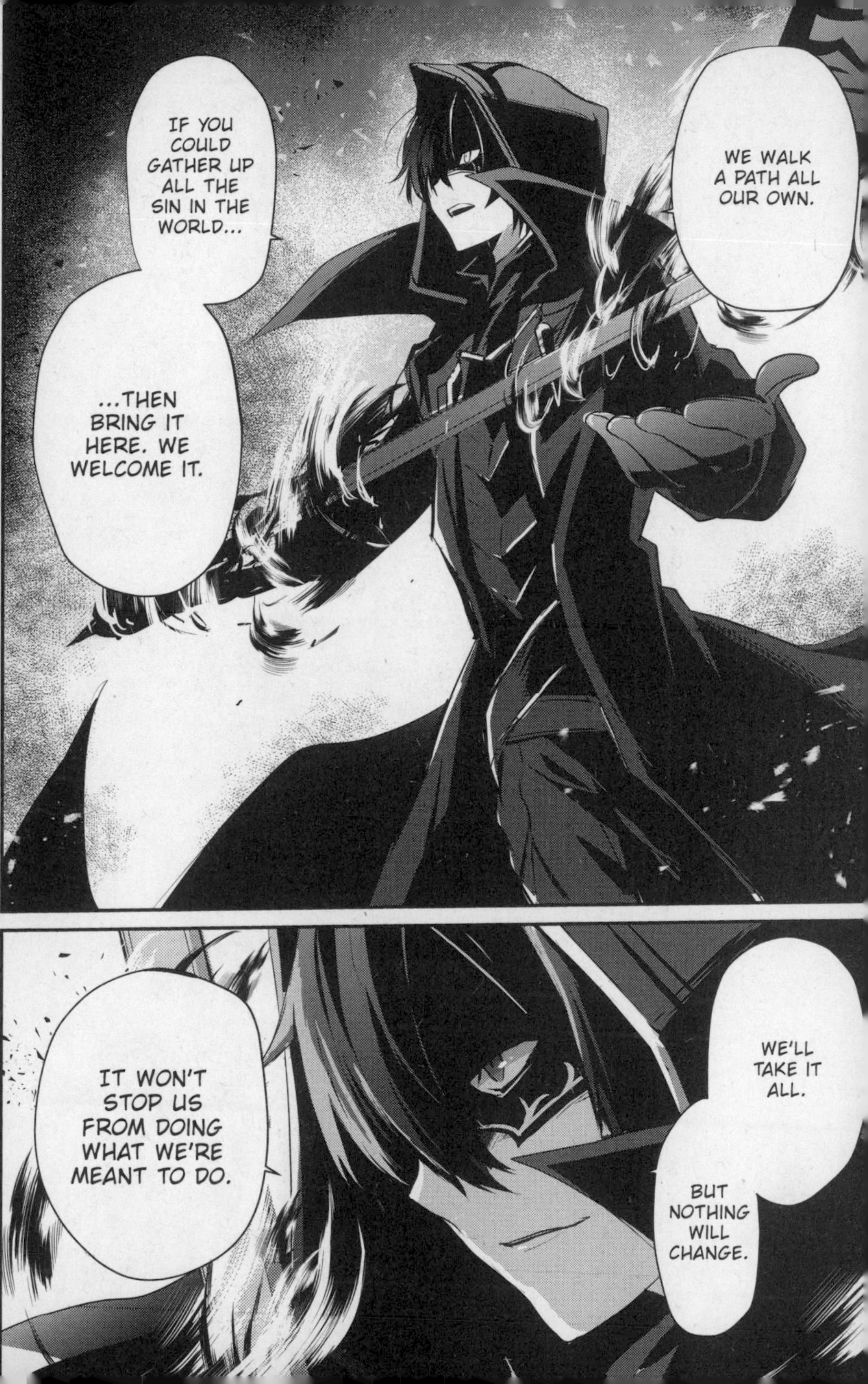
WE WALK A PATH ALL OUR OWN.
IF YOU COULD GATHER UP ALL THE SIN IN THE WORLD...
...THEN BRING IT HERE. WE WELCOME IT.
WE'LL TAKE IT ALL.
BUT NOTHING WILL CHANGE.
IT WON'T STOP US FROM DOING WHAT WE'RE MEANT TO DO.

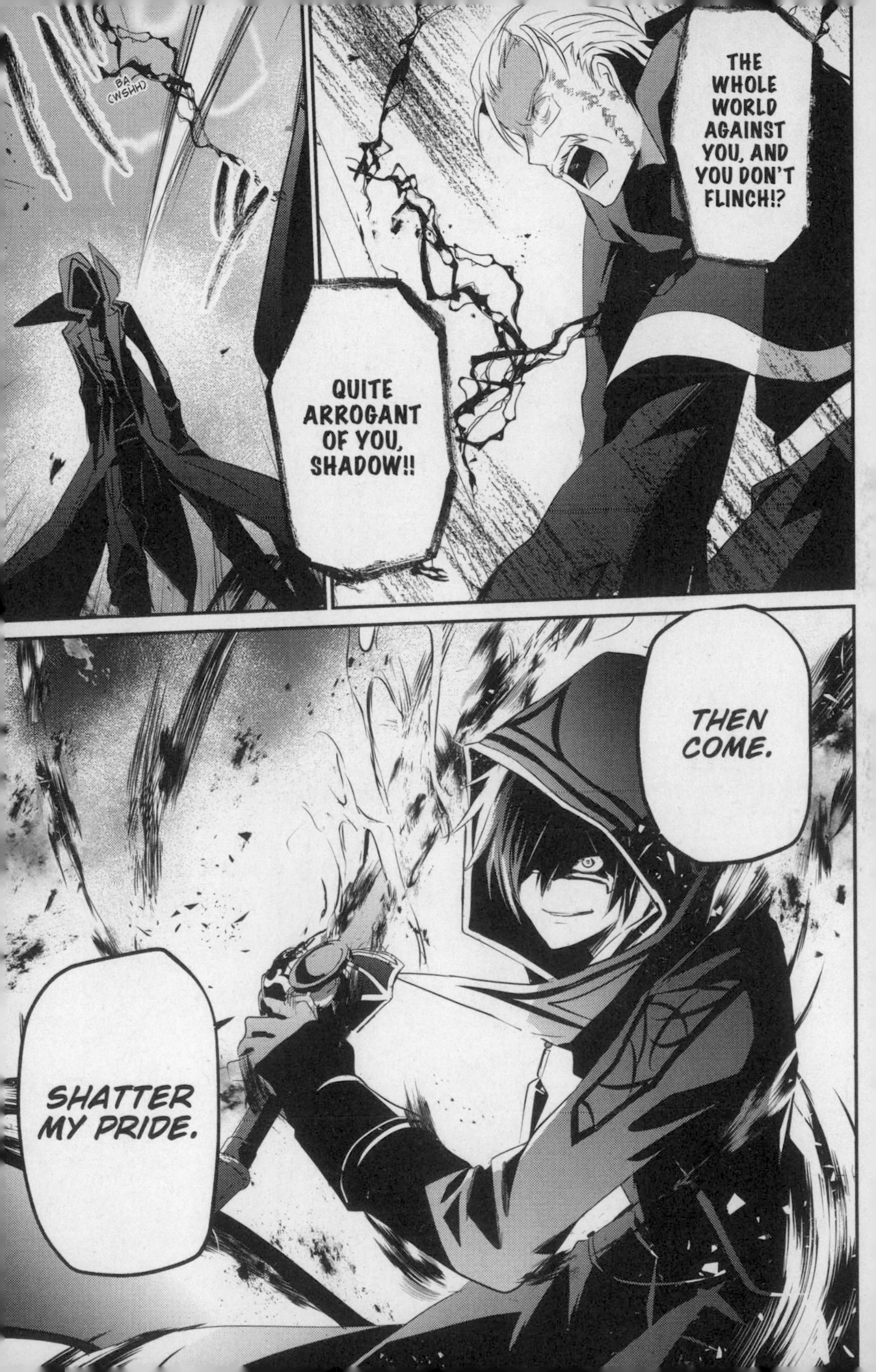
THE WHOLE WORLD AGAINST YOU, AND YOU DON'T FLINCH!?
QUITE ARROGANT OF YOU, SHADOW!!
BA (WSHH)
THEN COME.
SHATTER MY PRIDE.

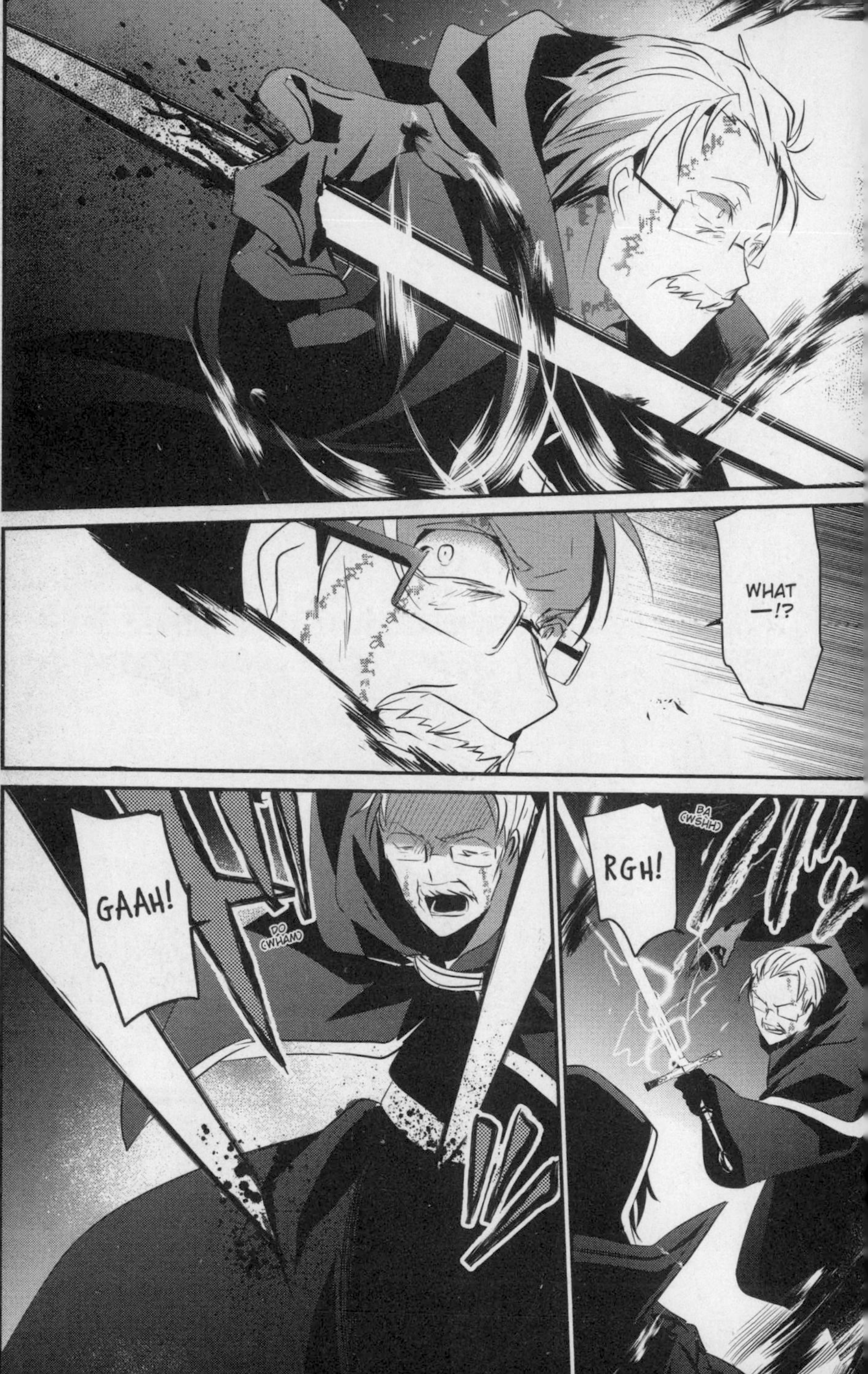
WHAT—!?
BA (WSHH)
RGH!
GAAH!
DO (WHAM)

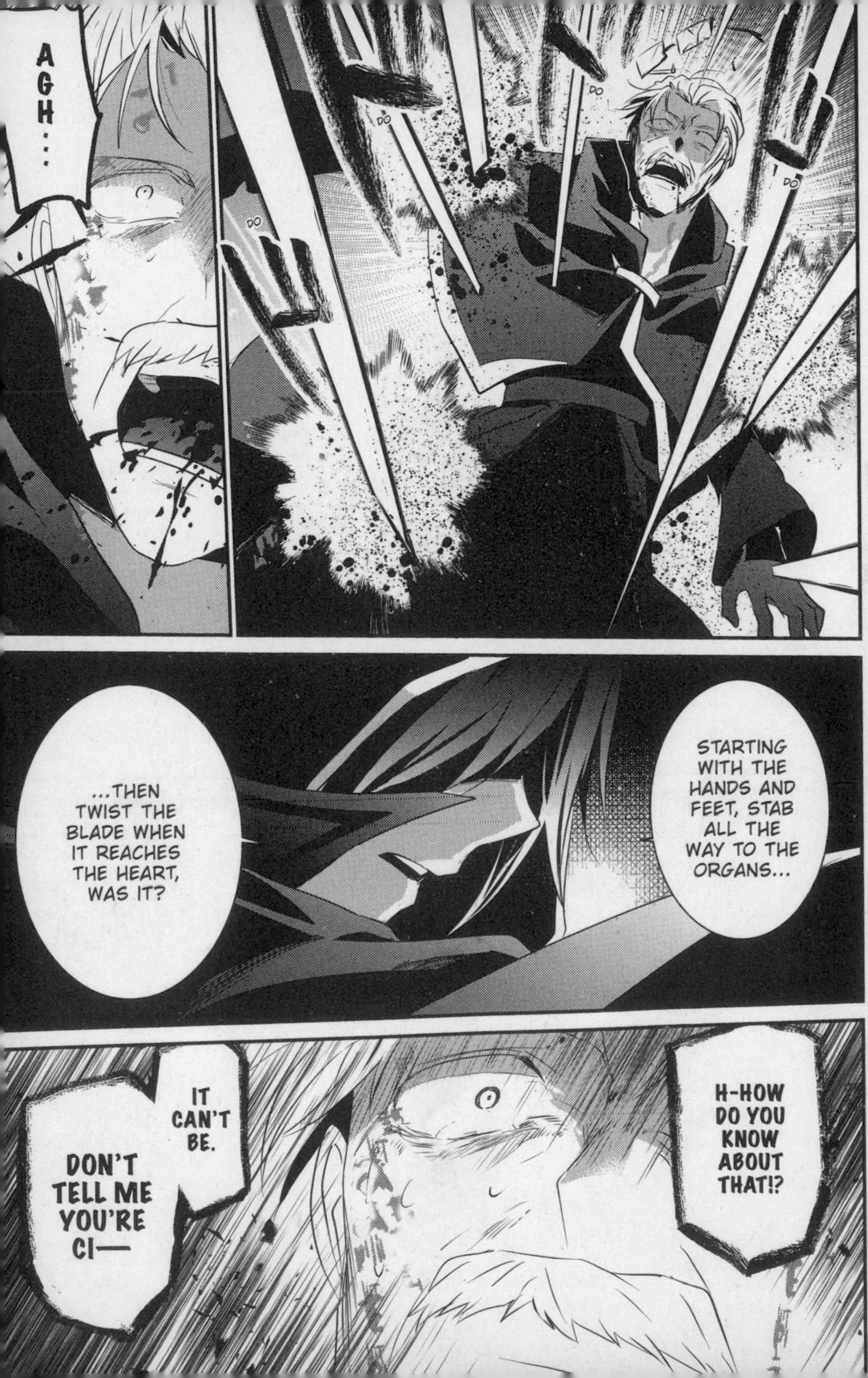
DO
DO
DO
DO
AGH...
STARTING WITH THE HANDS AND FEET, STAB ALL THE WAY TO THE ORGANS...
...THEN TWIST THE BLADE WHEN IT REACHES THE HEART, WAS IT?
H-HOW DO YOU KNOW ABOUT THAT!?
IT CAN'T BE.
DON'T TELL ME YOU'RE CI—

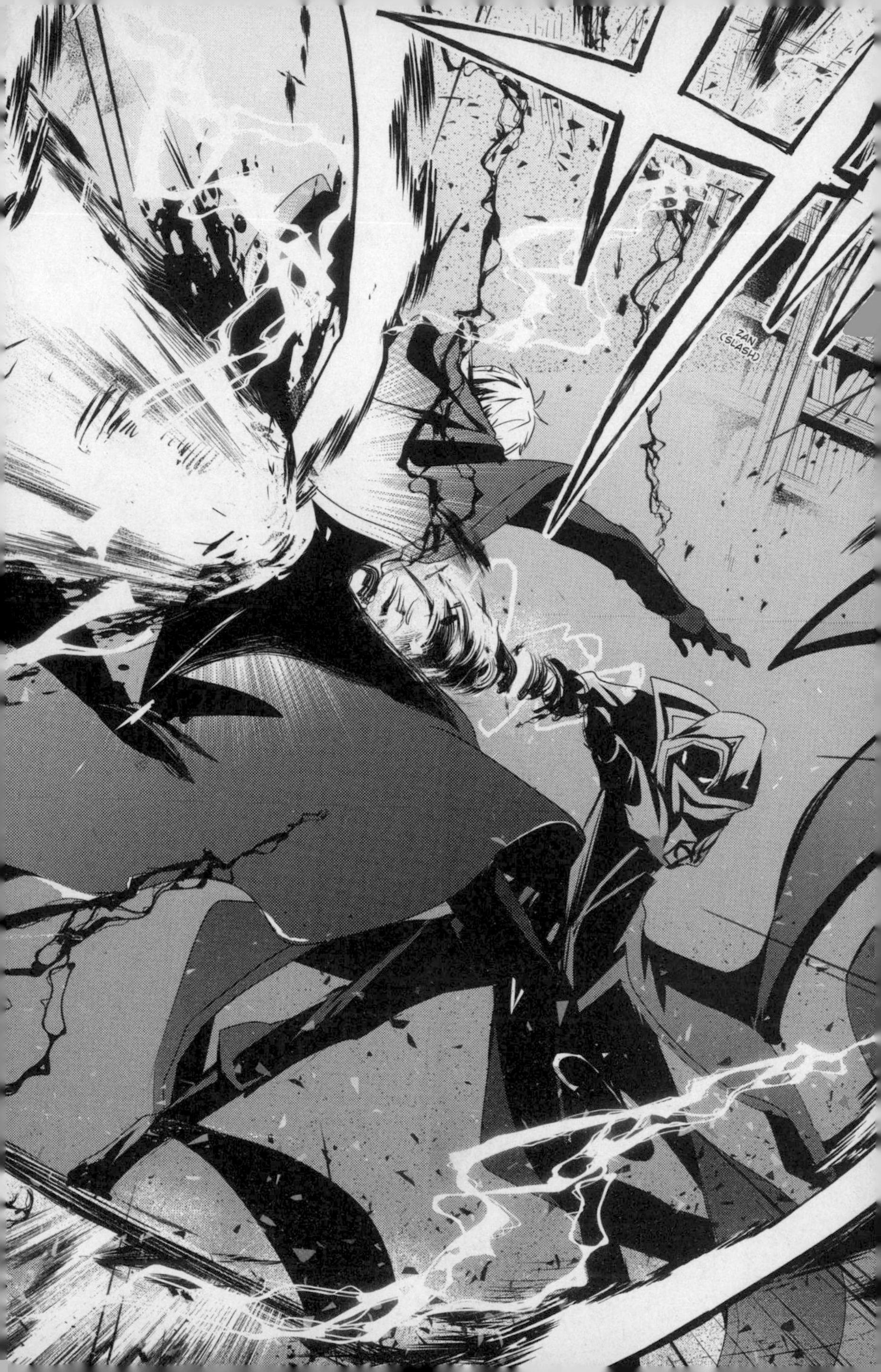
ZAN
(SLASH)

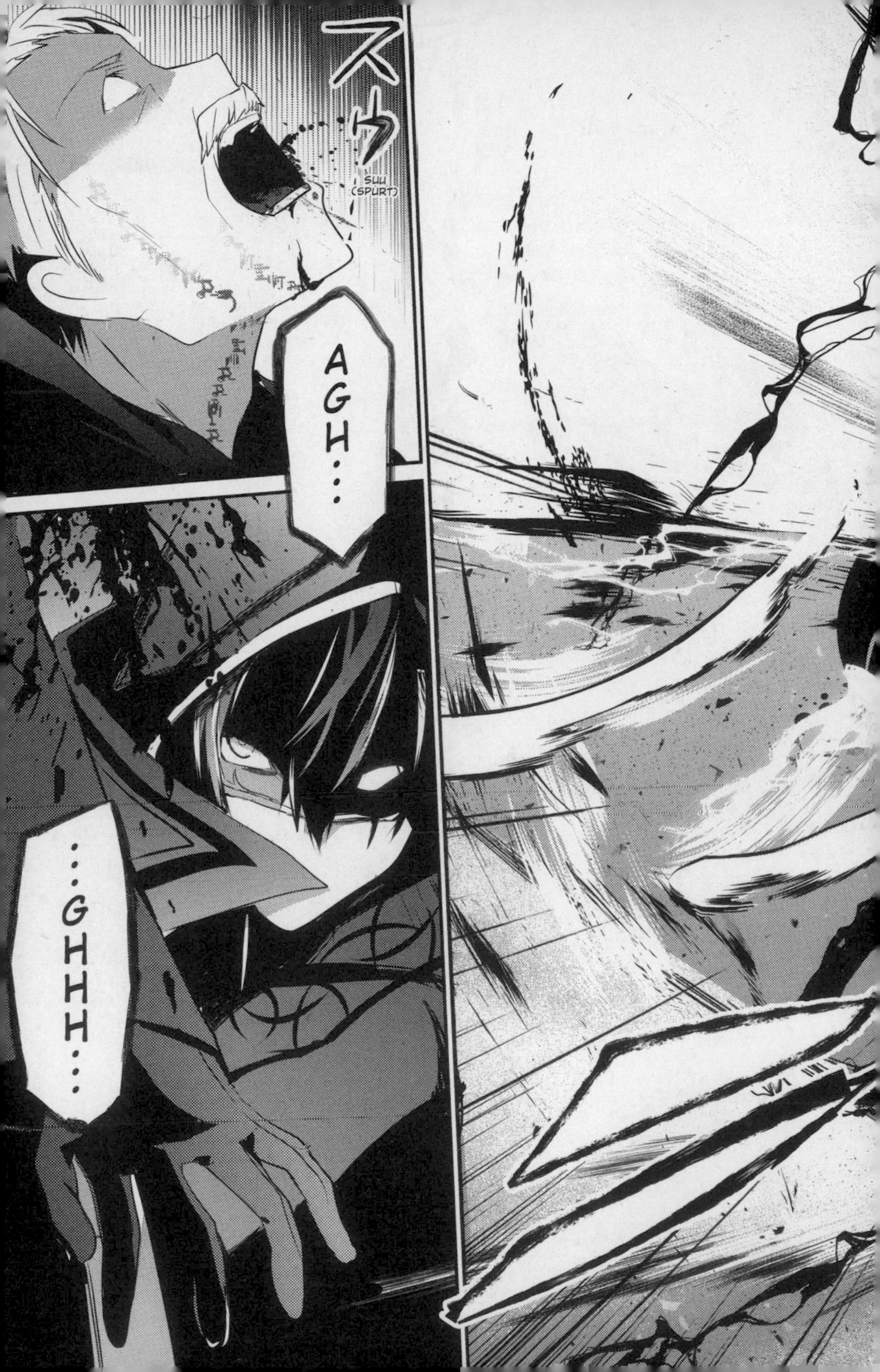
スゥ
SUU (SPURT)
AGH...
...GHHH...

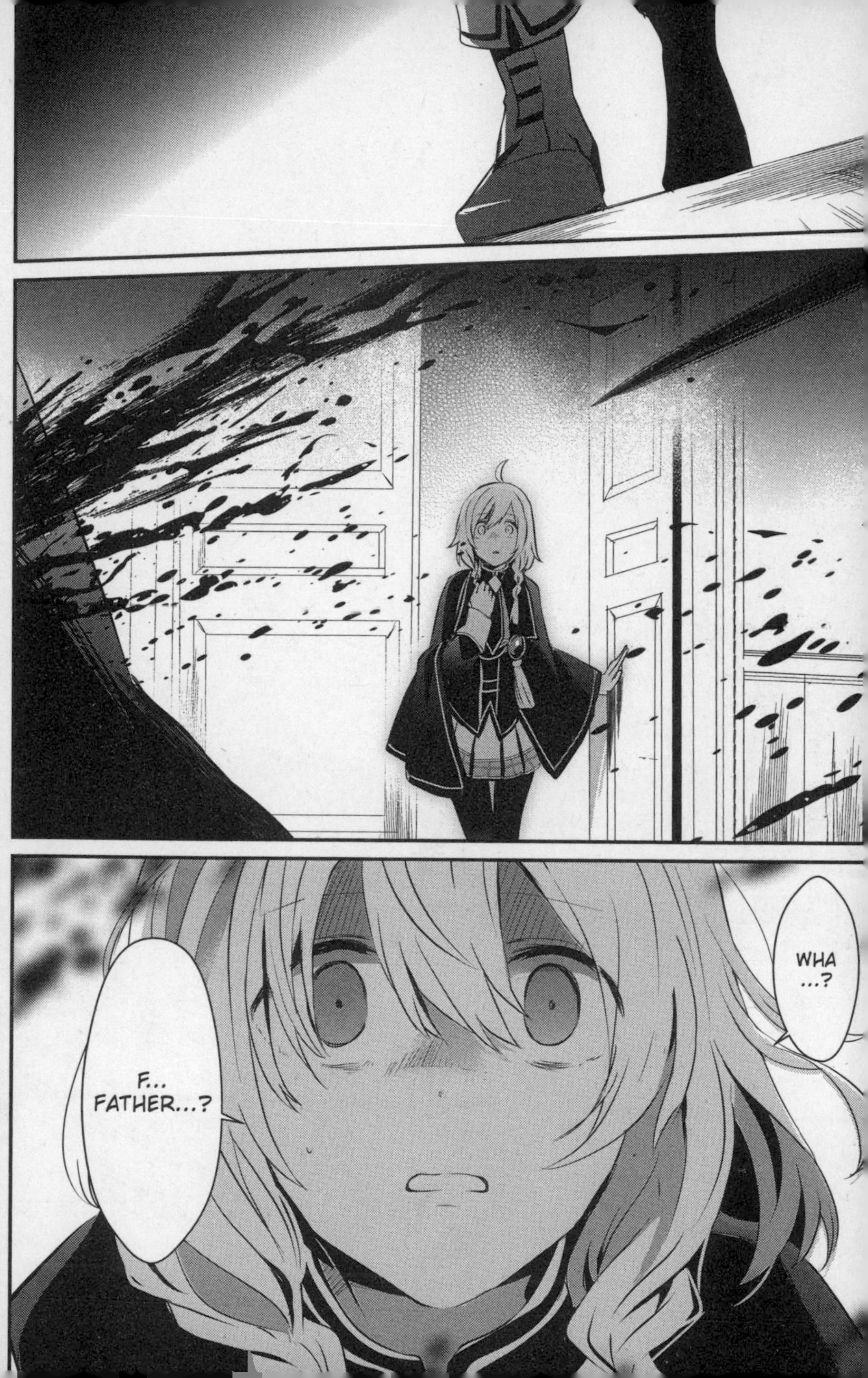
WHA ...?
F... FATHER...?

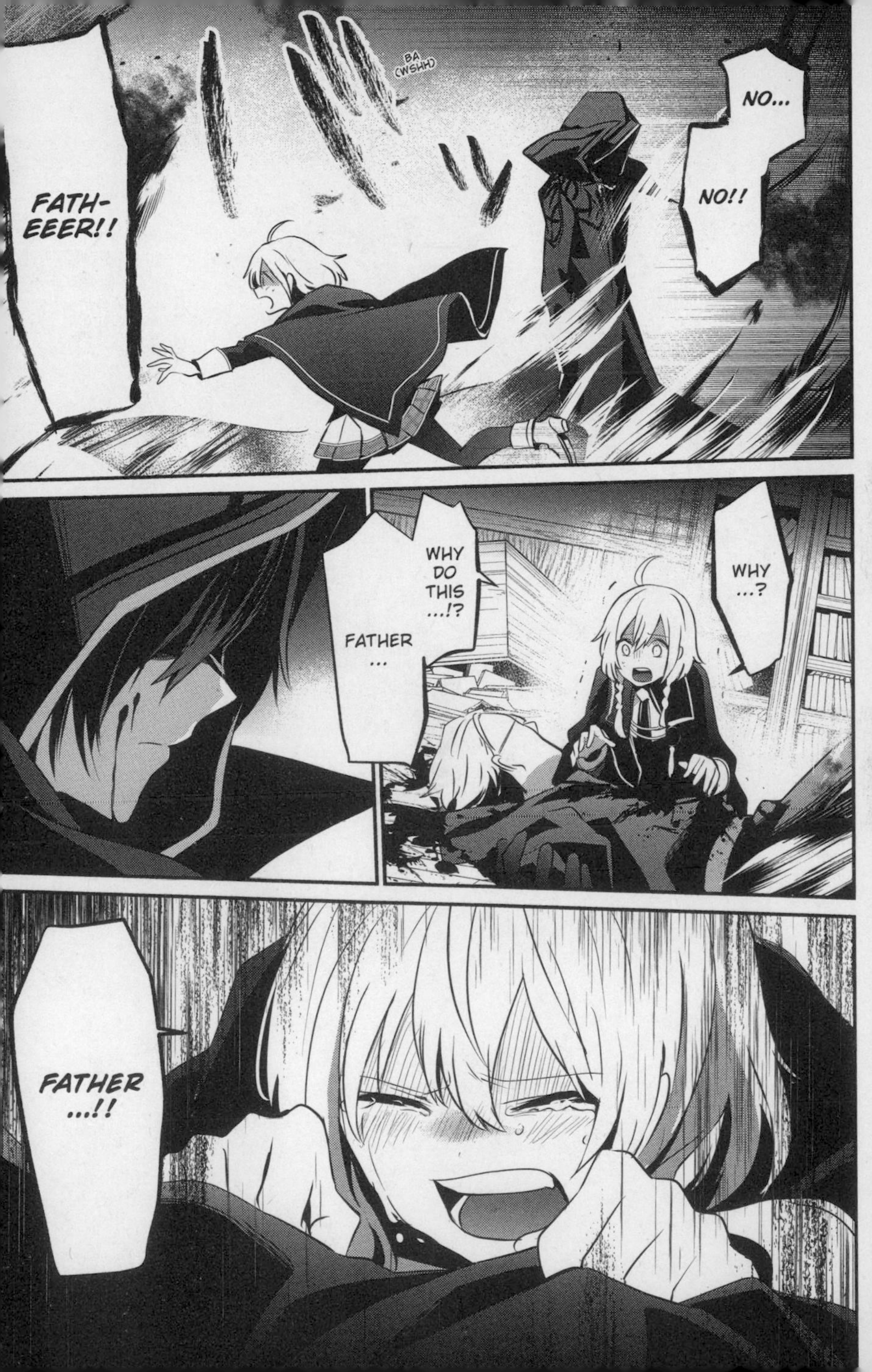
NO...
NO!!
BA (WSHH)
FATH-EEER!!
WHY ...?
WHY DO THIS ...!?
FATHER ...
FATHER ...!!

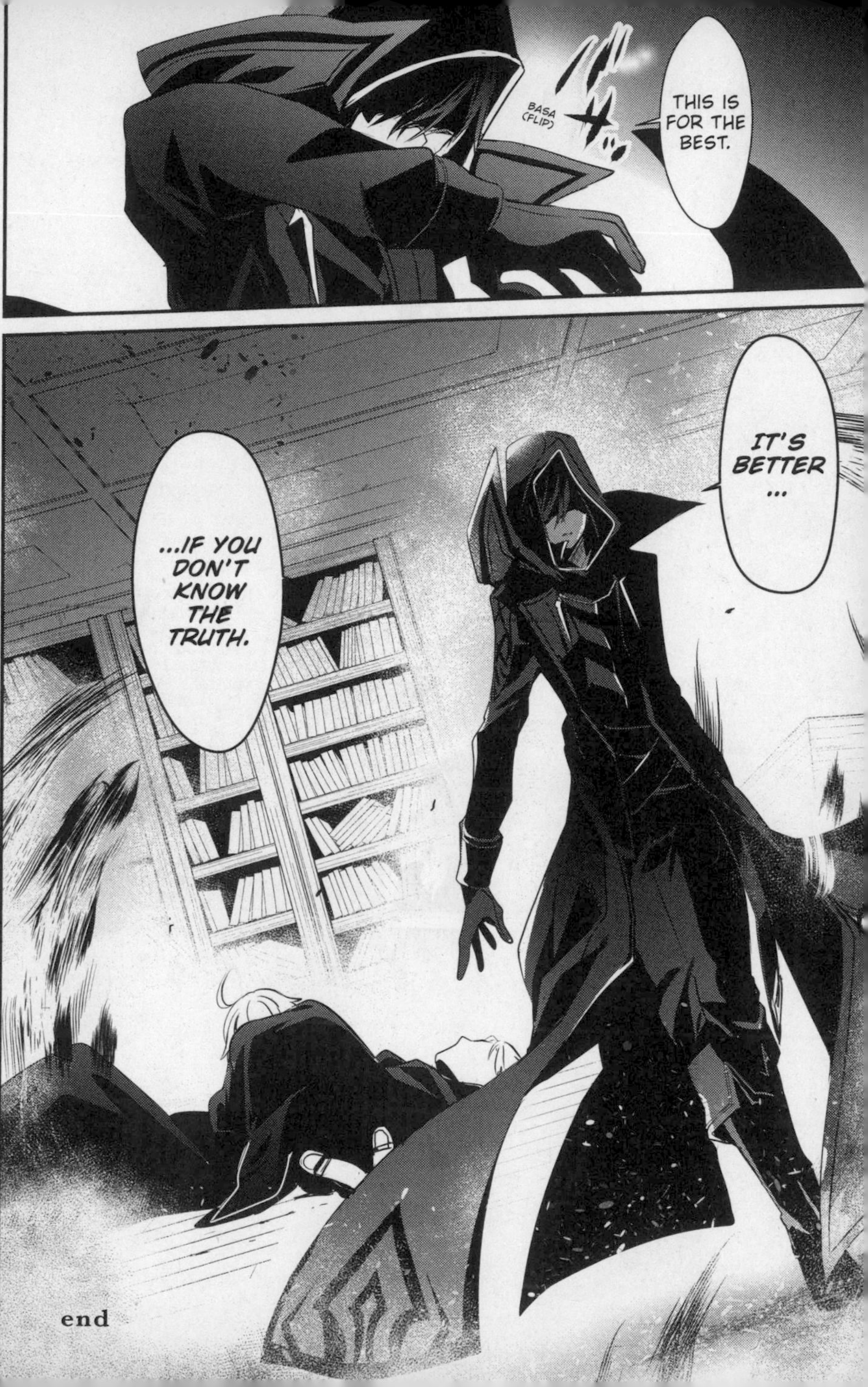
THIS IS FOR THE BEST.
BASA (FLIP)
IT'S BETTER ...
...IF YOU DON'T KNOW THE TRUTH.
end

Episode.14

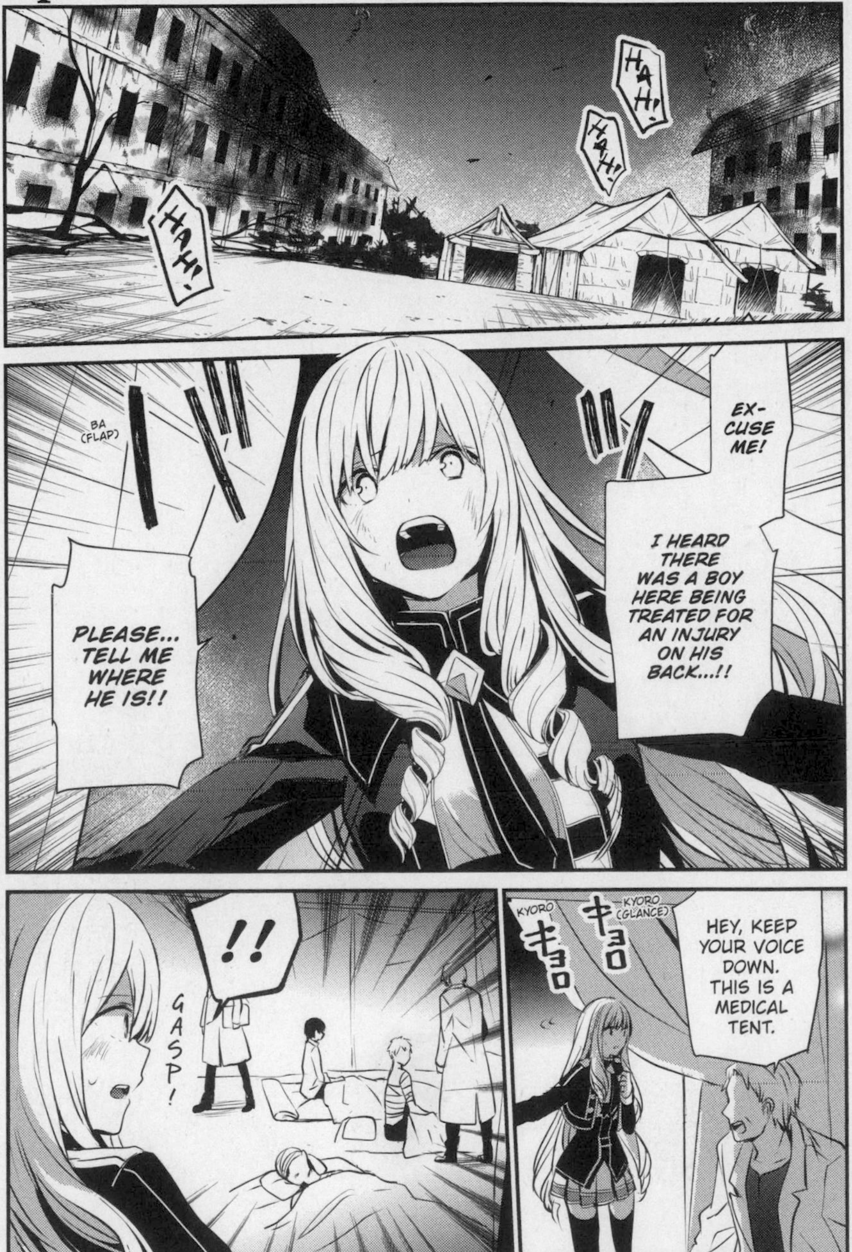
HAH!
HAH!
HAH!
EX-CUSE ME!
BA (FLAP)
I HEARD THERE WAS A BOY HERE BEING TREATED FOR AN INJURY ON HIS BACK...!!
PLEASE... TELL ME WHERE HE IS!!
KYORO (GLANCE)
KYORO
HEY, KEEP YOUR VOICE DOWN. THIS IS A MEDICAL TENT.
!!
GASP!

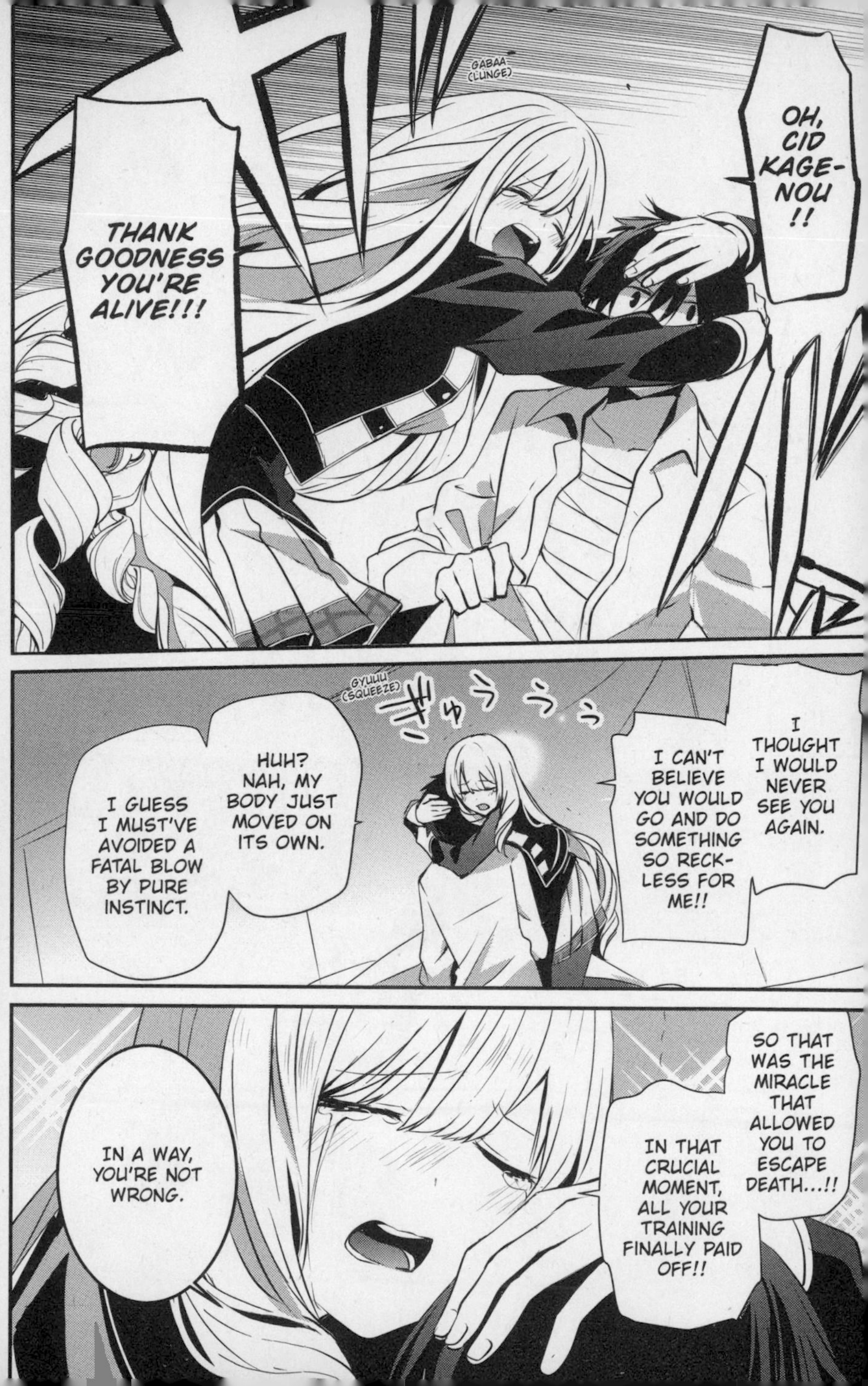
OH, CID KAGE-NOU!!
GABAA (LUNGE)
THANK GOODNESS YOU'RE ALIVE!!!
I THOUGHT I WOULD NEVER SEE YOU AGAIN.
I CAN'T BELIEVE YOU WOULD GO AND DO SOMETHING SO RECK-LESS FOR ME!!
GYUUU (SQUEEZE)
HUH? NAH, MY BODY JUST MOVED ON ITS OWN.
I GUESS I MUST'VE AVOIDED A FATAL BLOW BY PURE INSTINCT.
SO THAT WAS THE MIRACLE THAT ALLOWED YOU TO ESCAPE DEATH...!!
IN THAT CRUCIAL MOMENT, ALL YOUR TRAINING FINALLY PAID OFF!!
IN A WAY, YOU'RE NOT WRONG.

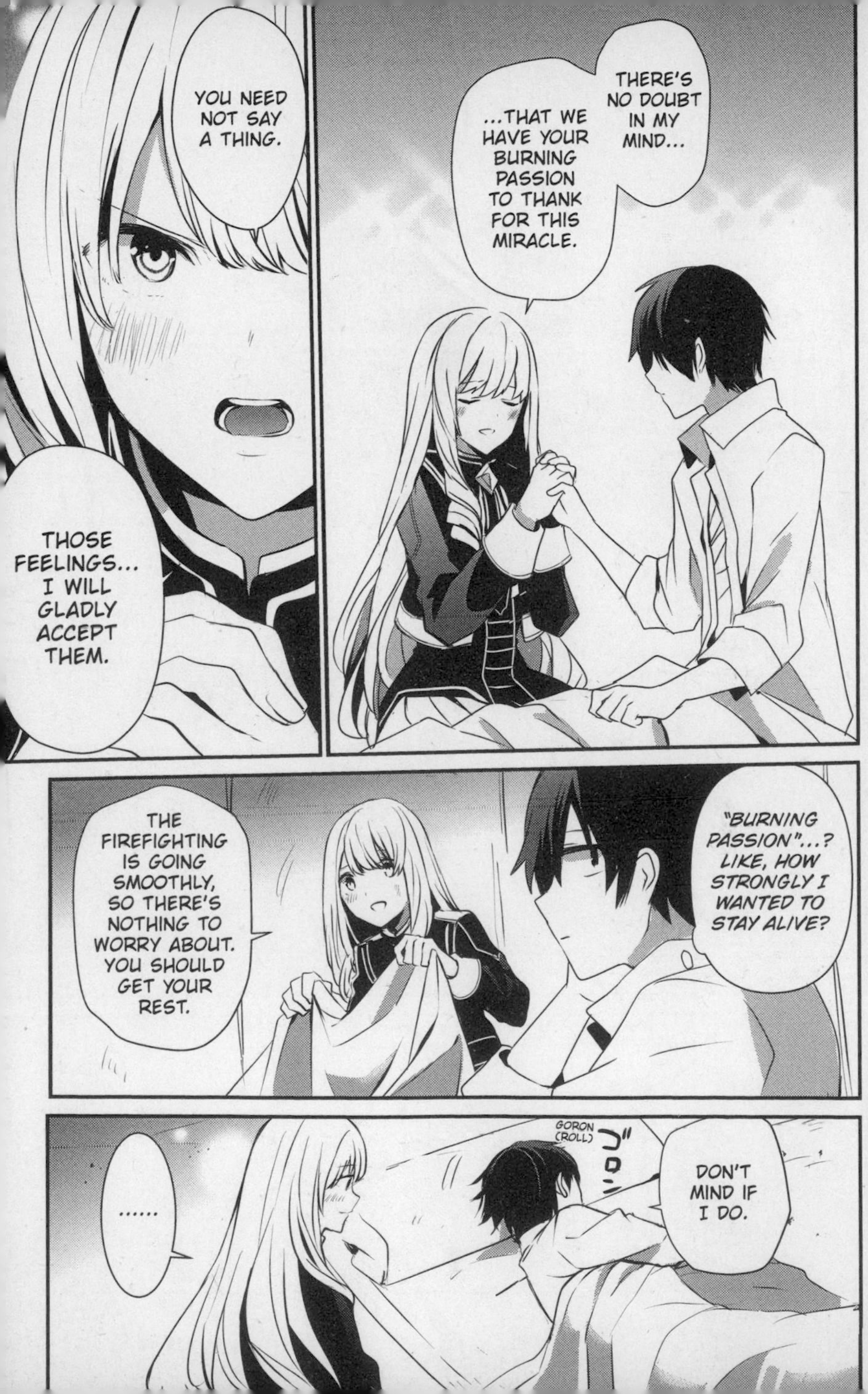
THERE'S NO DOUBT IN MY MIND...
...THAT WE HAVE YOUR BURNING PASSION TO THANK FOR THIS MIRACLE.
YOU NEED NOT SAY A THING.
THOSE FEELINGS... I WILL GLADLY ACCEPT THEM.
"BURNING PASSION"...? LIKE, HOW STRONGLY I WANTED TO STAY ALIVE?
THE FIREFIGHTING IS GOING SMOOTHLY, SO THERE'S NOTHING TO WORRY ABOUT. YOU SHOULD GET YOUR REST.
GORON (ROLL)
DON'T MIND IF I DO.
......

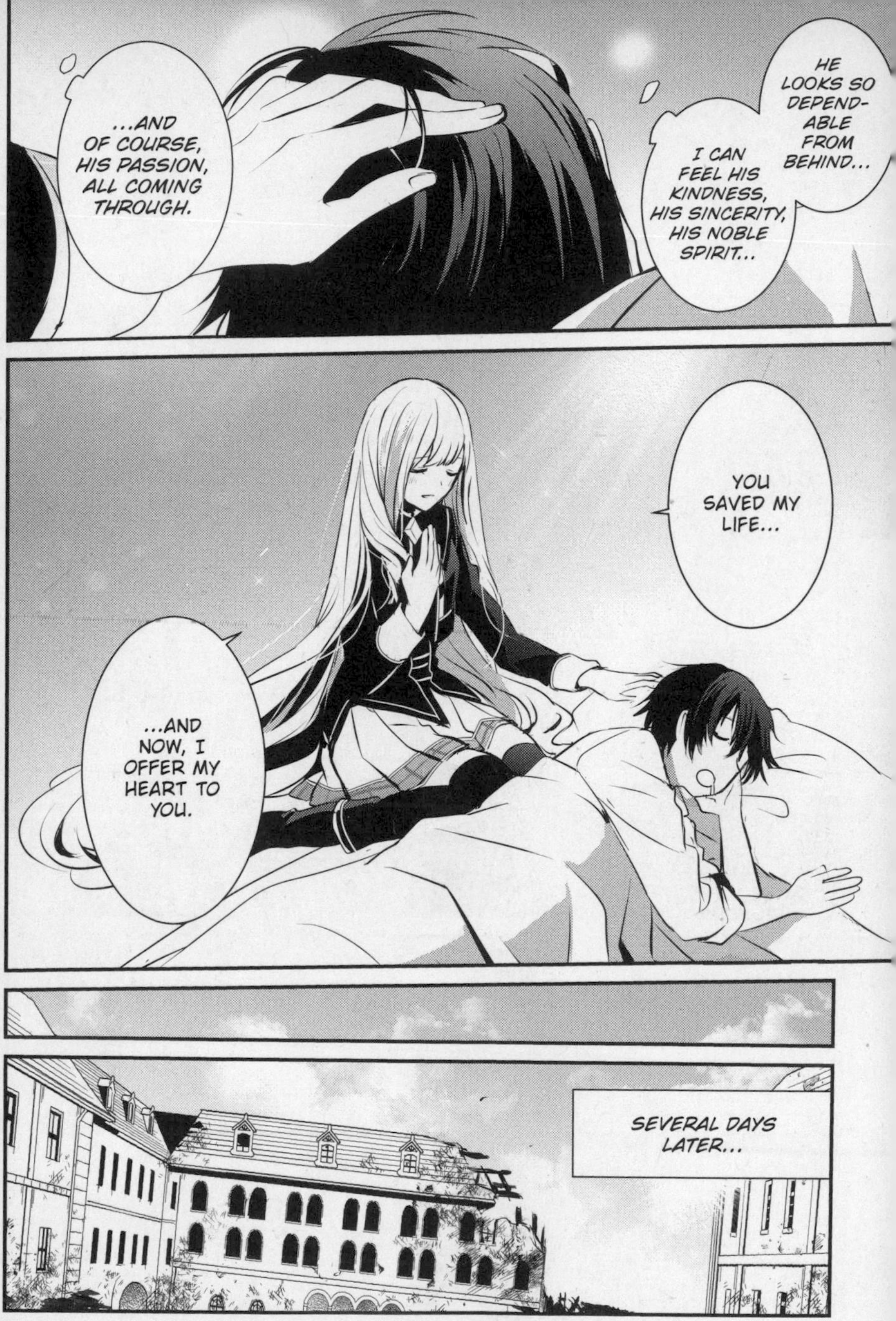
HE LOOKS SO DEPEND-ABLE FROM BEHIND...
I CAN FEEL HIS KINDNESS, HIS SINCERITY, HIS NOBLE SPIRIT...
...AND OF COURSE, HIS PASSION, ALL COMING THROUGH.
YOU SAVED MY LIFE...
...AND NOW, I OFFER MY HEART TO YOU.
SEVERAL DAYS LATER...

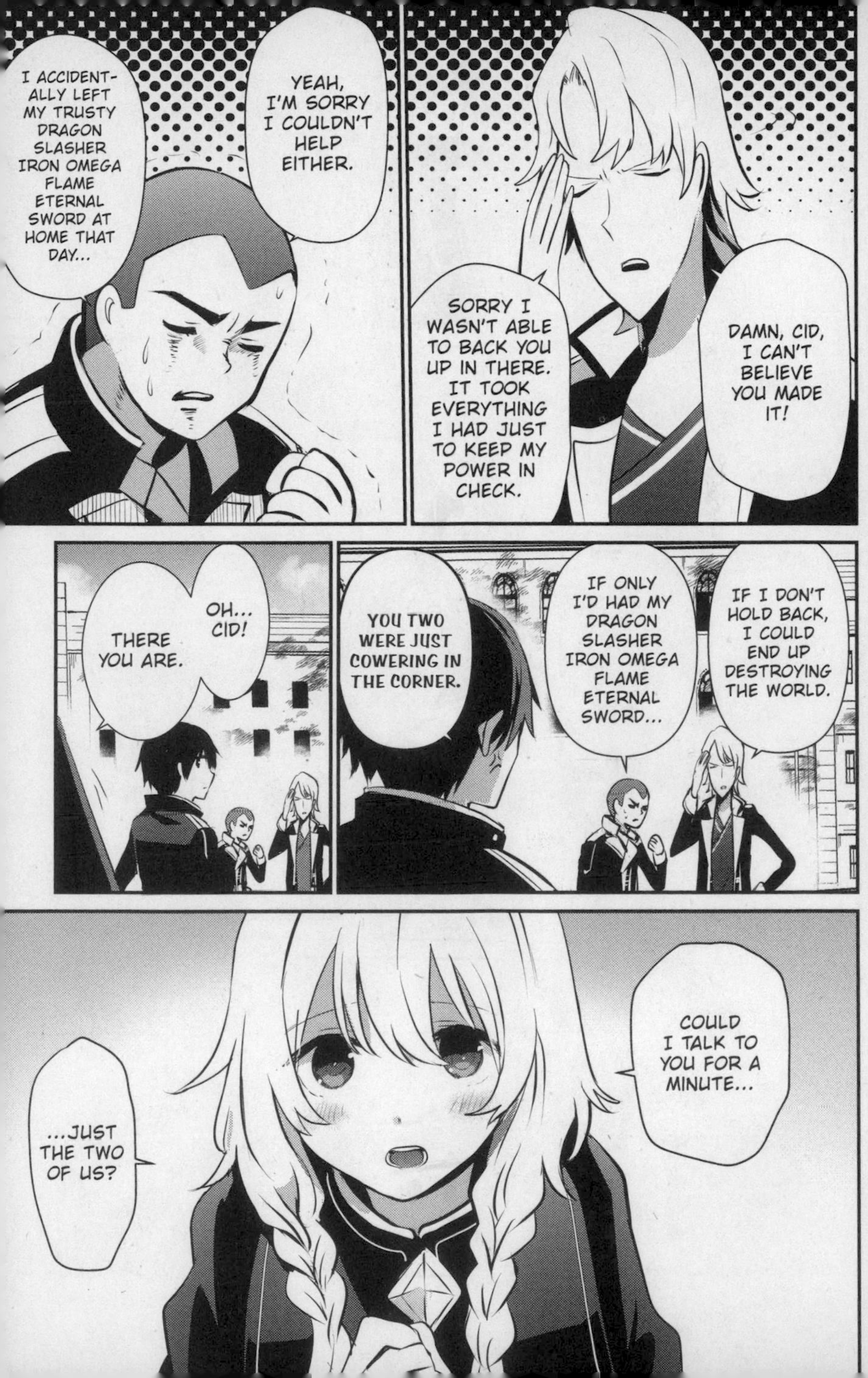
DAMN, CID, I CAN'T BELIEVE YOU MADE IT!
SORRY I WASN'T ABLE TO BACK YOU UP IN THERE. IT TOOK EVERYTHING I HAD JUST TO KEEP MY POWER IN CHECK.
YEAH, I'M SORRY I COULDN'T HELP EITHER.
I ACCIDENT-ALLY LEFT MY TRUSTY DRAGON SLASHER IRON OMEGA FLAME ETERNAL SWORD AT HOME THAT DAY...
IF I DON'T HOLD BACK, I COULD END UP DESTROYING THE WORLD.
IF ONLY I'D HAD MY DRAGON SLASHER IRON OMEGA FLAME ETERNAL SWORD...
YOU TWO WERE JUST COWERING IN THE CORNER.
OH... CID!
THERE YOU ARE.
COULD I TALK TO YOU FOR A MINUTE...
...JUST THE TWO OF US?

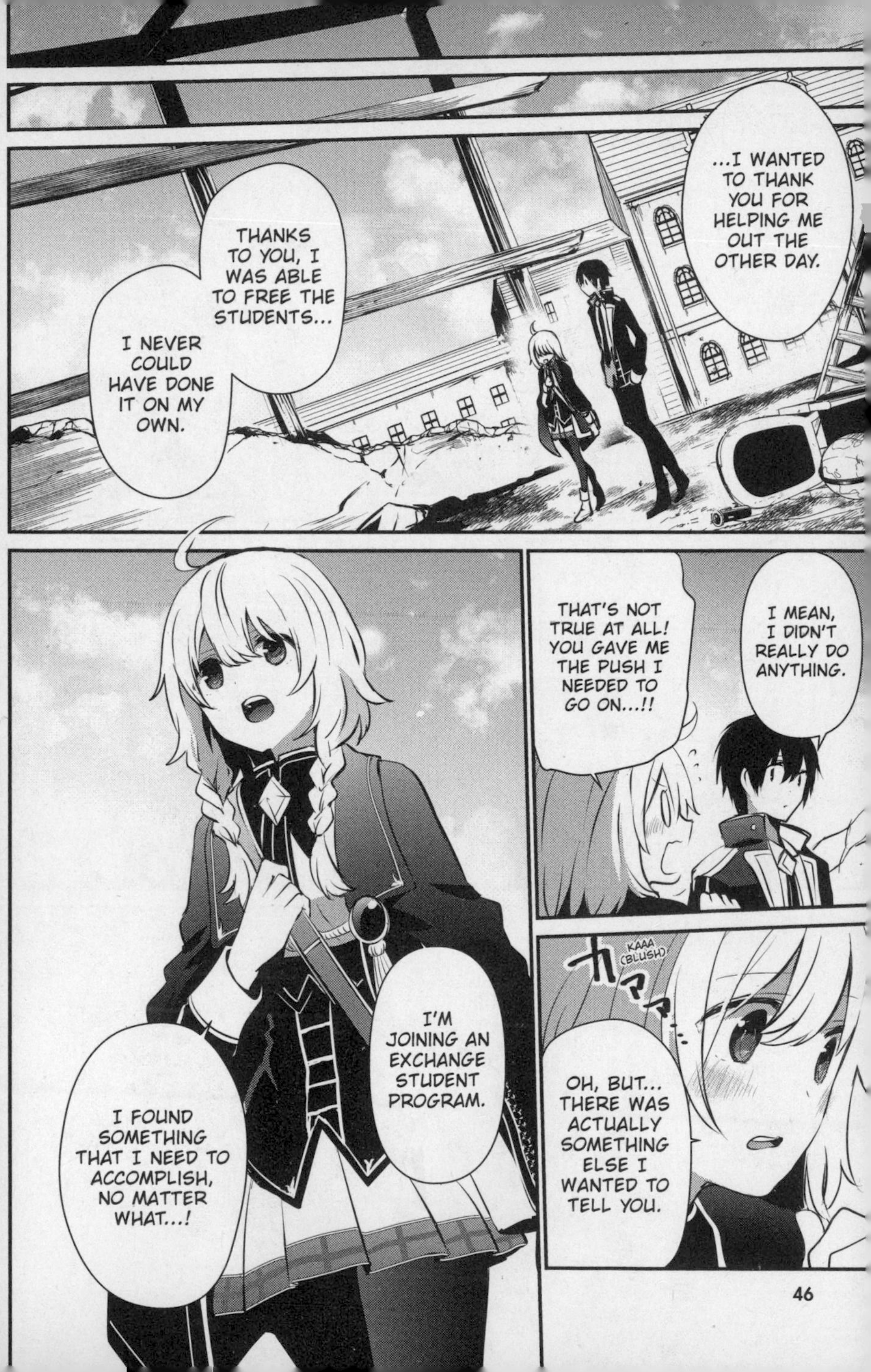
...I WANTED TO THANK YOU FOR HELPING ME OUT THE OTHER DAY.
THANKS TO YOU, I WAS ABLE TO FREE THE STUDENTS...
I NEVER COULD HAVE DONE IT ON MY OWN.
I MEAN, I DIDN'T REALLY DO ANYTHING.
THAT'S NOT TRUE AT ALL! YOU GAVE ME THE PUSH I NEEDED TO GO ON...!!
KAAA (BLUSH)
OH, BUT... THERE WAS ACTUALLY SOMETHING ELSE I WANTED TO TELL YOU.
I'M JOINING AN EXCHANGE STUDENT PROGRAM.
I FOUND SOMETHING THAT I NEED TO ACCOMPLISH, NO MATTER WHAT...!

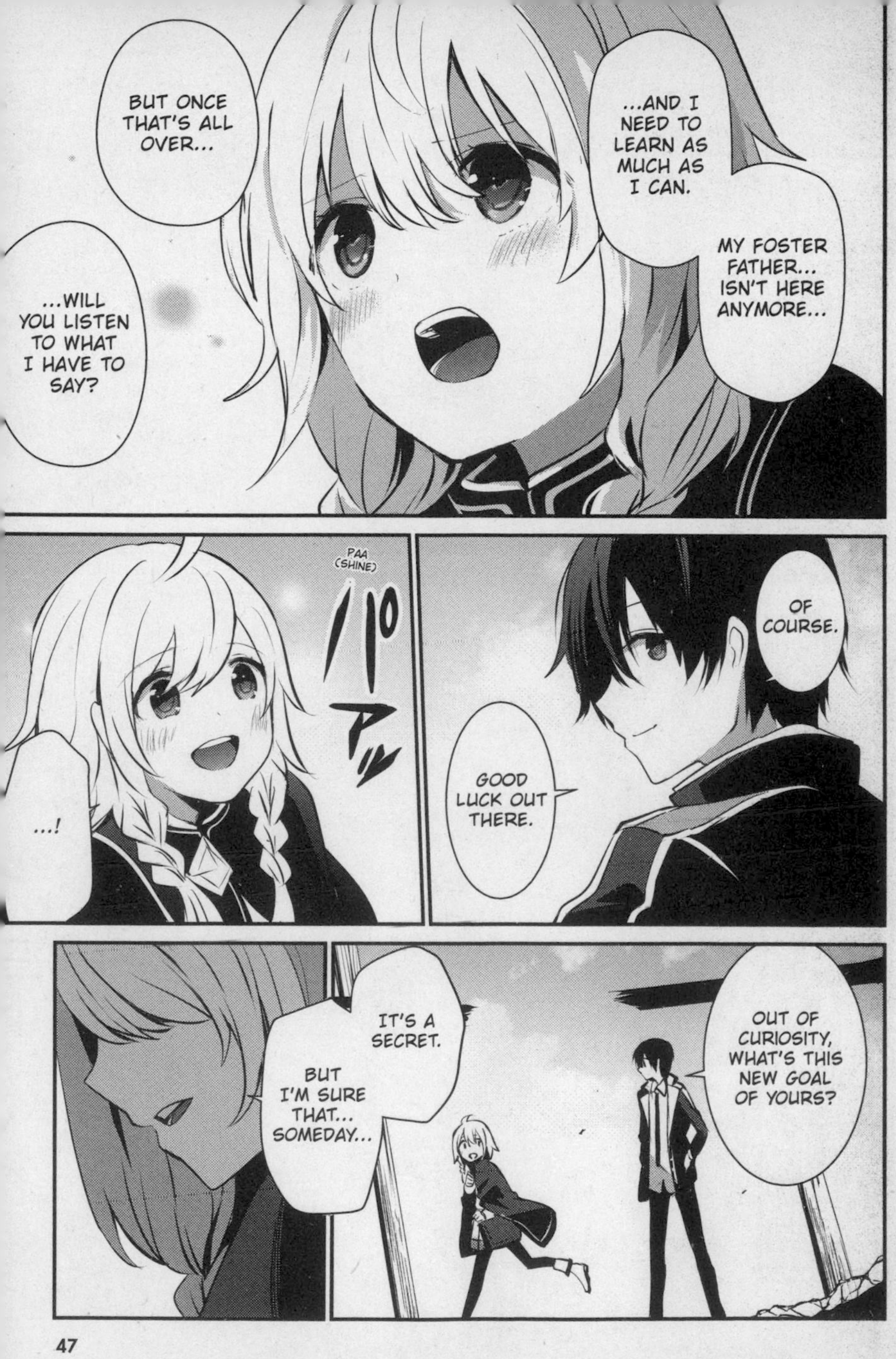
...AND I NEED TO LEARN AS MUCH AS I CAN.
MY FOSTER FATHER... ISN'T HERE ANYMORE...
BUT ONCE THAT'S ALL OVER...
...WILL YOU LISTEN TO WHAT I HAVE TO SAY?
OF COURSE.
GOOD LUCK OUT THERE.
PAA (SHINE)
...!
OUT OF CURIOSITY, WHAT'S THIS NEW GOAL OF YOURS?
IT'S A SECRET.
BUT I'M SURE THAT... SOMEDAY...

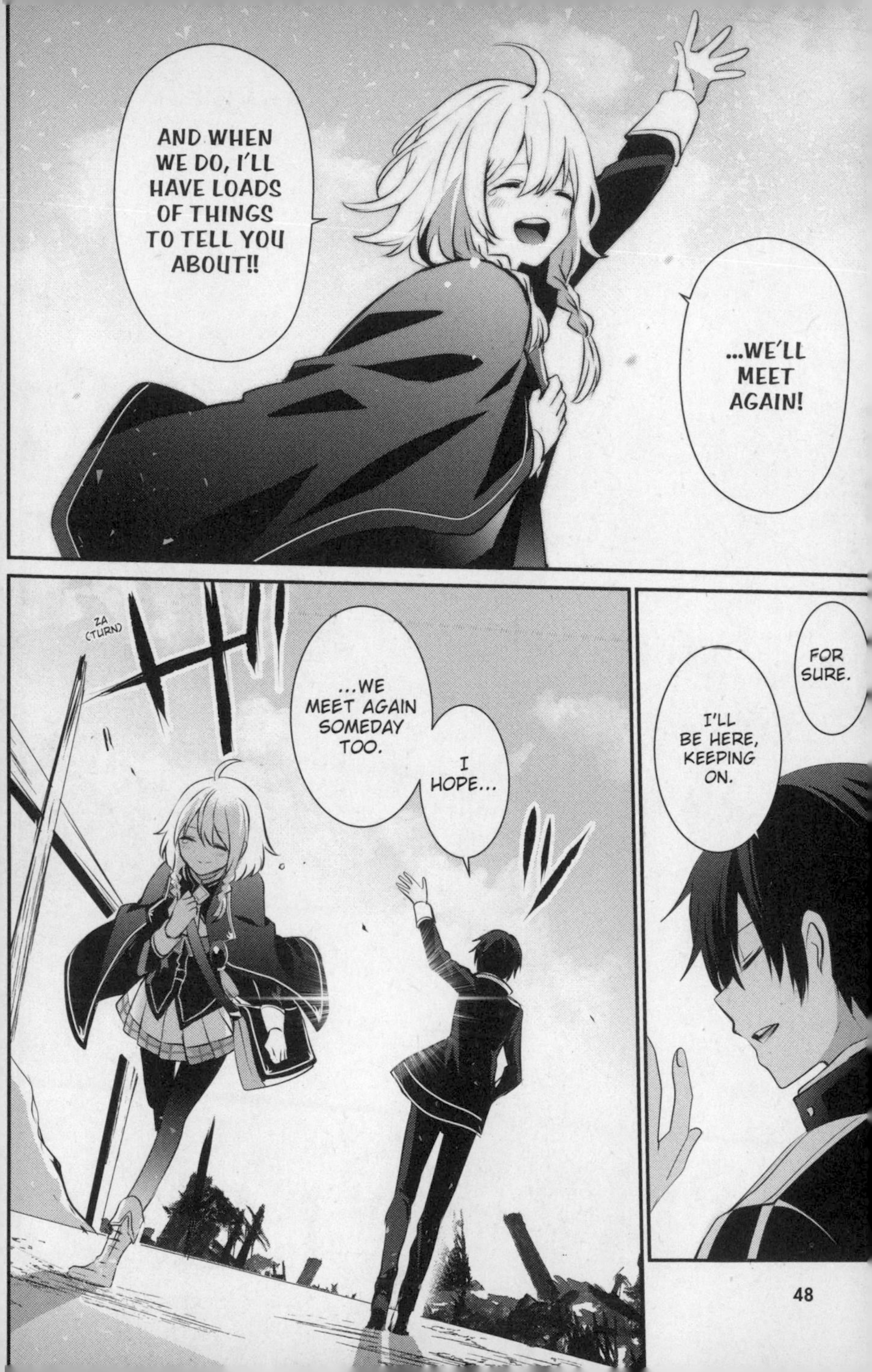

...WE'LL MEET AGAIN!
AND WHEN WE DO, I'LL HAVE LOADS OF THINGS TO TELL YOU ABOUT!!
FOR SURE.
I'LL BE HERE, KEEPING ON.
I HOPE...
...WE MEET AGAIN SOMEDAY TOO.
ZA (TURN)

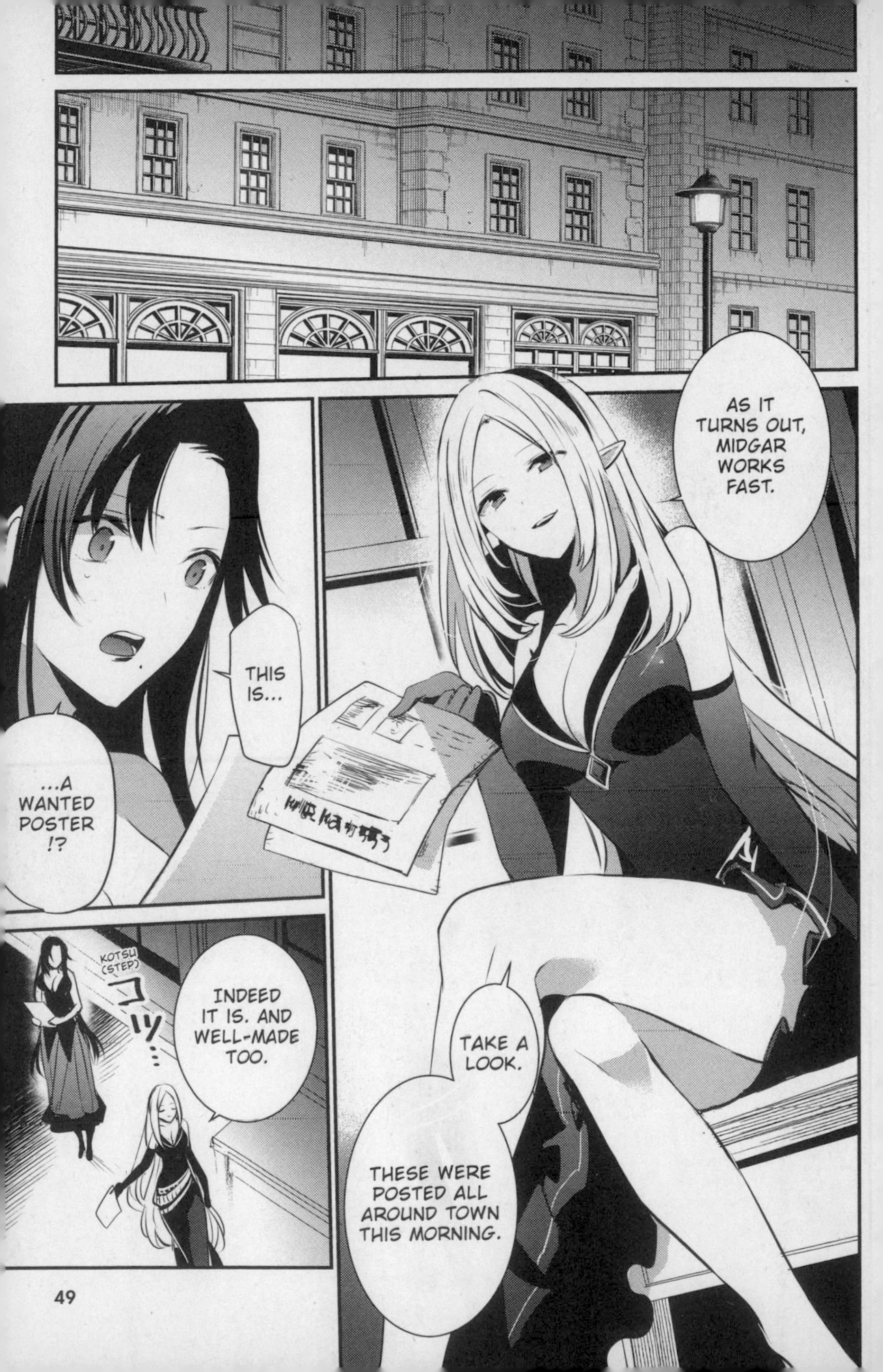

AS IT TURNS OUT, MIDGAR WORKS FAST.
TAKE A LOOK.
THESE WERE POSTED ALL AROUND TOWN THIS MORNING.
THIS IS...
...A WANTED POSTER!?
KOTSU (STEP)
INDEED IT IS. AND WELL-MADE TOO.

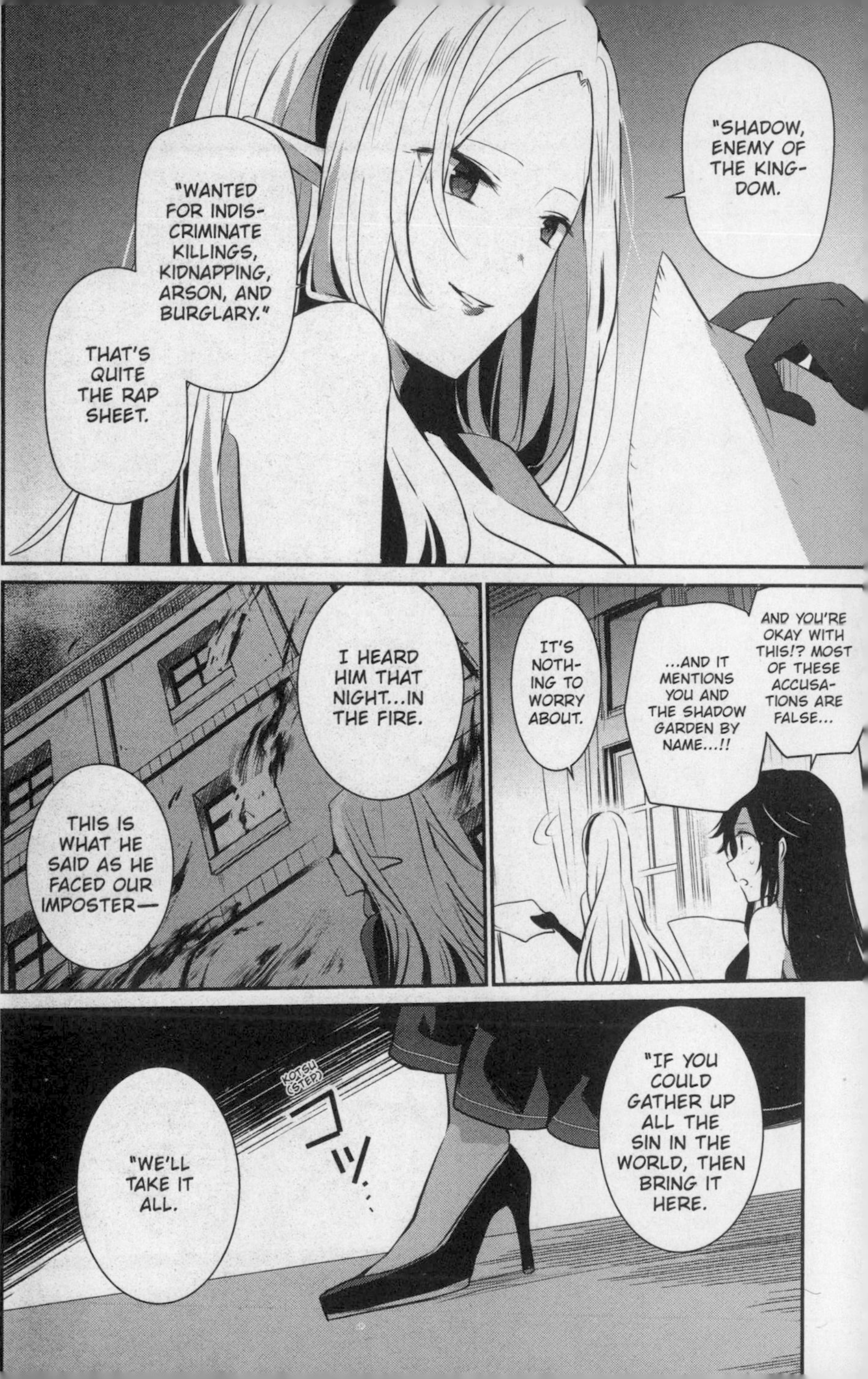
"SHADOW, ENEMY OF THE KINGDOM.
"WANTED FOR INDISCRIMINATE KILLINGS, KIDNAPPING, ARSON, AND BURGLARY."
THAT'S QUITE THE RAP SHEET.
AND YOU'RE OKAY WITH THIS!? MOST OF THESE ACCUSATIONS ARE FALSE...
...AND IT MENTIONS YOU AND THE SHADOW GARDEN BY NAME...!!
IT'S NOTHING TO WORRY ABOUT.
I HEARD HIM THAT NIGHT...IN THE FIRE.
THIS IS WHAT HE SAID AS HE FACED OUR IMPOSTER—
"IF YOU COULD GATHER UP ALL THE SIN IN THE WORLD, THEN BRING IT HERE.
KOTSU (STEP)
コツ
"WE'LL TAKE IT ALL.

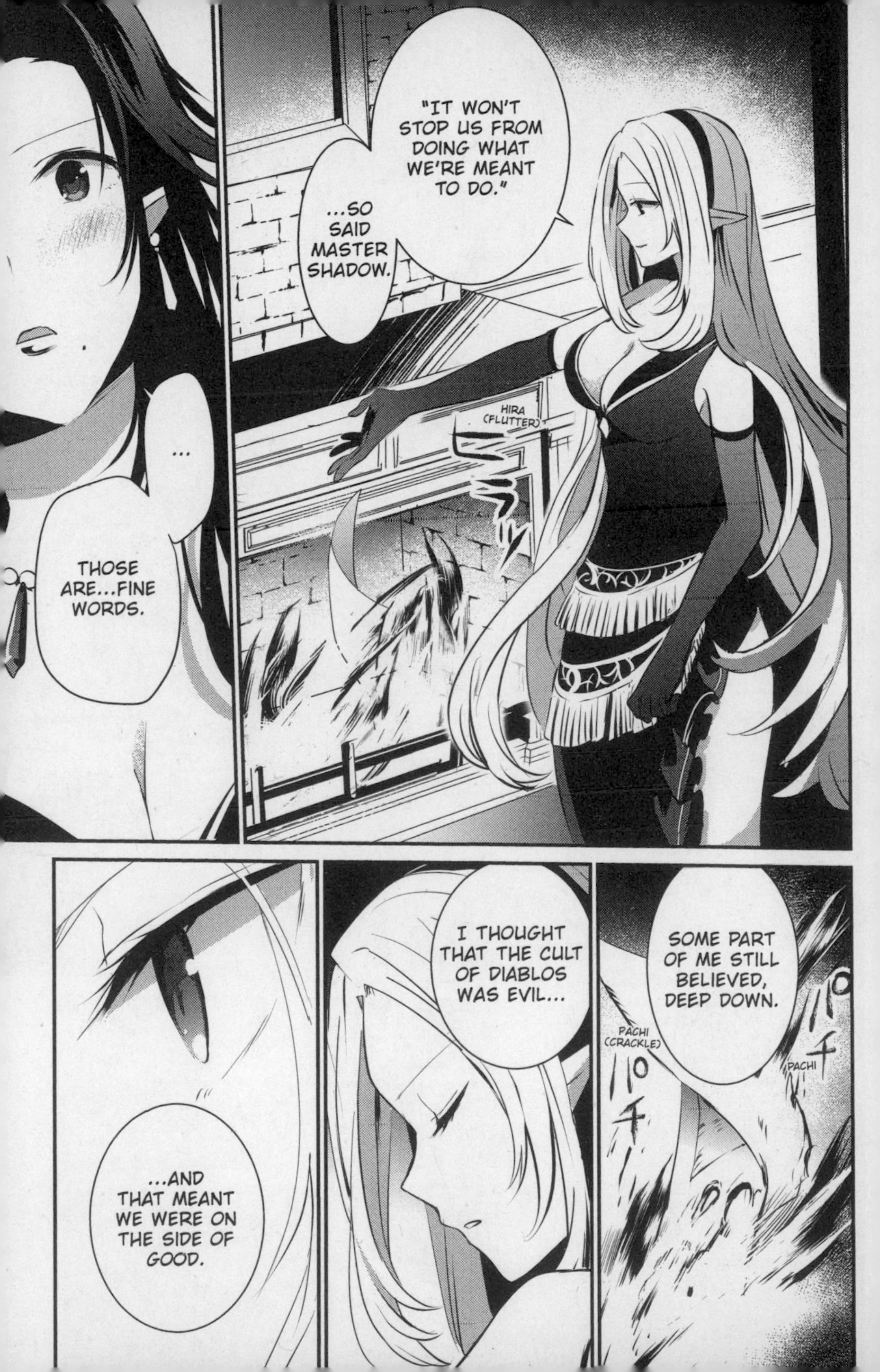
"IT WON'T STOP US FROM DOING WHAT WE'RE MEANT TO DO."
...SO SAID MASTER SHADOW.
HIRA (FLUTTER)
...
THOSE ARE...FINE WORDS.
SOME PART OF ME STILL BELIEVED, DEEP DOWN.
PACHI
PACHI (CRACKLE)
I THOUGHT THAT THE CULT OF DIABLOS WAS EVIL...
...AND THAT MEANT WE WERE ON THE SIDE OF GOOD.

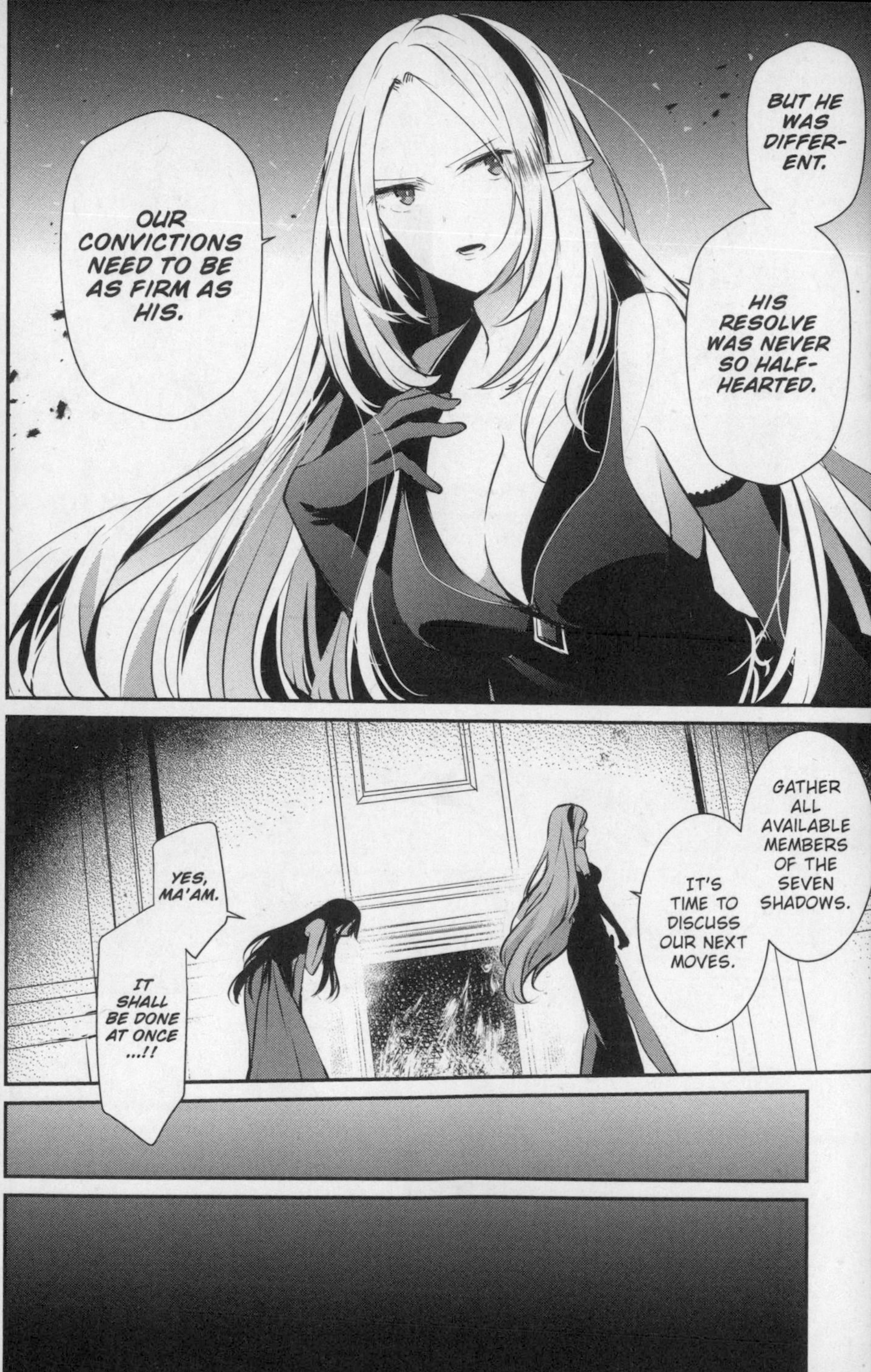
BUT HE WAS DIFFER-ENT.
HIS RESOLVE WAS NEVER SO HALF-HEARTED.
OUR CONVICTIONS NEED TO BE AS FIRM AS HIS.
GATHER ALL AVAILABLE MEMBERS OF THE SEVEN SHADOWS.
IT'S TIME TO DISCUSS OUR NEXT MOVES.
YES, MA'AM.
IT SHALL BE DONE AT ONCE ...!!

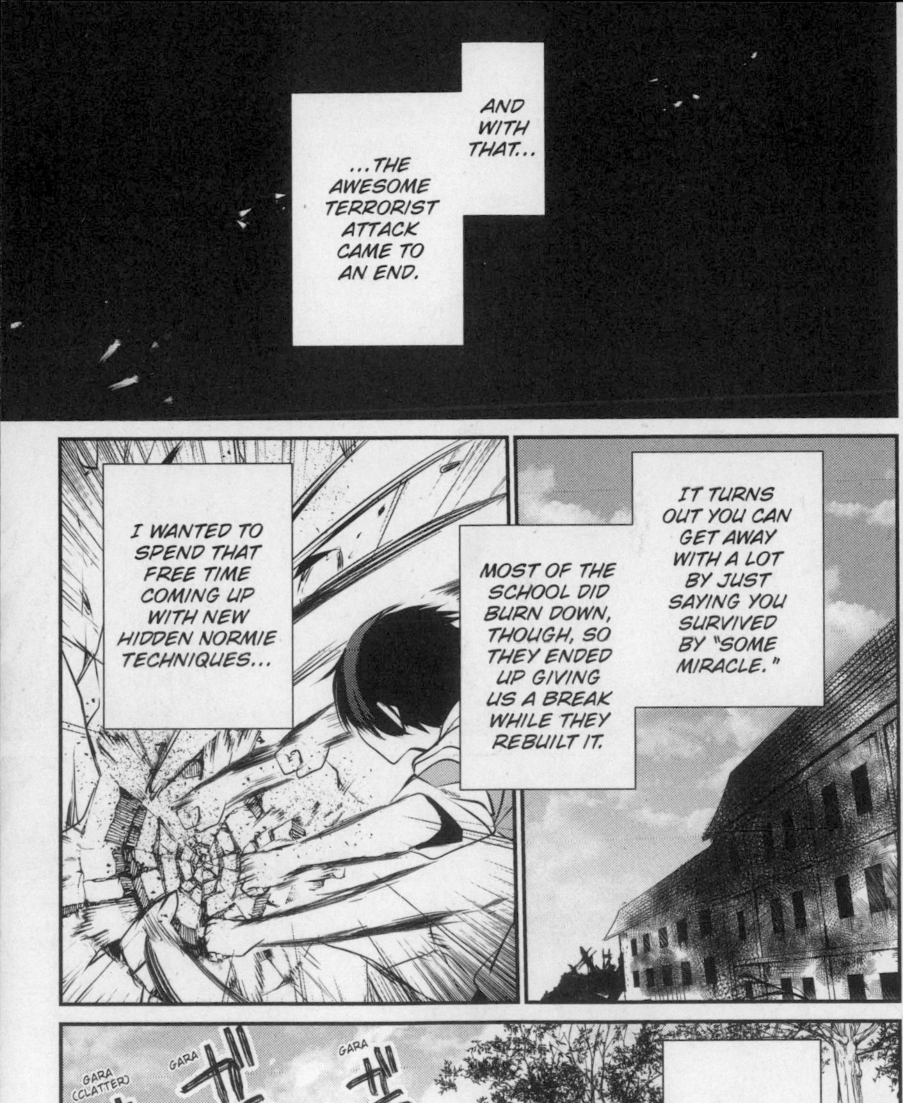
AND WITH THAT...
...THE AWESOME TERRORIST ATTACK CAME TO AN END.
IT TURNS OUT YOU CAN GET AWAY WITH A LOT BY JUST SAYING YOU SURVIVED BY "SOME MIRACLE."
MOST OF THE SCHOOL DID BURN DOWN, THOUGH, SO THEY ENDED UP GIVING US A BREAK WHILE THEY REBUILT IT.
I WANTED TO SPEND THAT FREE TIME COMING UP WITH NEW HIDDEN NORMIE TECHNIQUES...
...BUT MY PLANS GOT DERAILED.
GARA
GARA
GARA (CLATTER)

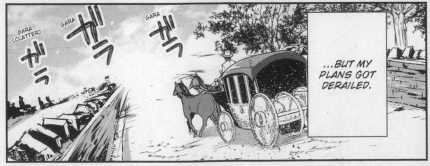

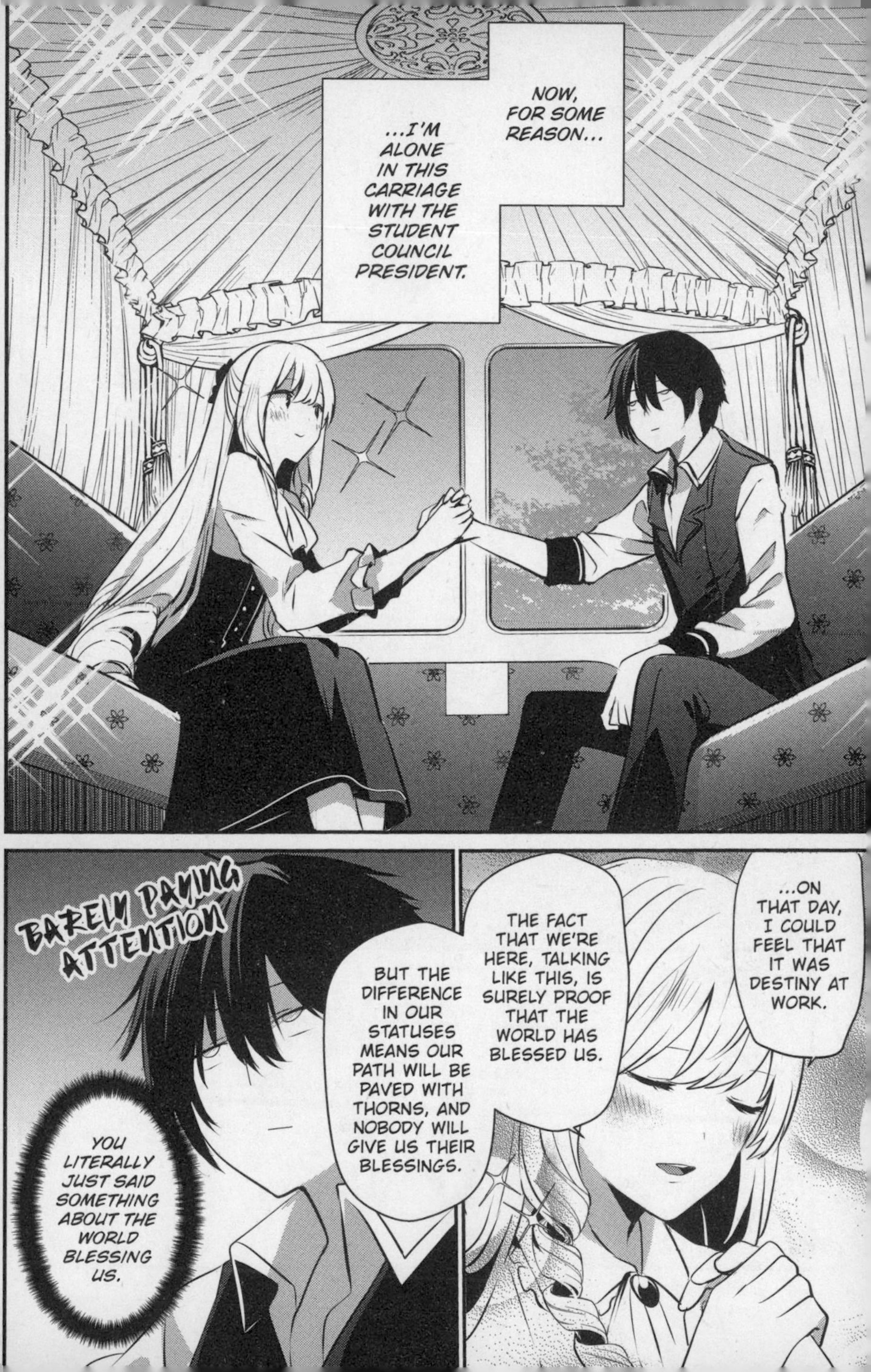
NOW, FOR SOME REASON...
...I'M ALONE IN THIS CARRIAGE WITH THE STUDENT COUNCIL PRESIDENT.
...ON THAT DAY, I COULD FEEL THAT IT WAS DESTINY AT WORK.
THE FACT THAT WE'RE HERE, TALKING LIKE THIS, IS SURELY PROOF THAT THE WORLD HAS BLESSED US.
BUT THE DIFFERENCE IN OUR STATUSES MEANS OUR PATH WILL BE PAVED WITH THORNS, AND NOBODY WILL GIVE US THEIR BLESSINGS.
BARELY PAYING ATTENTION
YOU LITERALLY JUST SAID SOMETHING ABOUT THE WORLD BLESSING US.

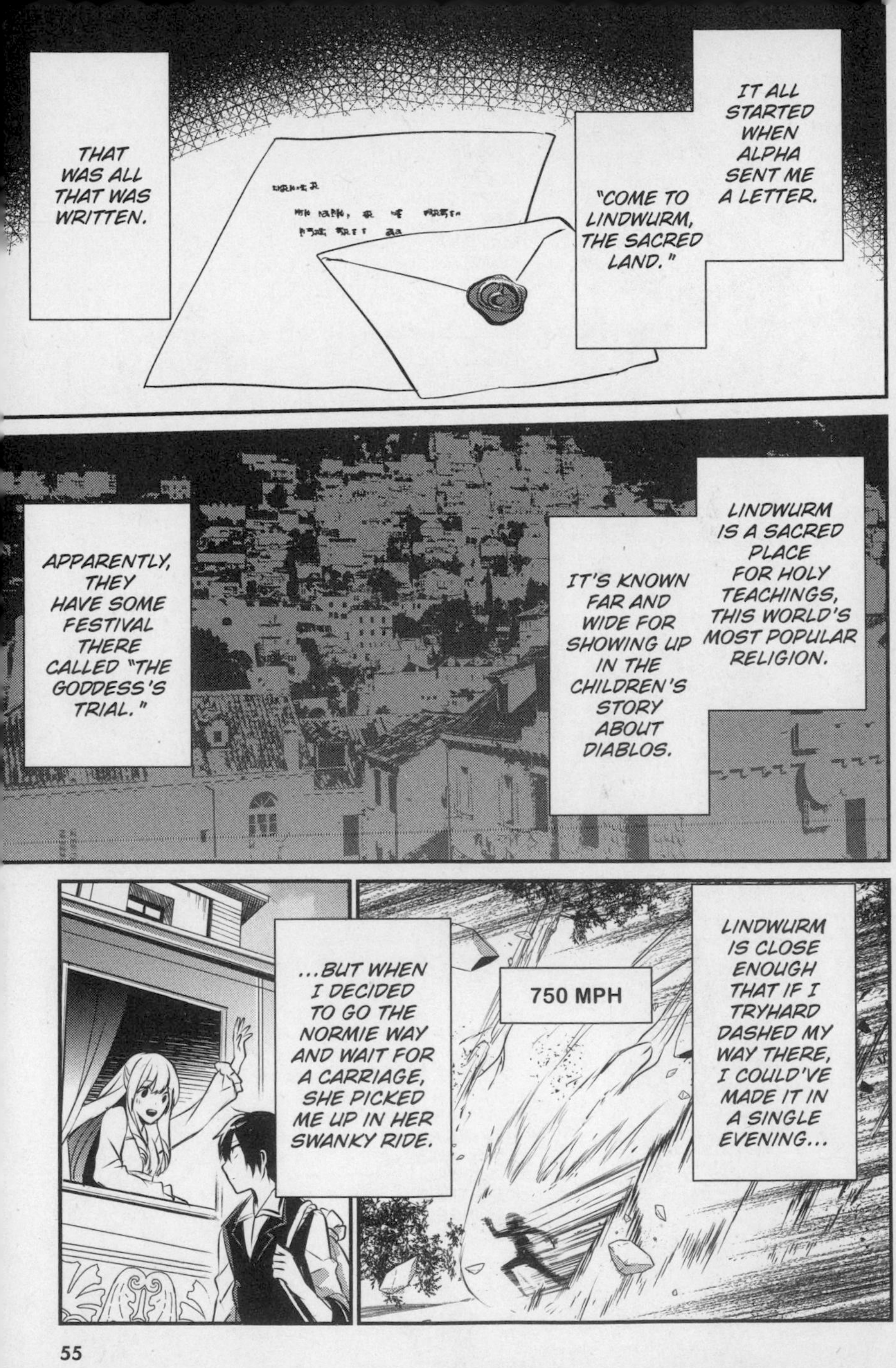
IT ALL STARTED WHEN ALPHA SENT ME A LETTER.
"COME TO LINDWURM, THE SACRED LAND."
THAT WAS ALL THAT WAS WRITTEN.
LINDWURM IS A SACRED PLACE FOR HOLY TEACHINGS, THIS WORLD'S MOST POPULAR RELIGION.
IT'S KNOWN FAR AND WIDE FOR SHOWING UP IN THE CHILDREN'S STORY ABOUT DIABLOS.
APPARENTLY, THEY HAVE SOME FESTIVAL THERE CALLED "THE GODDESS'S TRIAL."
LINDWURM IS CLOSE ENOUGH THAT IF I TRYHARD DASHED MY WAY THERE, I COULD'VE MADE IT IN A SINGLE EVENING...
750 MPH
...BUT WHEN I DECIDED TO GO THE NORMIE WAY AND WAIT FOR A CARRIAGE, SHE PICKED ME UP IN HER SWANKY RIDE.

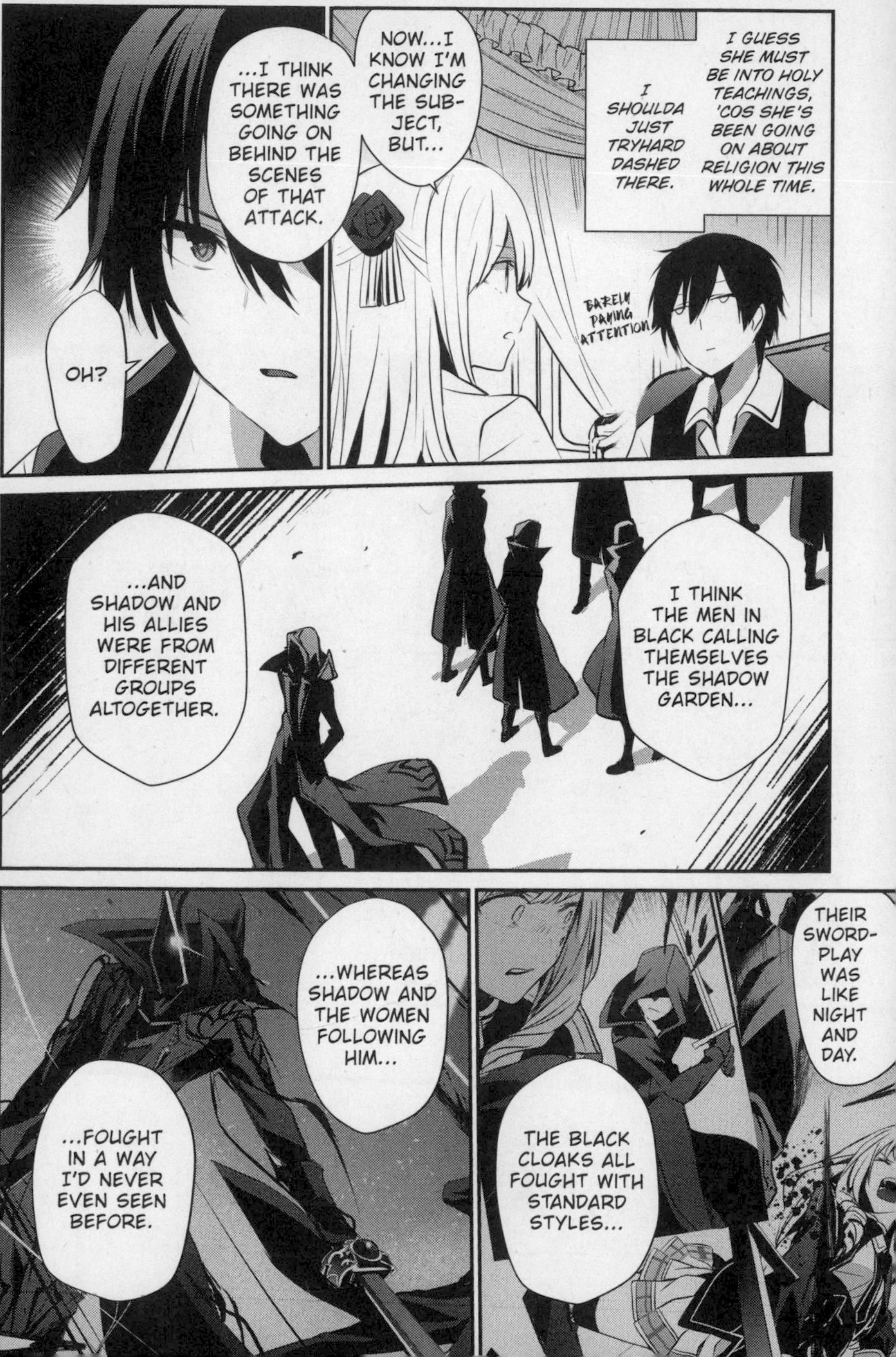
I GUESS SHE MUST BE INTO HOLY TEACHINGS, 'COS SHE'S BEEN GOING ON ABOUT RELIGION THIS WHOLE TIME.
I SHOULDA JUST TRYHARD DASHED THERE.
NOW...I KNOW I'M CHANGING THE SUB-JECT, BUT...
BARELY PAYING ATTENTION
...I THINK THERE WAS SOMETHING GOING ON BEHIND THE SCENES OF THAT ATTACK.
OH?
I THINK THE MEN IN BLACK CALLING THEMSELVES THE SHADOW GARDEN...
...AND SHADOW AND HIS ALLIES WERE FROM DIFFERENT GROUPS ALTOGETHER.
THEIR SWORD-PLAY WAS LIKE NIGHT AND DAY.
THE BLACK CLOAKS ALL FOUGHT WITH STANDARD STYLES...
...WHEREAS SHADOW AND THE WOMEN FOLLOWING HIM...
...FOUGHT IN A WAY I'D NEVER EVEN SEEN BEFORE.

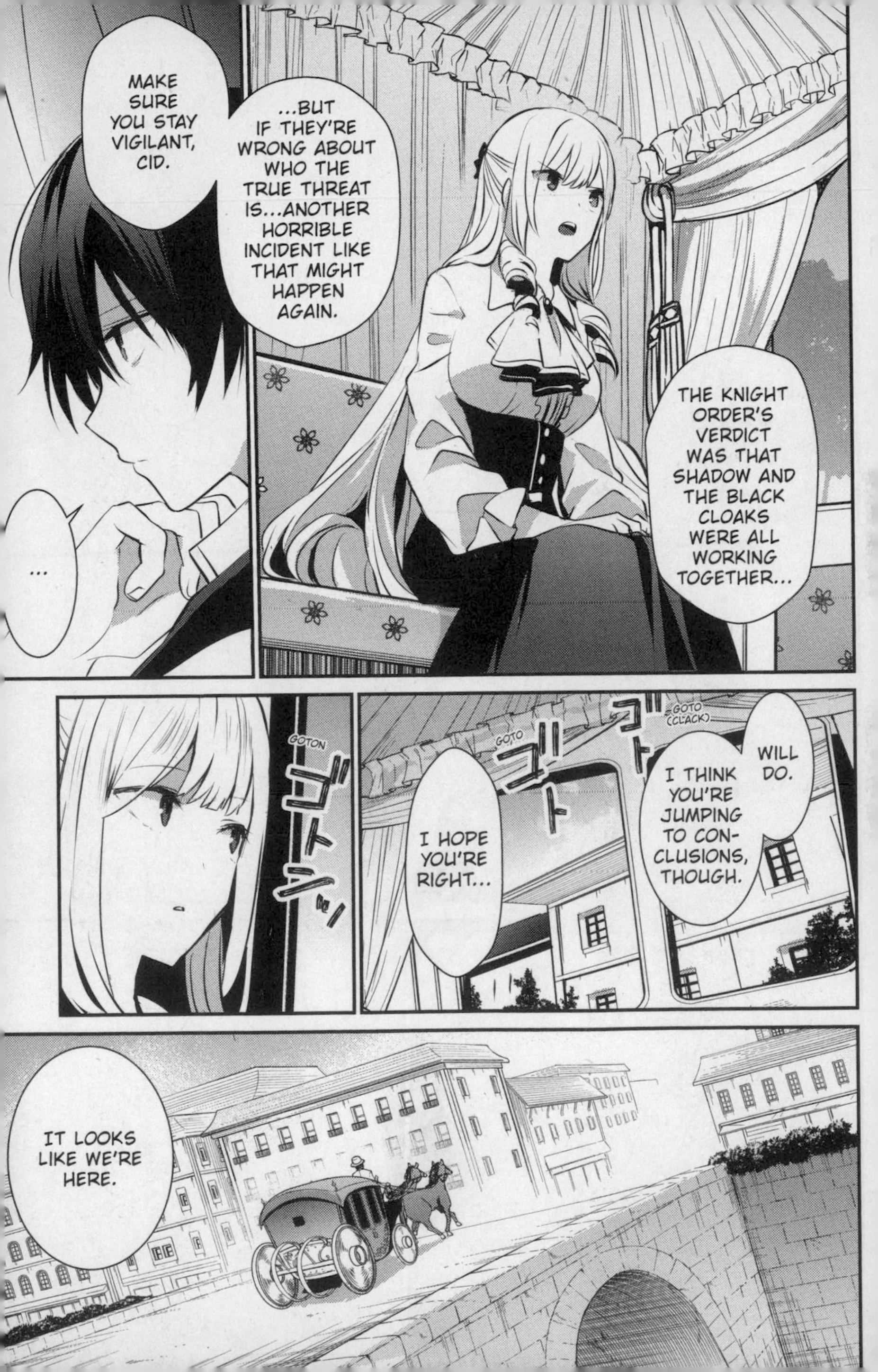
THE KNIGHT ORDER'S VERDICT WAS THAT SHADOW AND THE BLACK CLOAKS WERE ALL WORKING TOGETHER...
...BUT IF THEY'RE WRONG ABOUT WHO THE TRUE THREAT IS...ANOTHER HORRIBLE INCIDENT LIKE THAT MIGHT HAPPEN AGAIN.
MAKE SURE YOU STAY VIGILANT, CID.
...
WILL DO.
I THINK YOU'RE JUMPING TO CONCLUSIONS, THOUGH.
GOTO (CLACK)
GOTO
I HOPE YOU'RE RIGHT...
GOTON
IT LOOKS LIKE WE'RE HERE.

LINDWURM, THE SACRED LAND!

ZAA
(GLEAM)

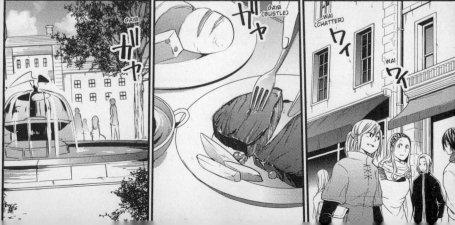

GAYA

GAYA
(BUSTLE)

WAI
(CHATTER)

WAI

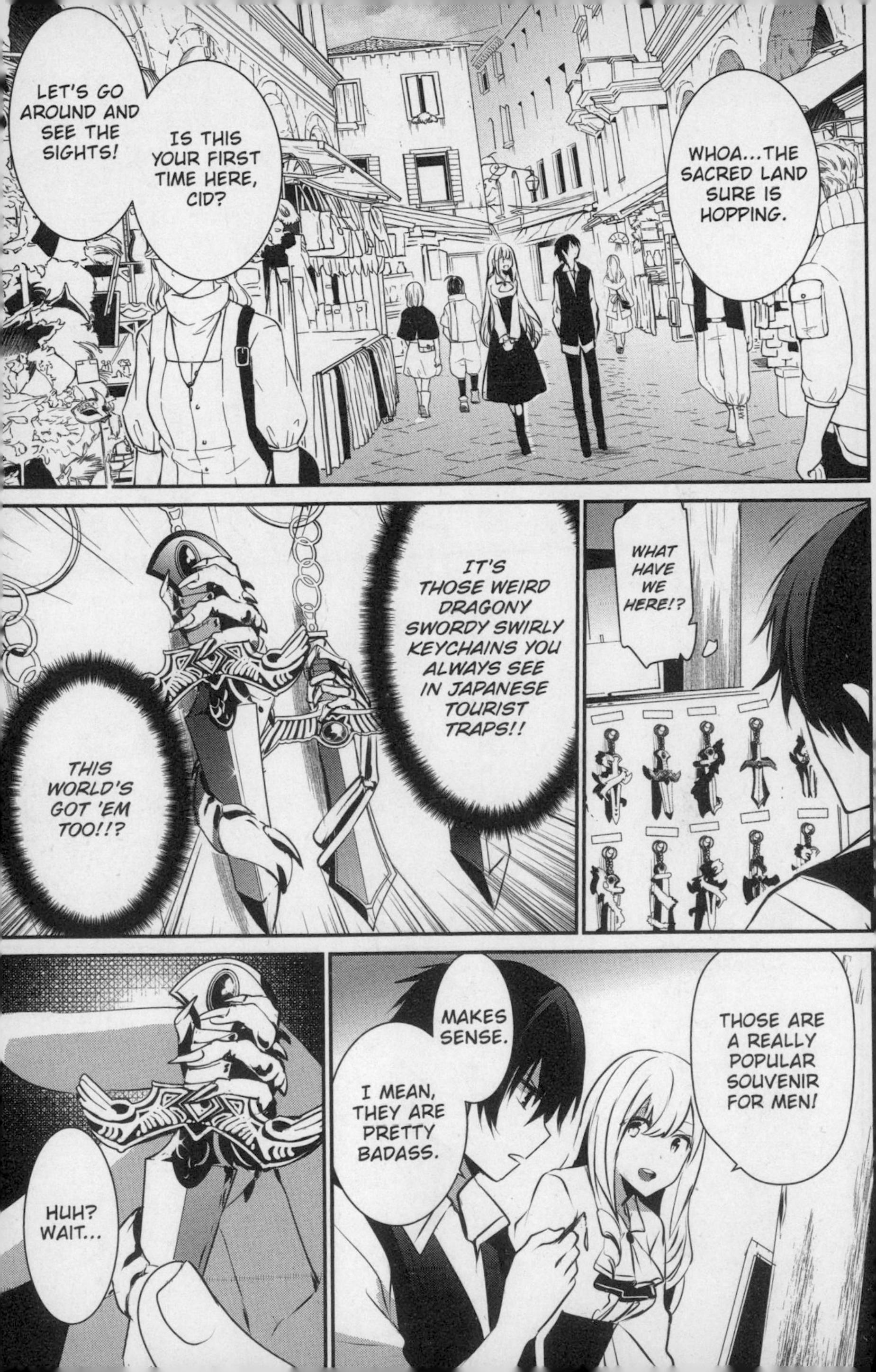
WHOA...THE SACRED LAND SURE IS HOPPING.
IS THIS YOUR FIRST TIME HERE, CID?
LET'S GO AROUND AND SEE THE SIGHTS!
WHAT HAVE WE HERE!?
IT'S THOSE WEIRD DRAGONY SWORDY SWIRLY KEYCHAINS YOU ALWAYS SEE IN JAPANESE TOURIST TRAPS!!
THIS WORLD'S GOT 'EM TOO!!?
THOSE ARE A REALLY POPULAR SOUVENIR FOR MEN!
MAKES SENSE.
I MEAN, THEY ARE PRETTY BADASS.
HUH? WAIT...

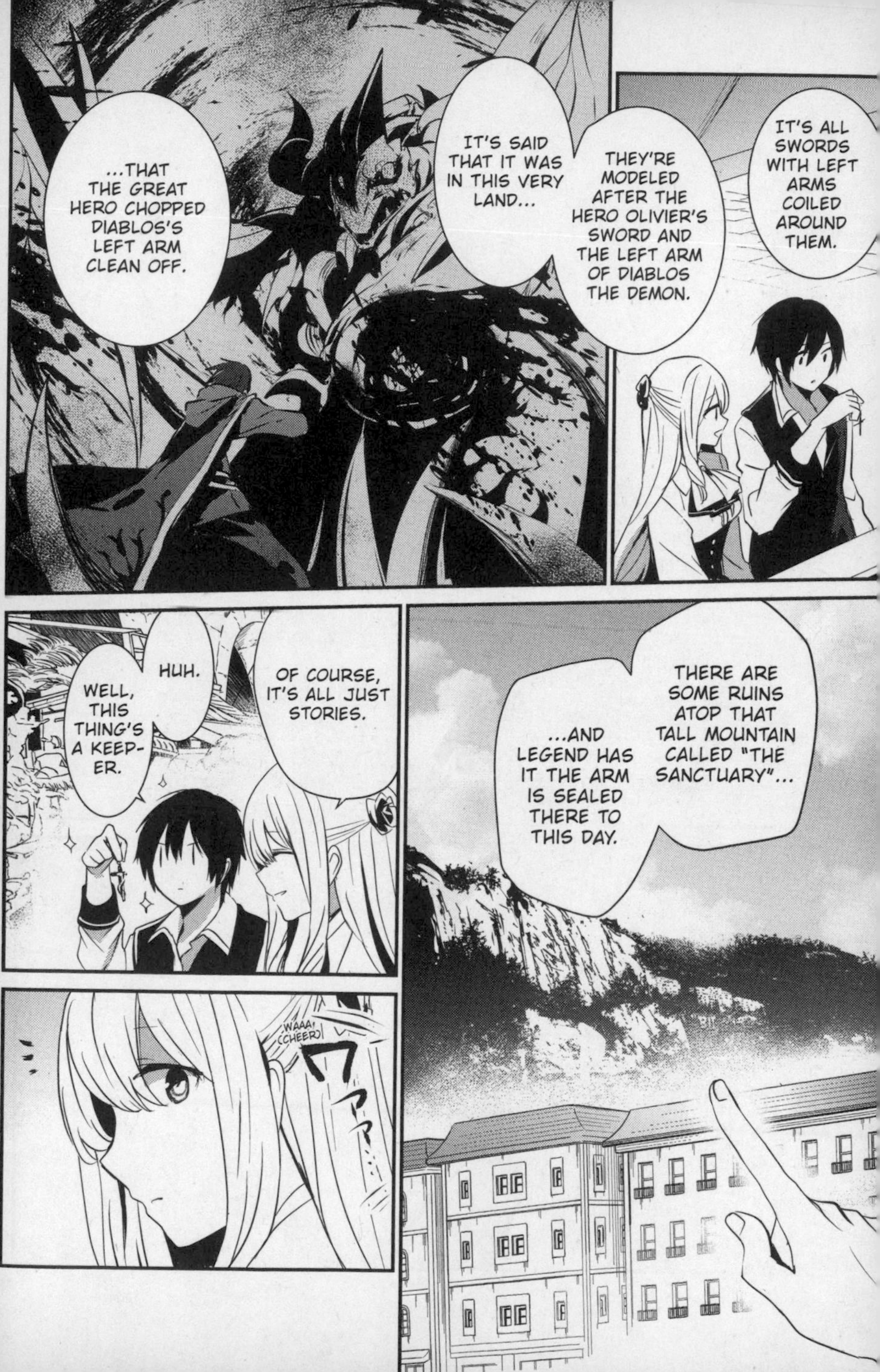
IT'S ALL SWORDS WITH LEFT ARMS COILED AROUND THEM.
THEY'RE MODELED AFTER THE HERO OLIVIER'S SWORD AND THE LEFT ARM OF DIABLOS THE DEMON.
IT'S SAID THAT IT WAS IN THIS VERY LAND...
...THAT THE GREAT HERO CHOPPED DIABLOS'S LEFT ARM CLEAN OFF.
THERE ARE SOME RUINS ATOP THAT TALL MOUNTAIN CALLED "THE SANCTUARY"...
...AND LEGEND HAS IT THE ARM IS SEALED THERE TO THIS DAY.
OF COURSE, IT'S ALL JUST STORIES.
HUH.
WELL, THIS THING'S A KEEP-ER.
WAAA (CHEER)

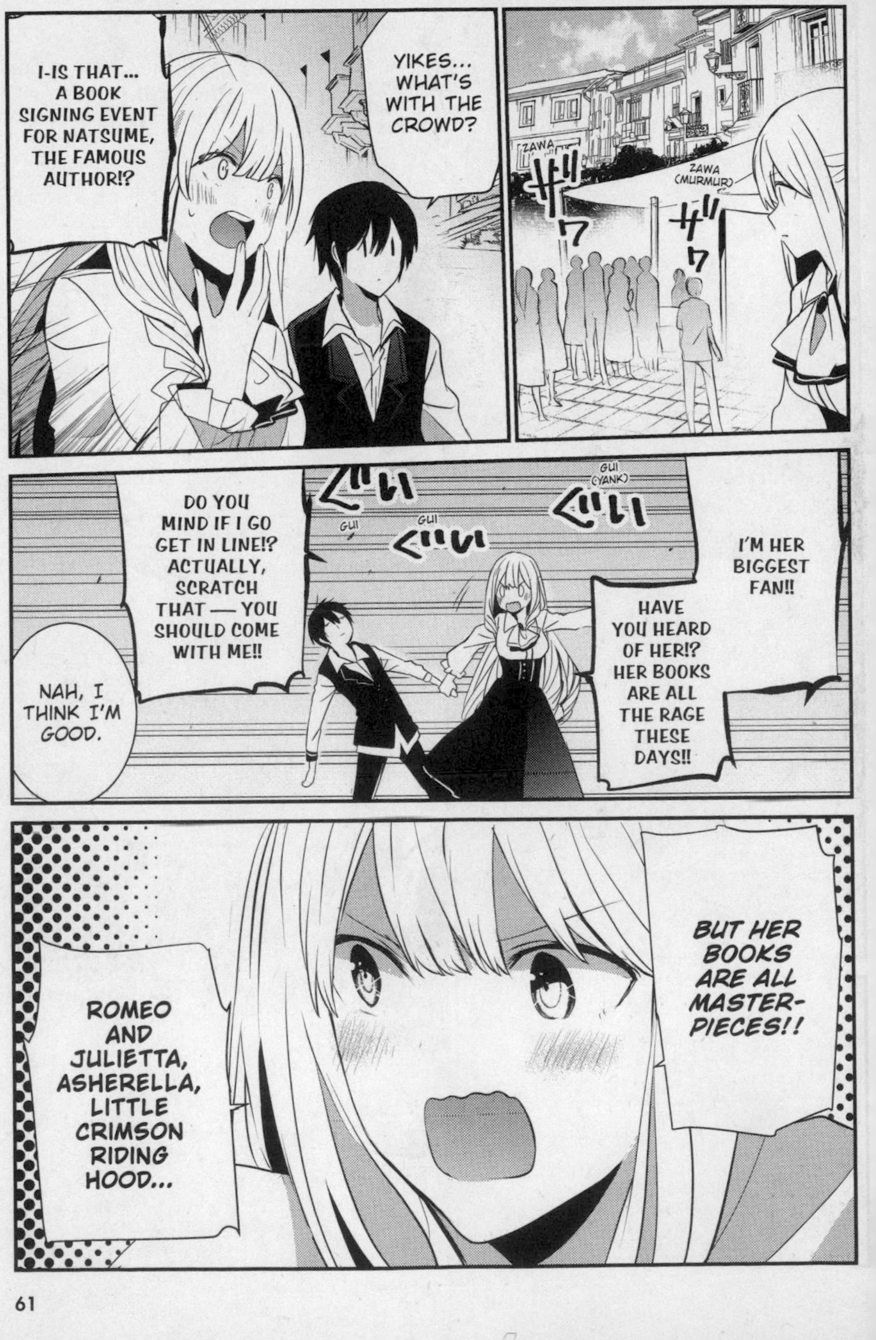
ZAWA
ザワ
ZAWA (MURMUR)
ザワ
YIKES... WHAT'S WITH THE CROWD?
I-IS THAT... A BOOK SIGNING EVENT FOR NATSUME, THE FAMOUS AUTHOR!?
I'M HER BIGGEST FAN!!
HAVE YOU HEARD OF HER!? HER BOOKS ARE ALL THE RAGE THESE DAYS!!
GUI (YANK)
ぐいい
GUI
ぐいい
ぐいい
DO YOU MIND IF I GO GET IN LINE!? ACTUALLY, SCRATCH THAT — YOU SHOULD COME WITH ME!!
NAH, I THINK I'M GOOD.
BUT HER BOOKS ARE ALL MASTER-PIECES!!
ROMEO AND JULIETTA, ASHERELLA, LITTLE CRIMSON RIDING HOOD...

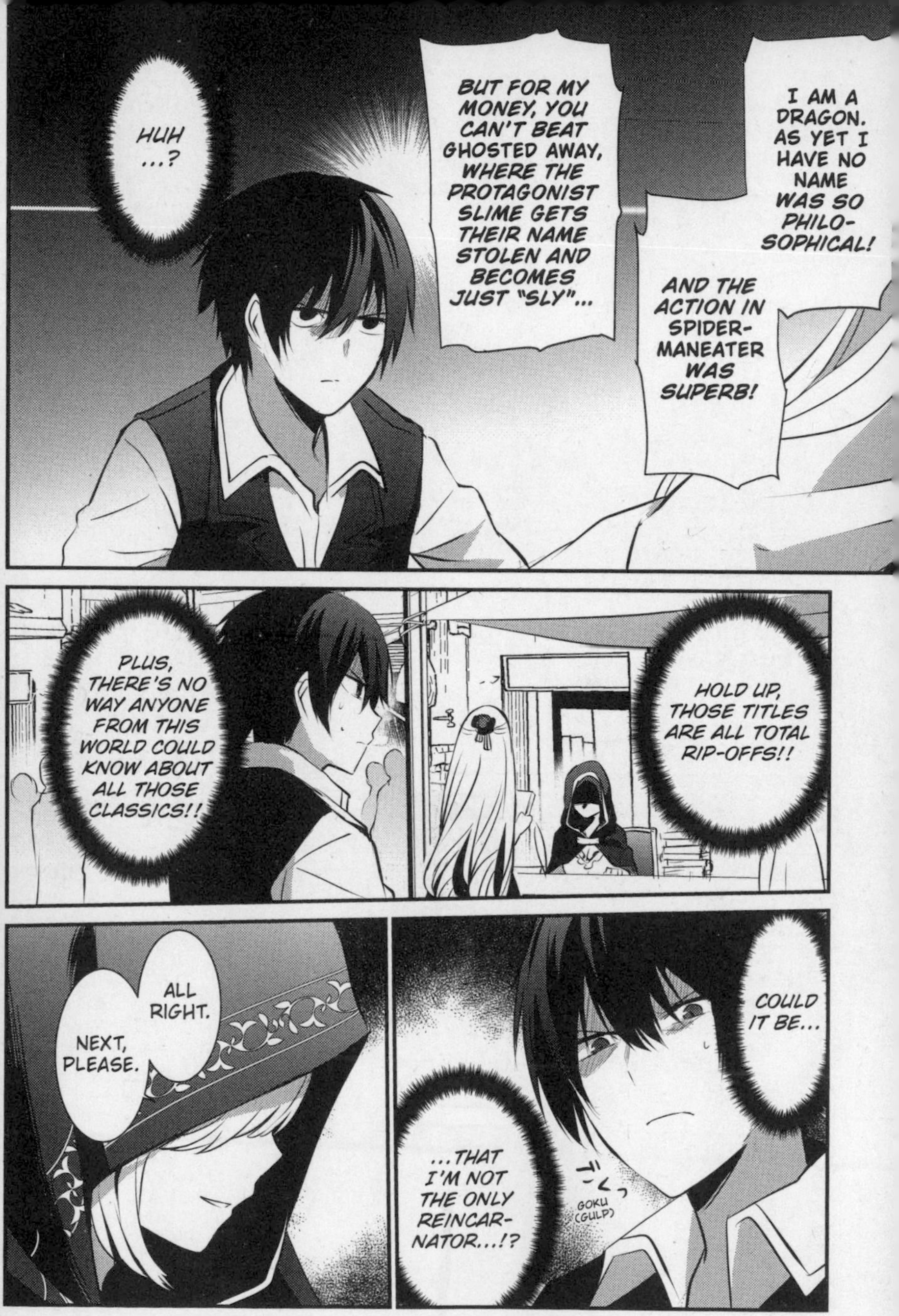
I AM A DRAGON. AS YET I HAVE NO NAME WAS SO PHILO-SOPHICAL!
AND THE ACTION IN SPIDER-MANEATER WAS SUPERB!
BUT FOR MY MONEY, YOU CAN'T BEAT GHOSTED AWAY, WHERE THE PROTAGONIST SLIME GETS THEIR NAME STOLEN AND BECOMES JUST "SLY"...
HUH ...?
HOLD UP, THOSE TITLES ARE ALL TOTAL RIP-OFFS!!
PLUS, THERE'S NO WAY ANYONE FROM THIS WORLD COULD KNOW ABOUT ALL THOSE CLASSICS!!
COULD IT BE...
...THAT I'M NOT THE ONLY REINCAR-NATOR...!?
ゴクッ
GOKU (GULP)
ALL RIGHT.
NEXT, PLEASE.

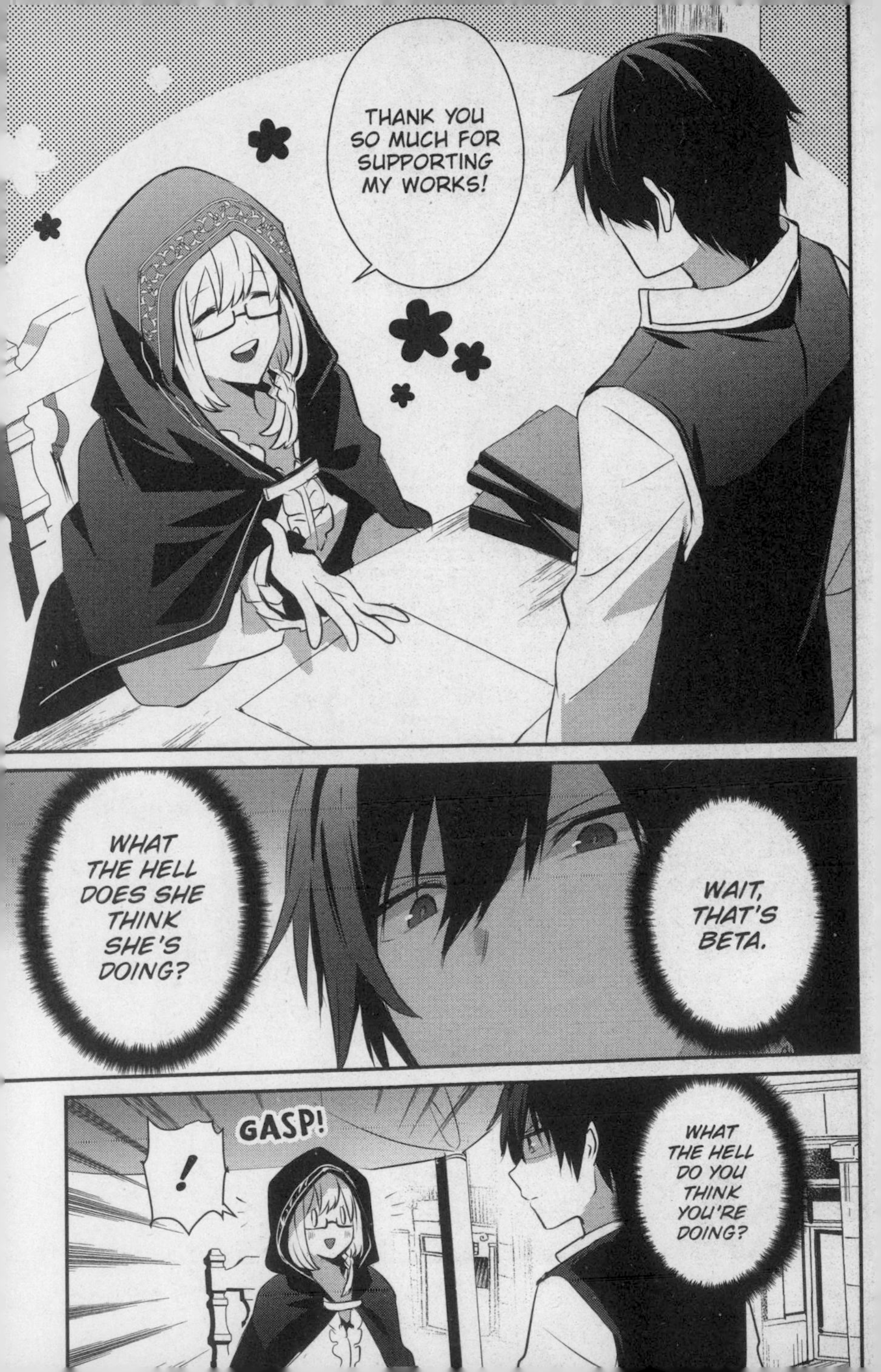
THANK YOU SO MUCH FOR SUPPORTING MY WORKS!
WAIT, THAT'S BETA.
WHAT THE HELL DOES SHE THINK SHE'S DOING?
WHAT THE HELL DO YOU THINK YOU'RE DOING?
GASP!
!

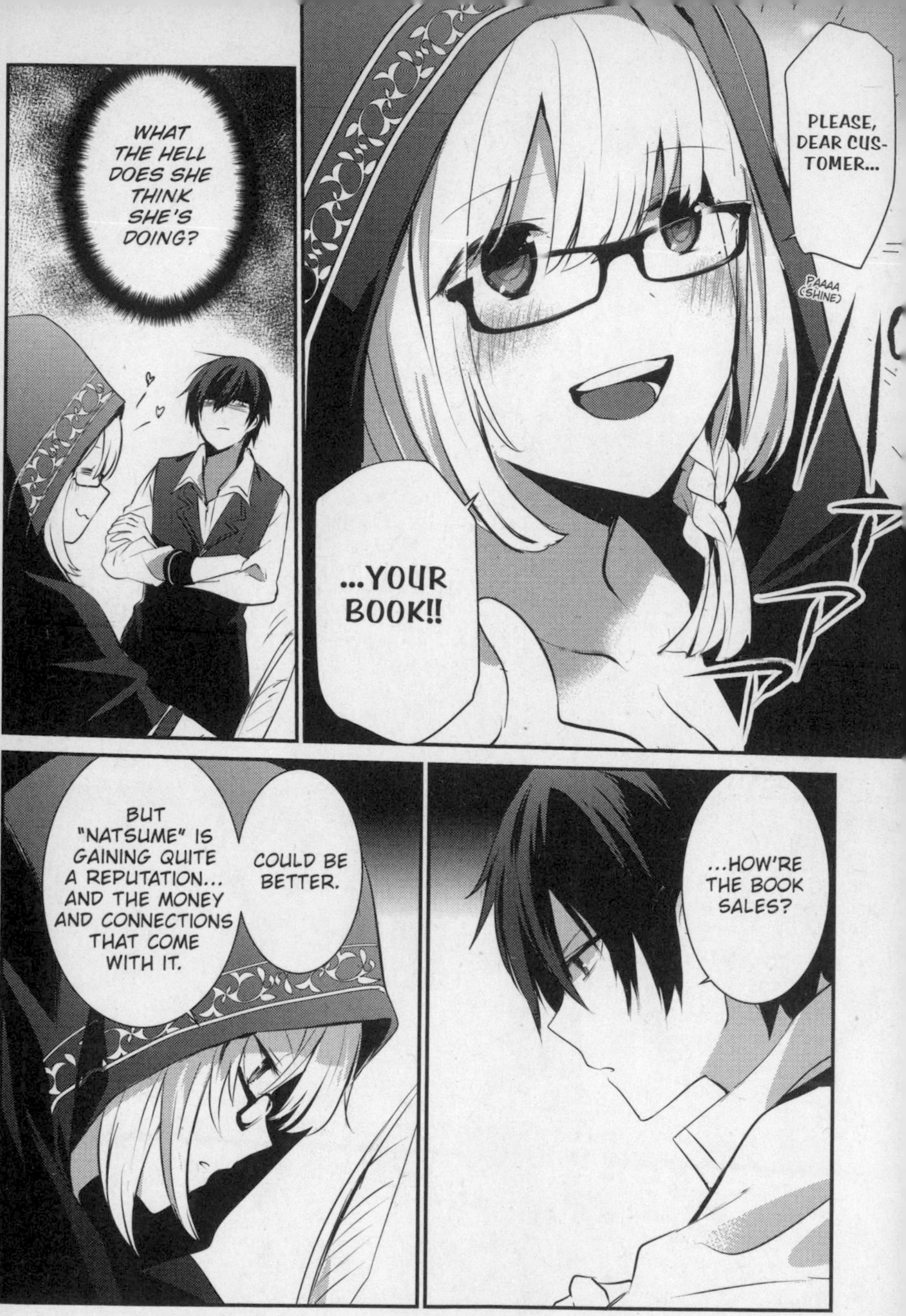
PLEASE, DEAR CUS-TOMER...
PAAAA (SHINE)
...YOUR BOOK!!
WHAT THE HELL DOES SHE THINK SHE'S DOING?
...HOW'RE THE BOOK SALES?
COULD BE BETTER.
BUT "NATSUME" IS GAINING QUITE A REPUTATION... AND THE MONEY AND CONNECTIONS THAT COME WITH IT.

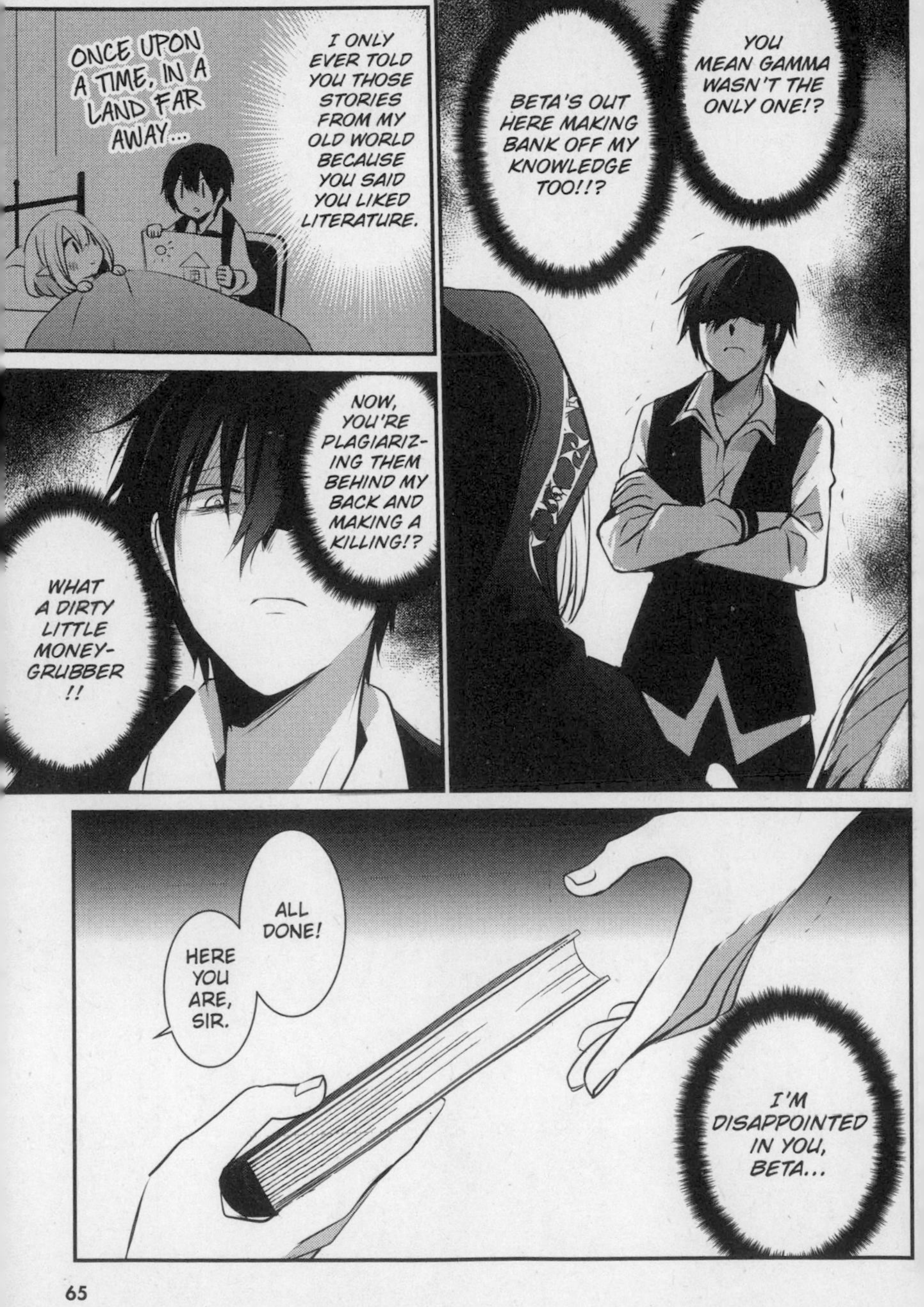
YOU MEAN GAMMA WASN'T THE ONLY ONE!?
BETA'S OUT HERE MAKING BANK OFF MY KNOWLEDGE TOO!!?
I ONLY EVER TOLD YOU THOSE STORIES FROM MY OLD WORLD BECAUSE YOU SAID YOU LIKED LITERATURE.
ONCE UPON A TIME, IN A LAND FAR AWAY...
NOW, YOU'RE PLAGIARIZING THEM BEHIND MY BACK AND MAKING A KILLING!?
WHAT A DIRTY LITTLE MONEY-GRUBBER!!
ALL DONE!
HERE YOU ARE, SIR.
I'M DISAPPOINTED IN YOU, BETA...

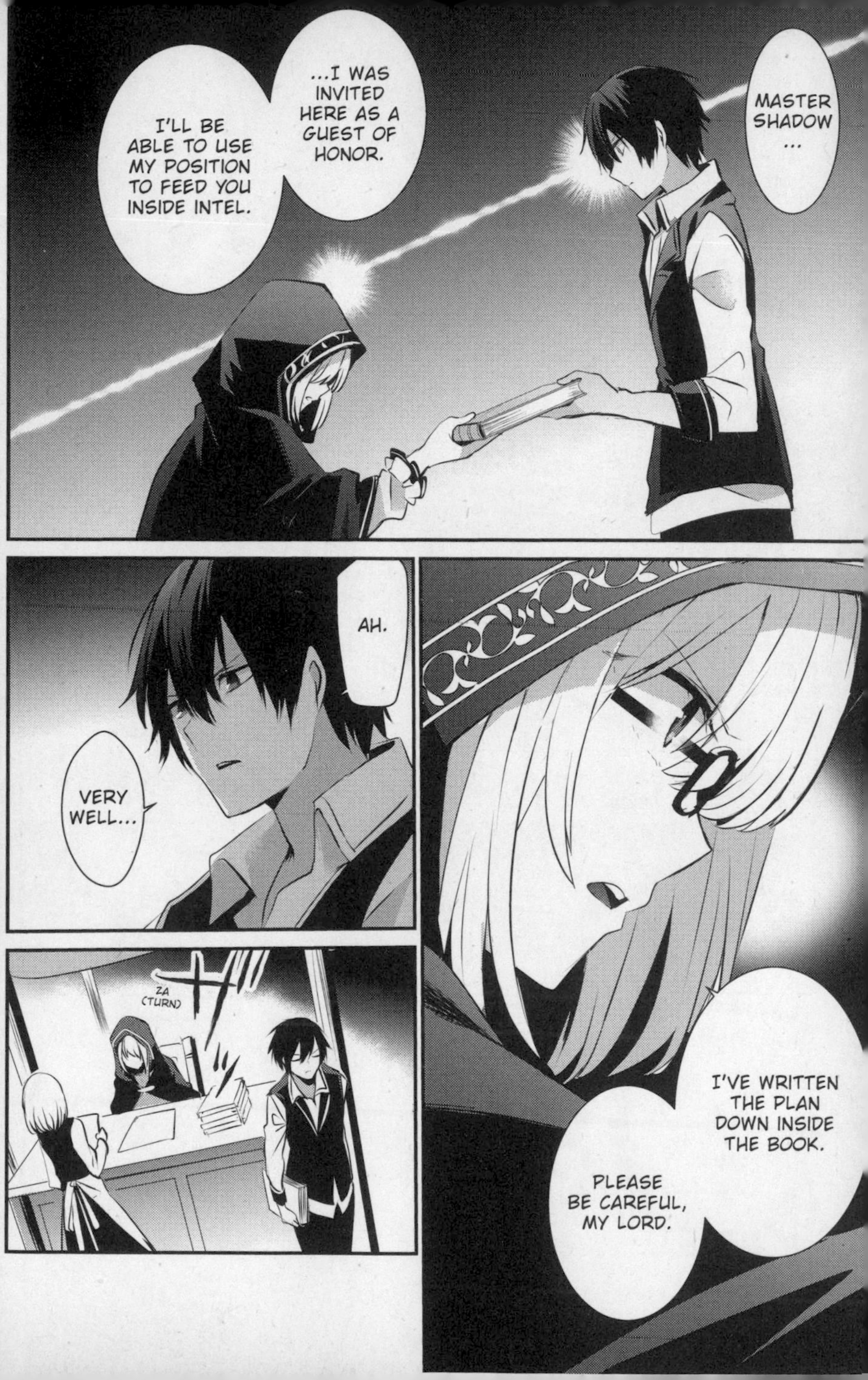
MASTER SHADOW ...
...I WAS INVITED HERE AS A GUEST OF HONOR.
I'LL BE ABLE TO USE MY POSITION TO FEED YOU INSIDE INTEL.
I'VE WRITTEN THE PLAN DOWN INSIDE THE BOOK.
PLEASE BE CAREFUL, MY LORD.
AH.
VERY WELL...
ZA (TURN)

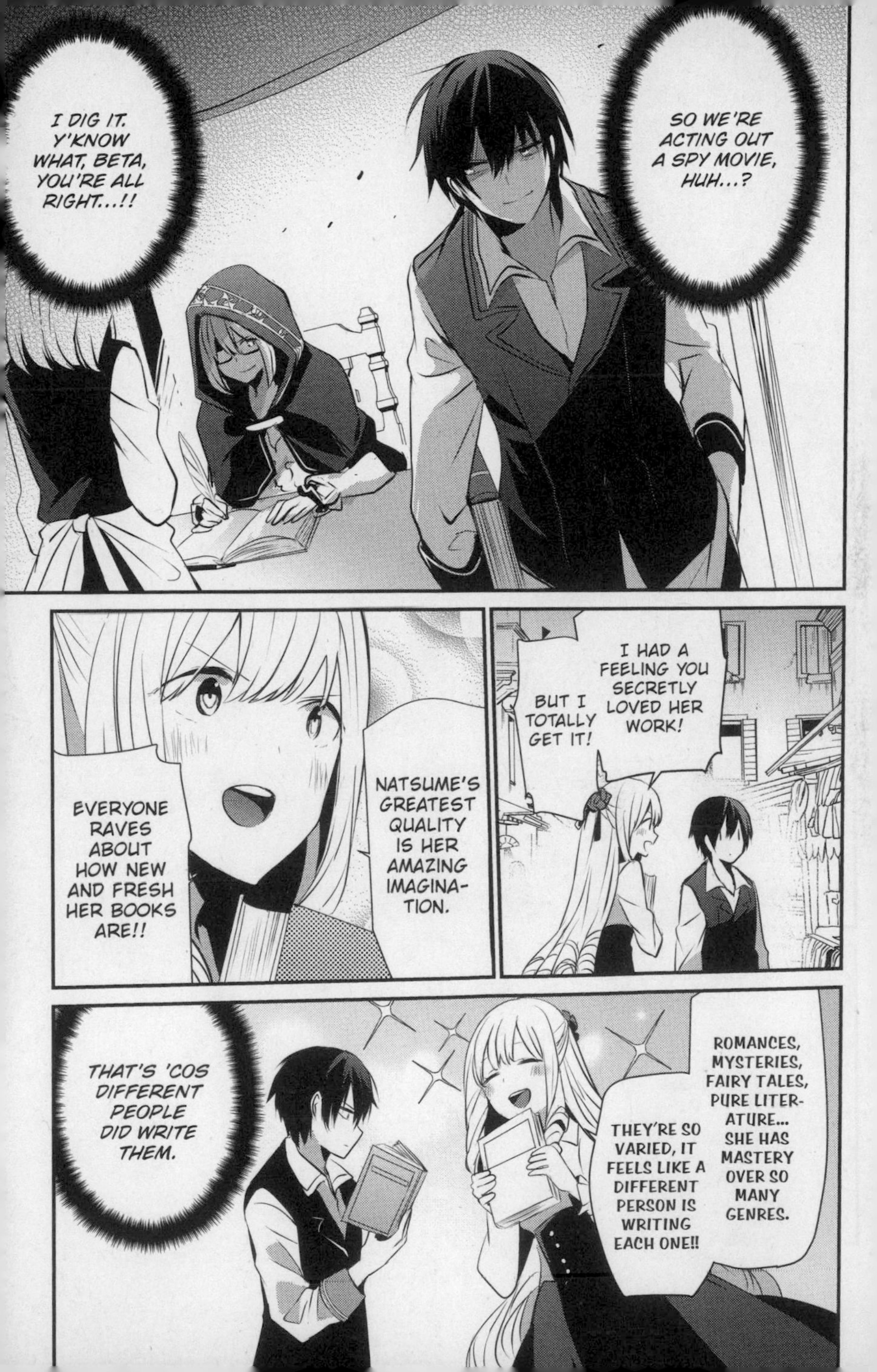
SO WE'RE ACTING OUT A SPY MOVIE, HUH...?
I DIG IT. Y'KNOW WHAT, BETA, YOU'RE ALL RIGHT...!!
I HAD A FEELING YOU SECRETLY LOVED HER WORK!
BUT I TOTALLY GET IT!
NATSUME'S GREATEST QUALITY IS HER AMAZING IMAGINA-TION.
EVERYONE RAVES ABOUT HOW NEW AND FRESH HER BOOKS ARE!!
ROMANCES, MYSTERIES, FAIRY TALES, PURE LITER-ATURE... SHE HAS MASTERY OVER SO MANY GENRES.
THEY'RE SO VARIED, IT FEELS LIKE A DIFFERENT PERSON IS WRITING EACH ONE!!
THAT'S 'COS DIFFERENT PEOPLE DID WRITE THEM.

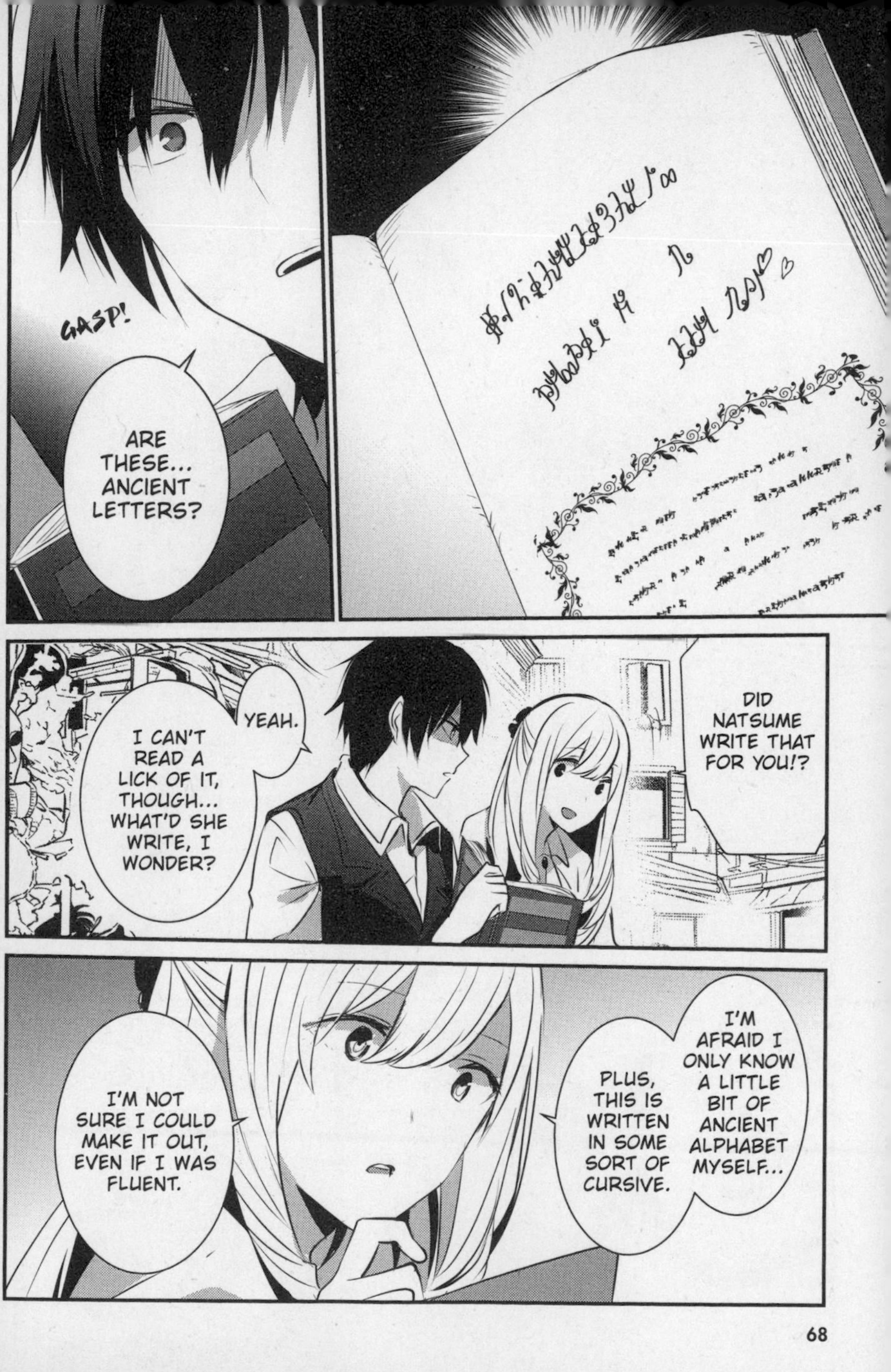
GASP!
ARE THESE... ANCIENT LETTERS?
DID NATSUME WRITE THAT FOR YOU!?
YEAH.
I CAN'T READ A LICK OF IT, THOUGH... WHAT'D SHE WRITE, I WONDER?
I'M AFRAID I ONLY KNOW A LITTLE BIT OF ANCIENT ALPHABET MYSELF...
PLUS, THIS IS WRITTEN IN SOME SORT OF CURSIVE.
I'M NOT SURE I COULD MAKE IT OUT, EVEN IF I WAS FLUENT.

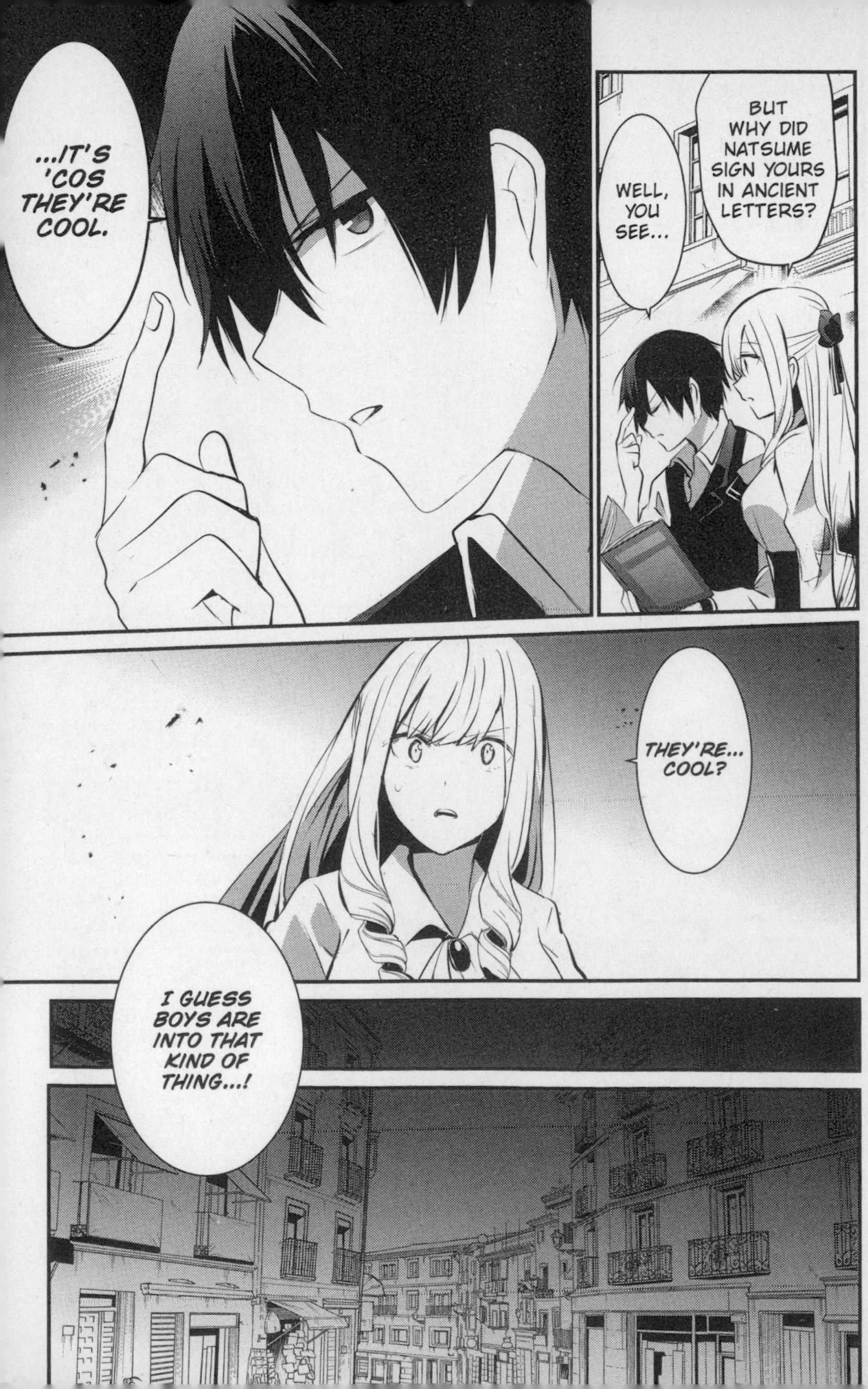
BUT WHY DID NATSUME SIGN YOURS IN ANCIENT LETTERS?
WELL, YOU SEE...
...IT'S 'COS THEY'RE COOL.
THEY'RE... COOL?
I GUESS BOYS ARE INTO THAT KIND OF THING...!

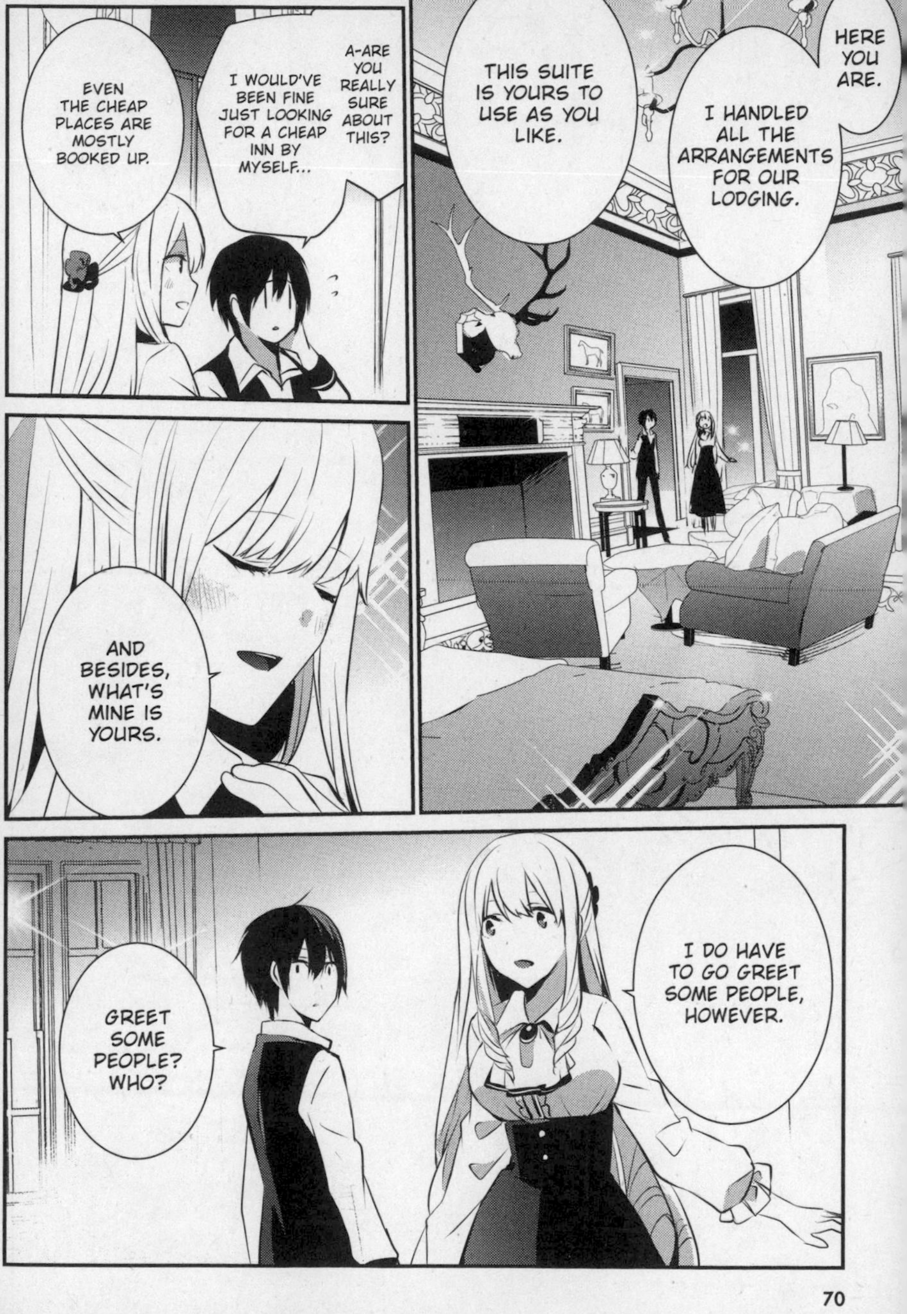
HERE YOU ARE.
I HANDLED ALL THE ARRANGEMENTS FOR OUR LODGING.
THIS SUITE IS YOURS TO USE AS YOU LIKE.
A-ARE YOU REALLY SURE ABOUT THIS?
I WOULD'VE BEEN FINE JUST LOOKING FOR A CHEAP INN BY MYSELF...
EVEN THE CHEAP PLACES ARE MOSTLY BOOKED UP.
AND BESIDES, WHAT'S MINE IS YOURS.
I DO HAVE TO GO GREET SOME PEOPLE, HOWEVER.
GREET SOME PEOPLE? WHO?

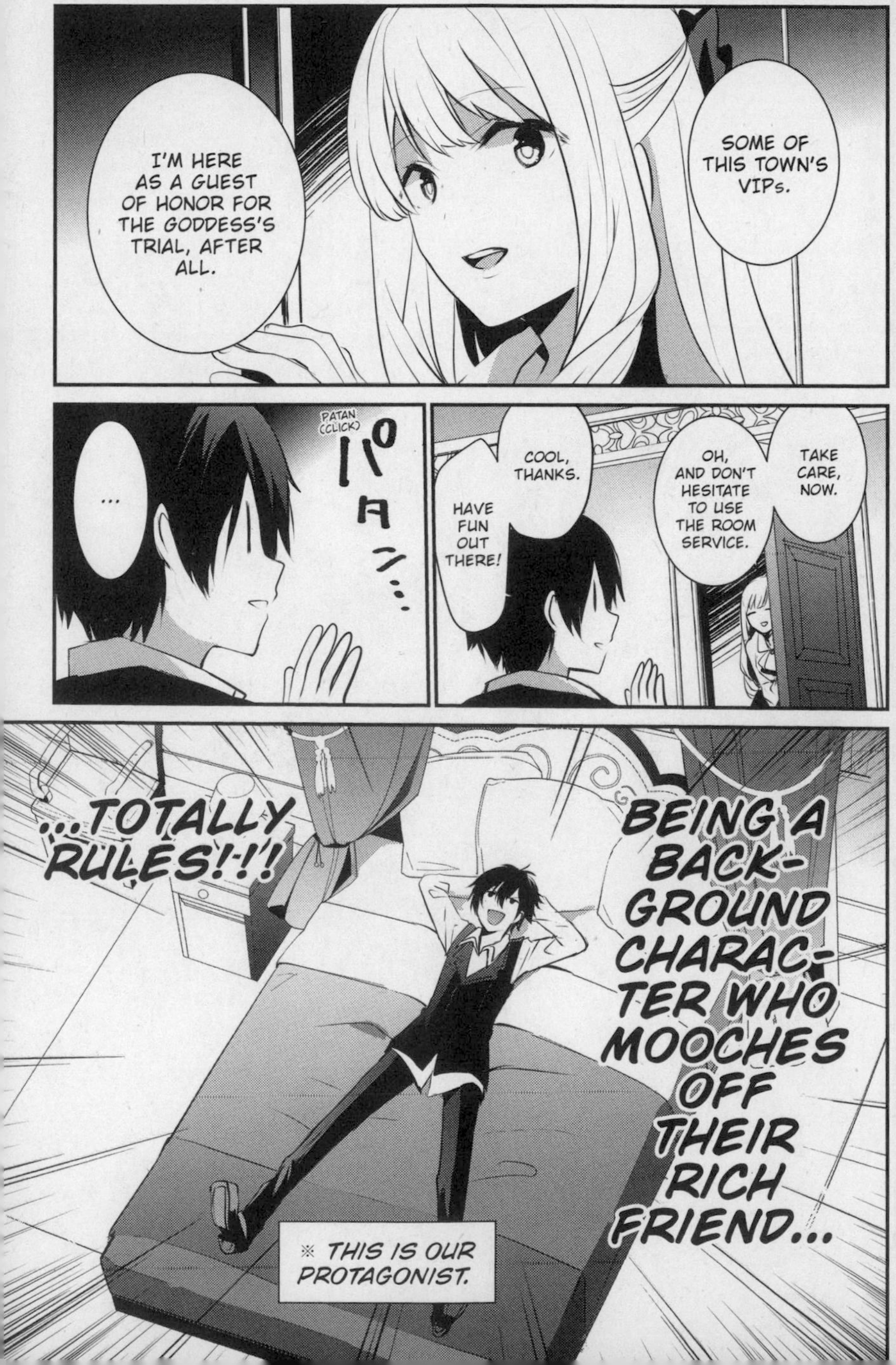
SOME OF THIS TOWN'S VIPs.
I'M HERE AS A GUEST OF HONOR FOR THE GODDESS'S TRIAL, AFTER ALL.
TAKE CARE, NOW.
OH, AND DON'T HESITATE TO USE THE ROOM SERVICE.
COOL, THANKS.
HAVE FUN OUT THERE!
PATAN (CLICK)
パタン…
...
BEING A BACK-GROUND CHARAC-TER WHO MOOCHES OFF THEIR RICH FRIEND...
...TOTALLY RULES!-!-!
※ THIS IS OUR PROTAGONIST.

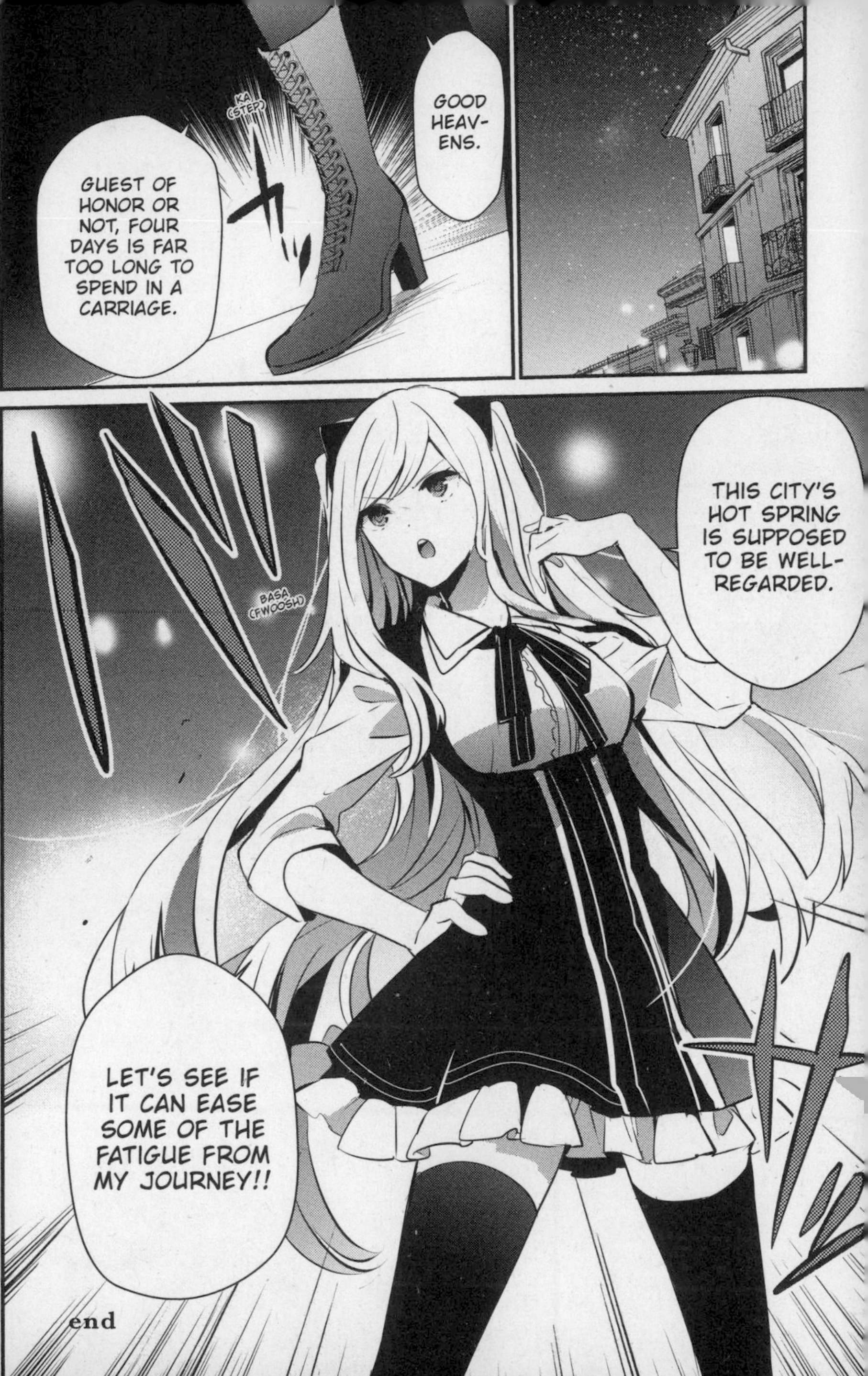
GOOD HEAV-ENS.
KA (STEP)
GUEST OF HONOR OR NOT, FOUR DAYS IS FAR TOO LONG TO SPEND IN A CARRIAGE.
THIS CITY'S HOT SPRING IS SUPPOSED TO BE WELL-REGARDED.
BASA (FWOOSH)
LET'S SEE IF IT CAN EASE SOME OF THE FATIGUE FROM MY JOURNEY!!
end

THE Eminence IN Shadow

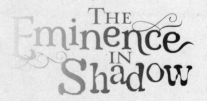

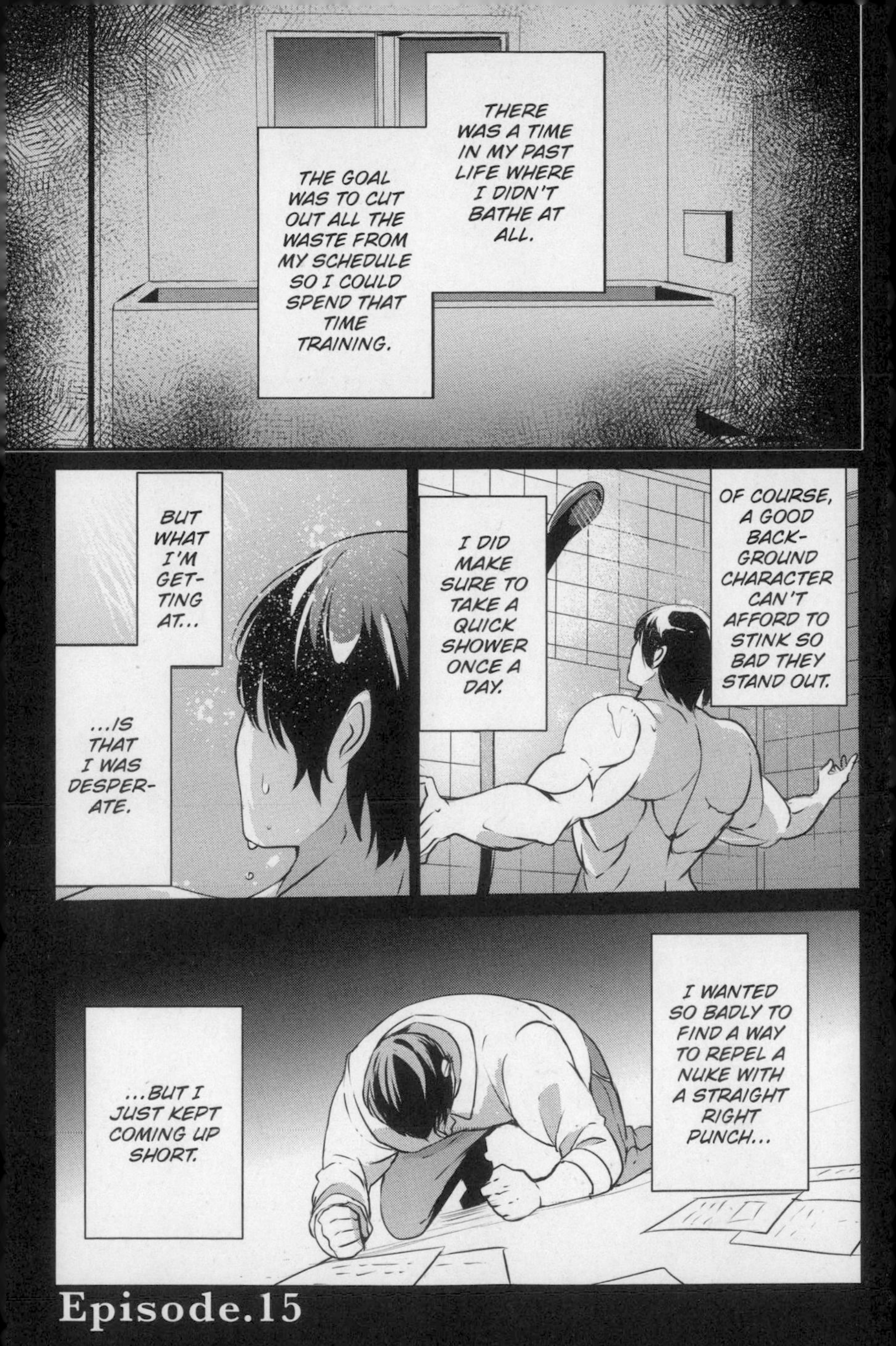
THERE WAS A TIME IN MY PAST LIFE WHERE I DIDN'T BATHE AT ALL.
THE GOAL WAS TO CUT OUT ALL THE WASTE FROM MY SCHEDULE SO I COULD SPEND THAT TIME TRAINING.
OF COURSE, A GOOD BACK-GROUND CHARACTER CAN'T AFFORD TO STINK SO BAD THEY STAND OUT.
I DID MAKE SURE TO TAKE A QUICK SHOWER ONCE A DAY.
BUT WHAT I'M GET-TING AT...
...IS THAT I WAS DESPER-ATE.
I WANTED SO BADLY TO FIND A WAY TO REPEL A NUKE WITH A STRAIGHT RIGHT PUNCH...
...BUT I JUST KEPT COMING UP SHORT.

Episode.15

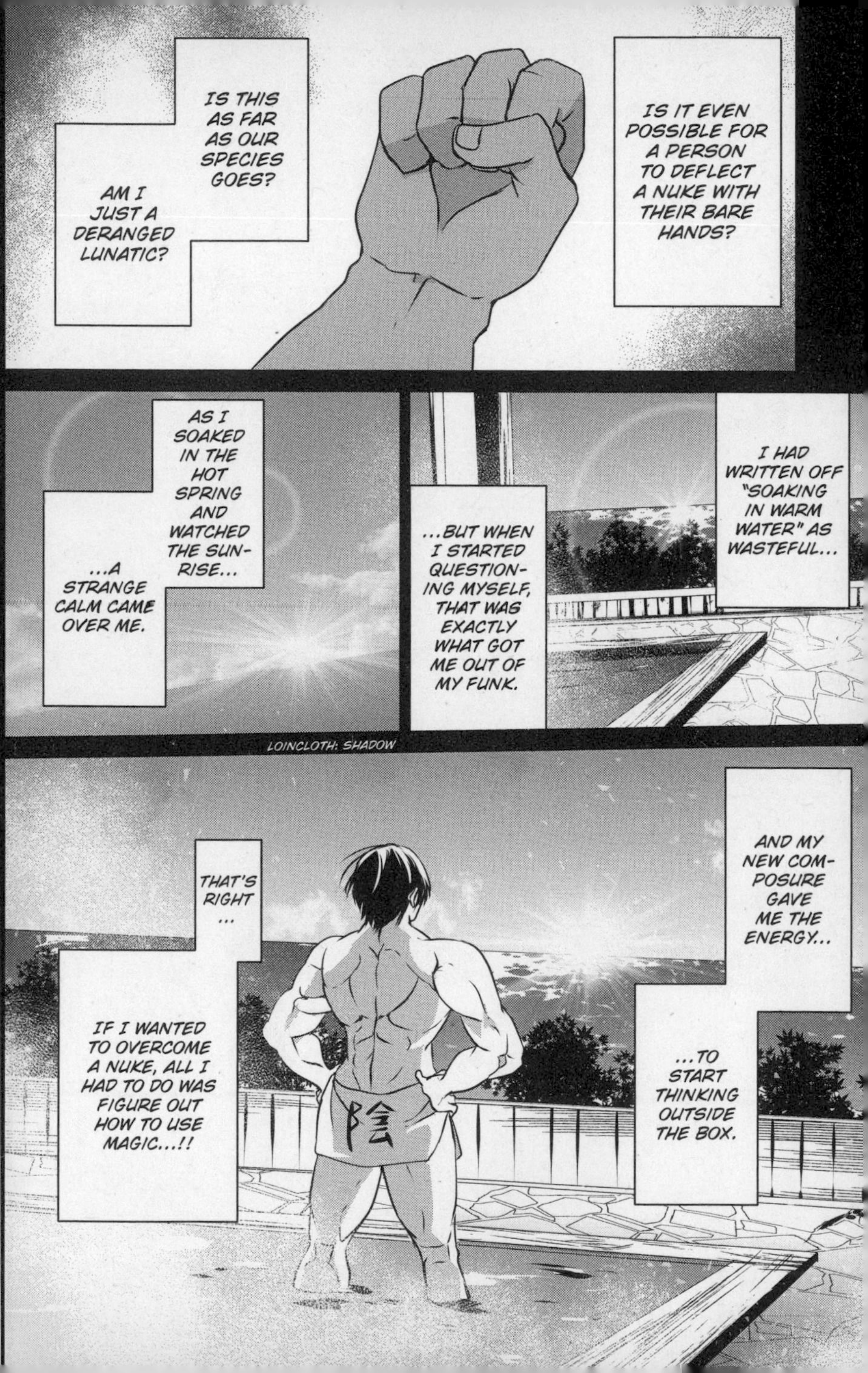
IS IT EVEN POSSIBLE FOR A PERSON TO DEFLECT A NUKE WITH THEIR BARE HANDS?
IS THIS AS FAR AS OUR SPECIES GOES?
AM I JUST A DERANGED LUNATIC?
I HAD WRITTEN OFF "SOAKING IN WARM WATER" AS WASTEFUL...
...BUT WHEN I STARTED QUESTION-ING MYSELF, THAT WAS EXACTLY WHAT GOT ME OUT OF MY FUNK.
AS I SOAKED IN THE HOT SPRING AND WATCHED THE SUN-RISE...
...A STRANGE CALM CAME OVER ME.
LOINCLOTH: SHADOW
AND MY NEW COM-POSURE GAVE ME THE ENERGY...
...TO START THINKING OUTSIDE THE BOX.
THAT'S RIGHT ...
IF I WANTED TO OVERCOME A NUKE, ALL I HAD TO DO WAS FIGURE OUT HOW TO USE MAGIC...!!

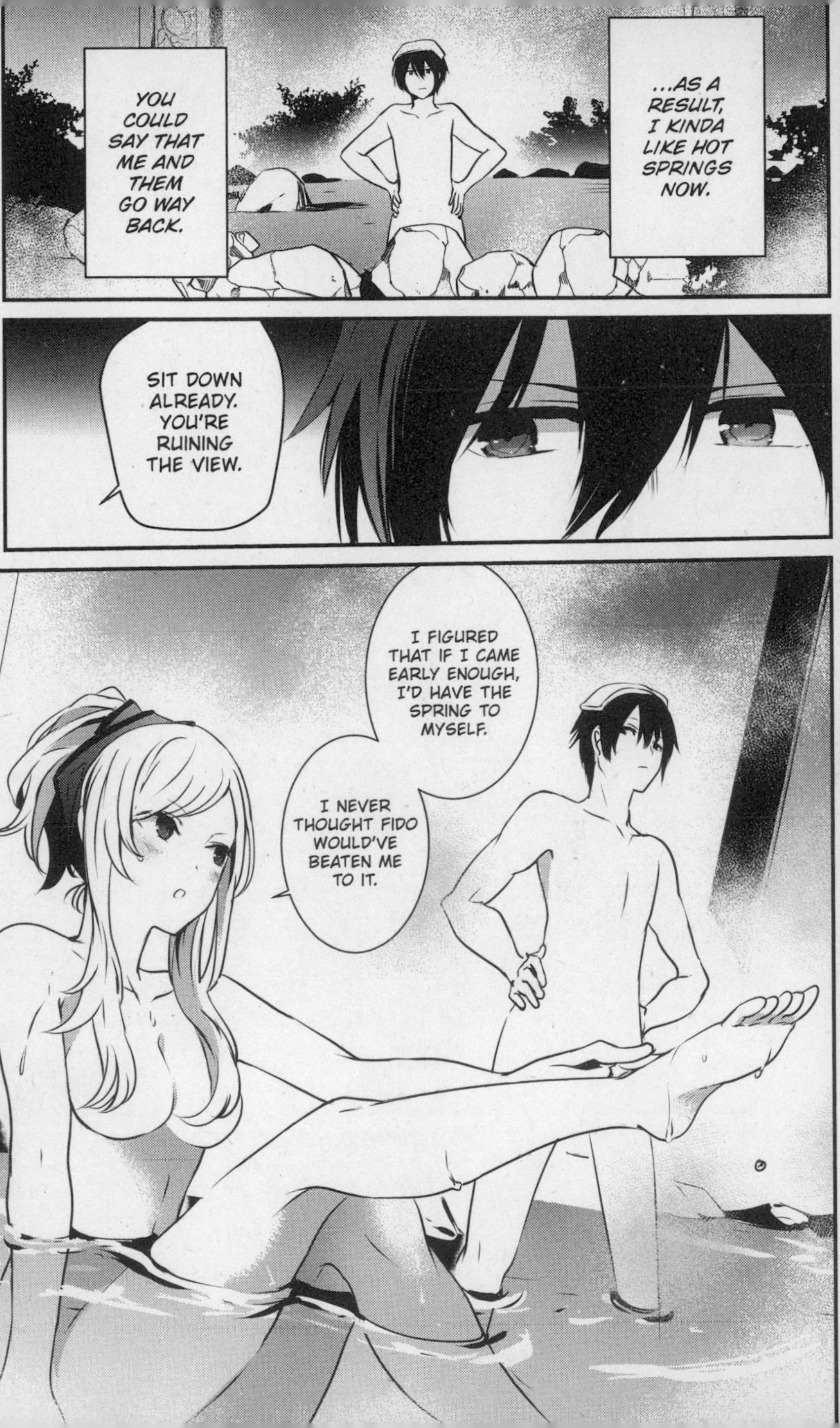
...AS A RESULT, I KINDA LIKE HOT SPRINGS NOW.
YOU COULD SAY THAT ME AND THEM GO WAY BACK.
SIT DOWN ALREADY. YOU'RE RUINING THE VIEW.
I FIGURED THAT IF I CAME EARLY ENOUGH, I'D HAVE THE SPRING TO MYSELF.
I NEVER THOUGHT FIDO WOULD'VE BEATEN ME TO IT.

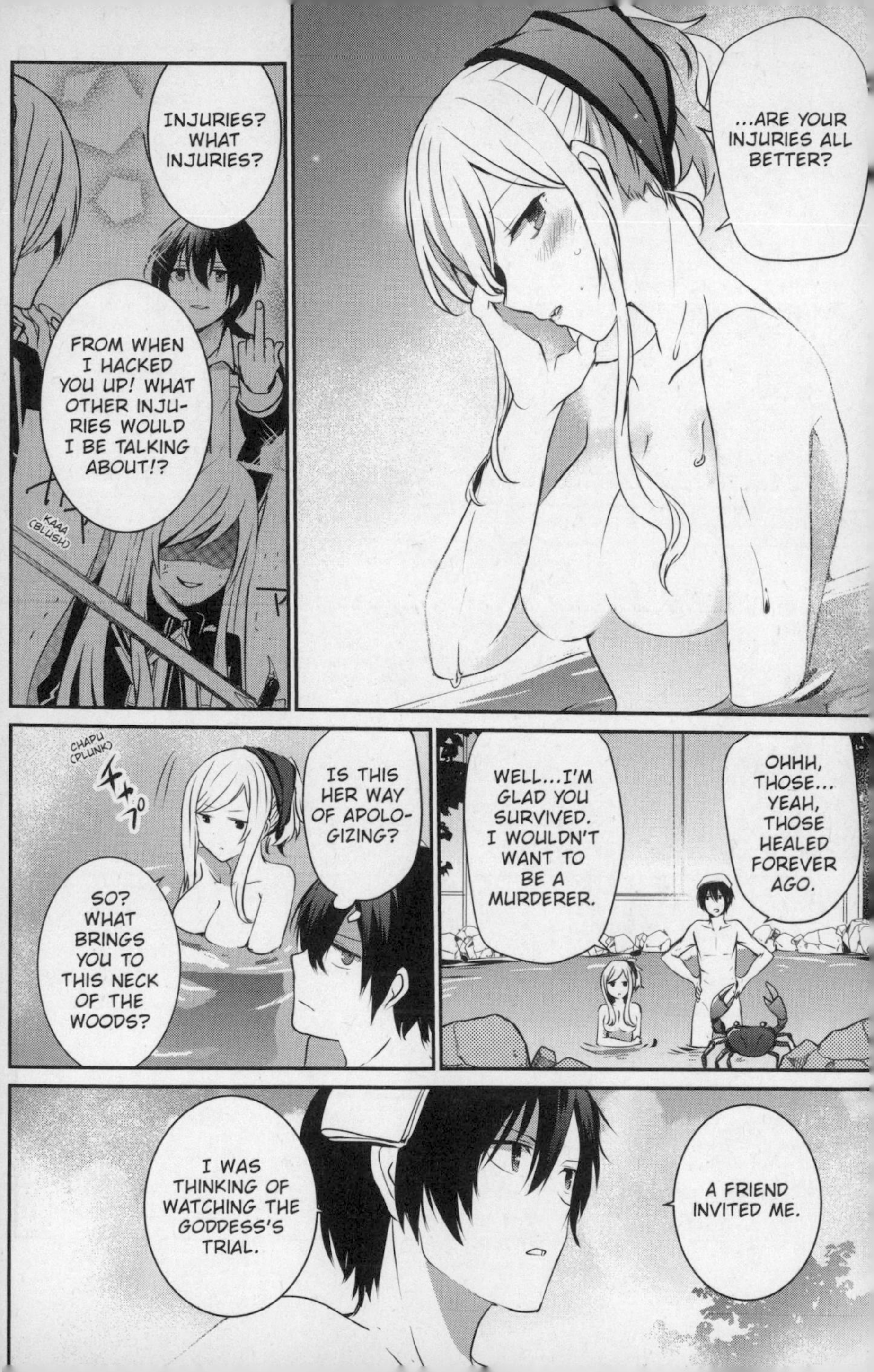
...ARE YOUR INJURIES ALL BETTER?
INJURIES? WHAT INJURIES?
FROM WHEN I HACKED YOU UP! WHAT OTHER INJURIES WOULD I BE TALKING ABOUT!?
KAAA (BLUSH)
OHHH, THOSE... YEAH, THOSE HEALED FOREVER AGO.
WELL...I'M GLAD YOU SURVIVED. I WOULDN'T WANT TO BE A MURDERER.
CHAPU (PLUNK)
チャプ
IS THIS HER WAY OF APOLOGIZING?
SO? WHAT BRINGS YOU TO THIS NECK OF THE WOODS?
A FRIEND INVITED ME.
I WAS THINKING OF WATCHING THE GODDESS'S TRIAL.

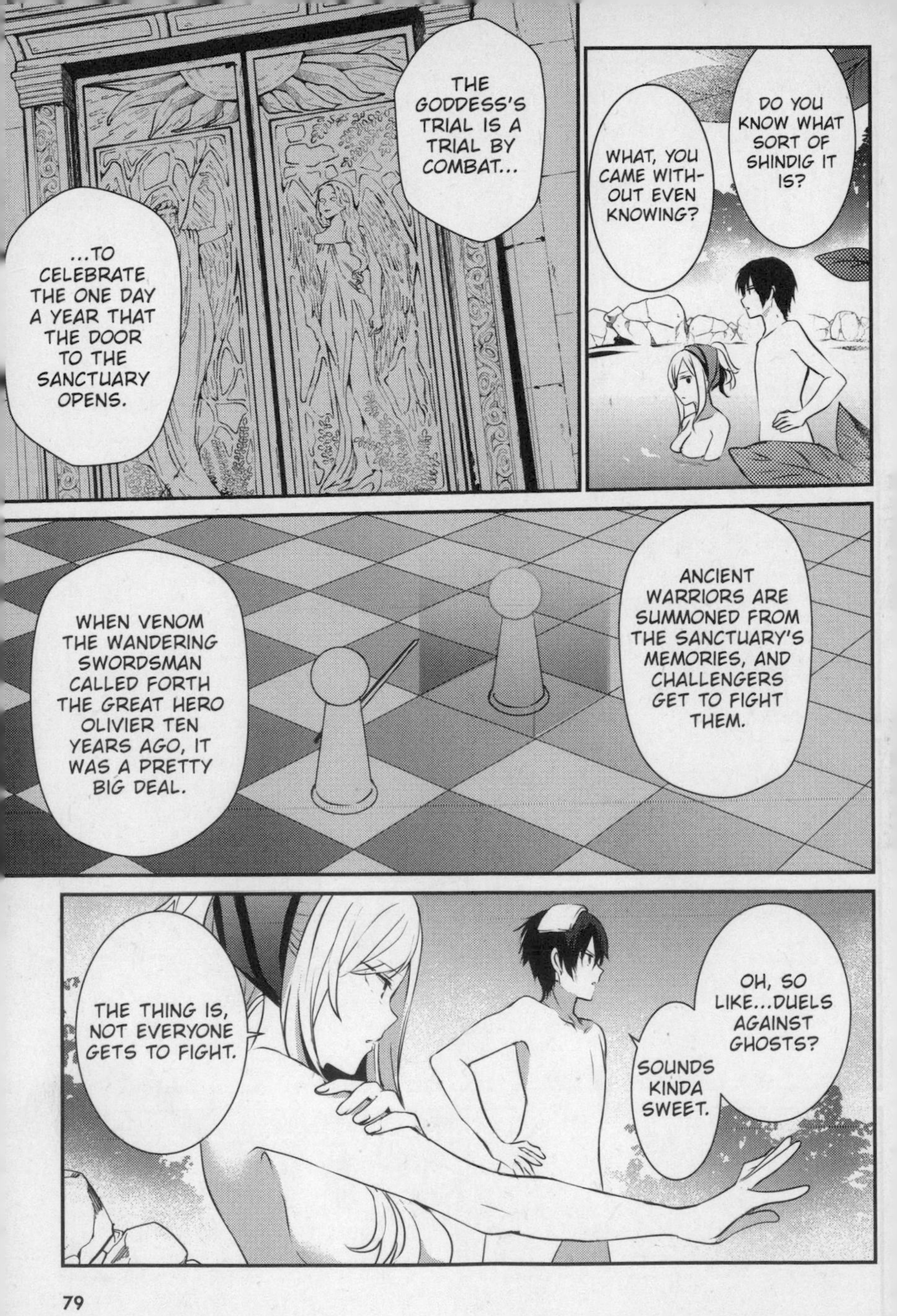
DO YOU KNOW WHAT SORT OF SHINDIG IT IS?
WHAT, YOU CAME WITHOUT EVEN KNOWING?
THE GODDESS'S TRIAL IS A TRIAL BY COMBAT...
...TO CELEBRATE THE ONE DAY A YEAR THAT THE DOOR TO THE SANCTUARY OPENS.
ANCIENT WARRIORS ARE SUMMONED FROM THE SANCTUARY'S MEMORIES, AND CHALLENGERS GET TO FIGHT THEM.
WHEN VENOM THE WANDERING SWORDSMAN CALLED FORTH THE GREAT HERO OLIVIER TEN YEARS AGO, IT WAS A PRETTY BIG DEAL.
OH, SO LIKE...DUELS AGAINST GHOSTS?
SOUNDS KINDA SWEET.
THE THING IS, NOT EVERYONE GETS TO FIGHT.

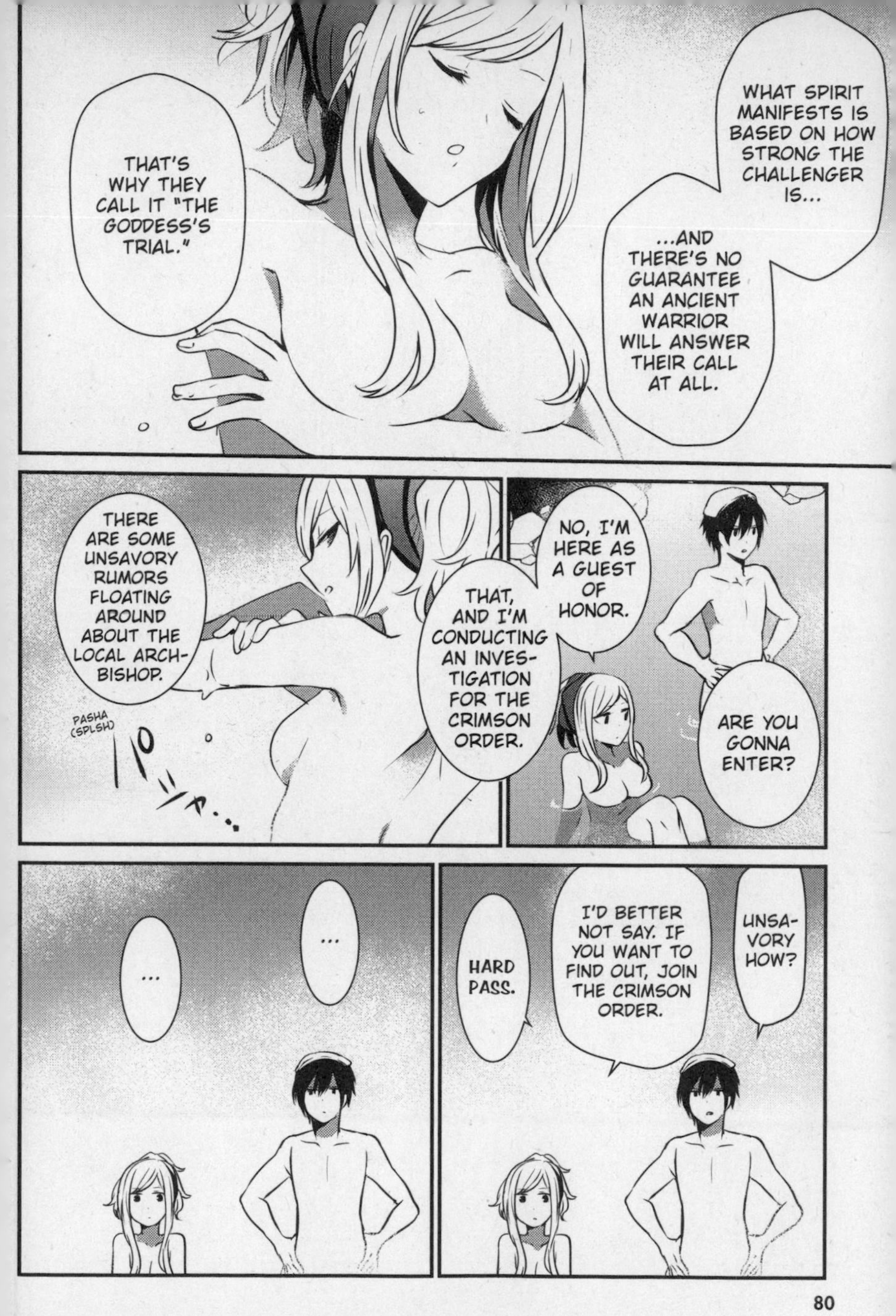
WHAT SPIRIT MANIFESTS IS BASED ON HOW STRONG THE CHALLENGER IS...
...AND THERE'S NO GUARANTEE AN ANCIENT WARRIOR WILL ANSWER THEIR CALL AT ALL.
THAT'S WHY THEY CALL IT "THE GODDESS'S TRIAL."
ARE YOU GONNA ENTER?
NO, I'M HERE AS A GUEST OF HONOR.
THAT, AND I'M CONDUCTING AN INVES-TIGATION FOR THE CRIMSON ORDER.
THERE ARE SOME UNSAVORY RUMORS FLOATING AROUND ABOUT THE LOCAL ARCH-BISHOP.
PASHA (SPLSH)
UNSA-VORY HOW?
I'D BETTER NOT SAY. IF YOU WANT TO FIND OUT, JOIN THE CRIMSON ORDER.
HARD PASS.
...
...

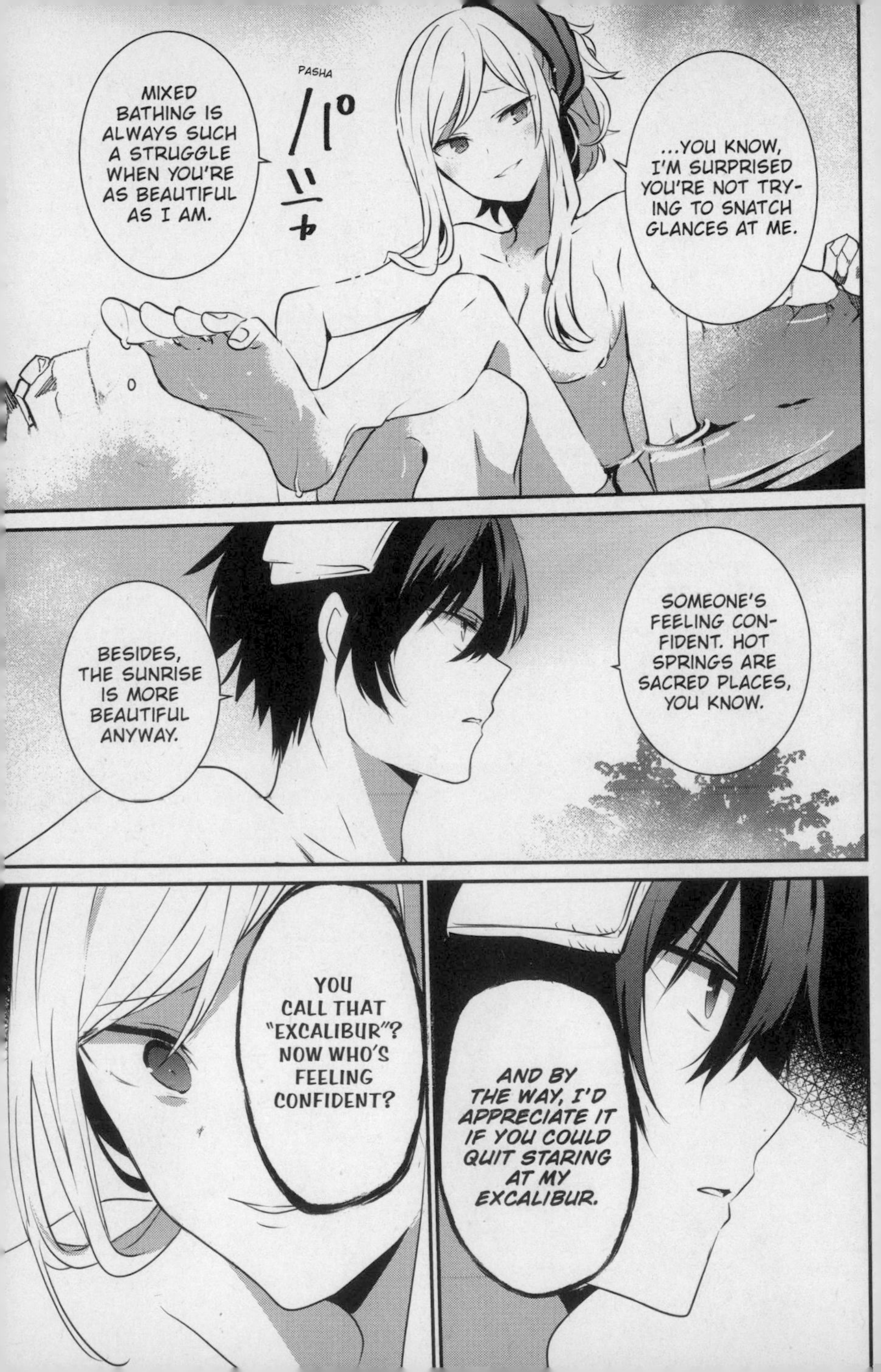
...YOU KNOW, I'M SURPRISED YOU'RE NOT TRY-ING TO SNATCH GLANCES AT ME.
PASHA
パシャ
MIXED BATHING IS ALWAYS SUCH A STRUGGLE WHEN YOU'RE AS BEAUTIFUL AS I AM.
SOMEONE'S FEELING CON-FIDENT. HOT SPRINGS ARE SACRED PLACES, YOU KNOW.
BESIDES, THE SUNRISE IS MORE BEAUTIFUL ANYWAY.
AND BY THE WAY, I'D APPRECIATE IT IF YOU COULD QUIT STARING AT MY EXCALIBUR.
YOU CALL THAT "EXCALIBUR"? NOW WHO'S FEELING CONFIDENT?

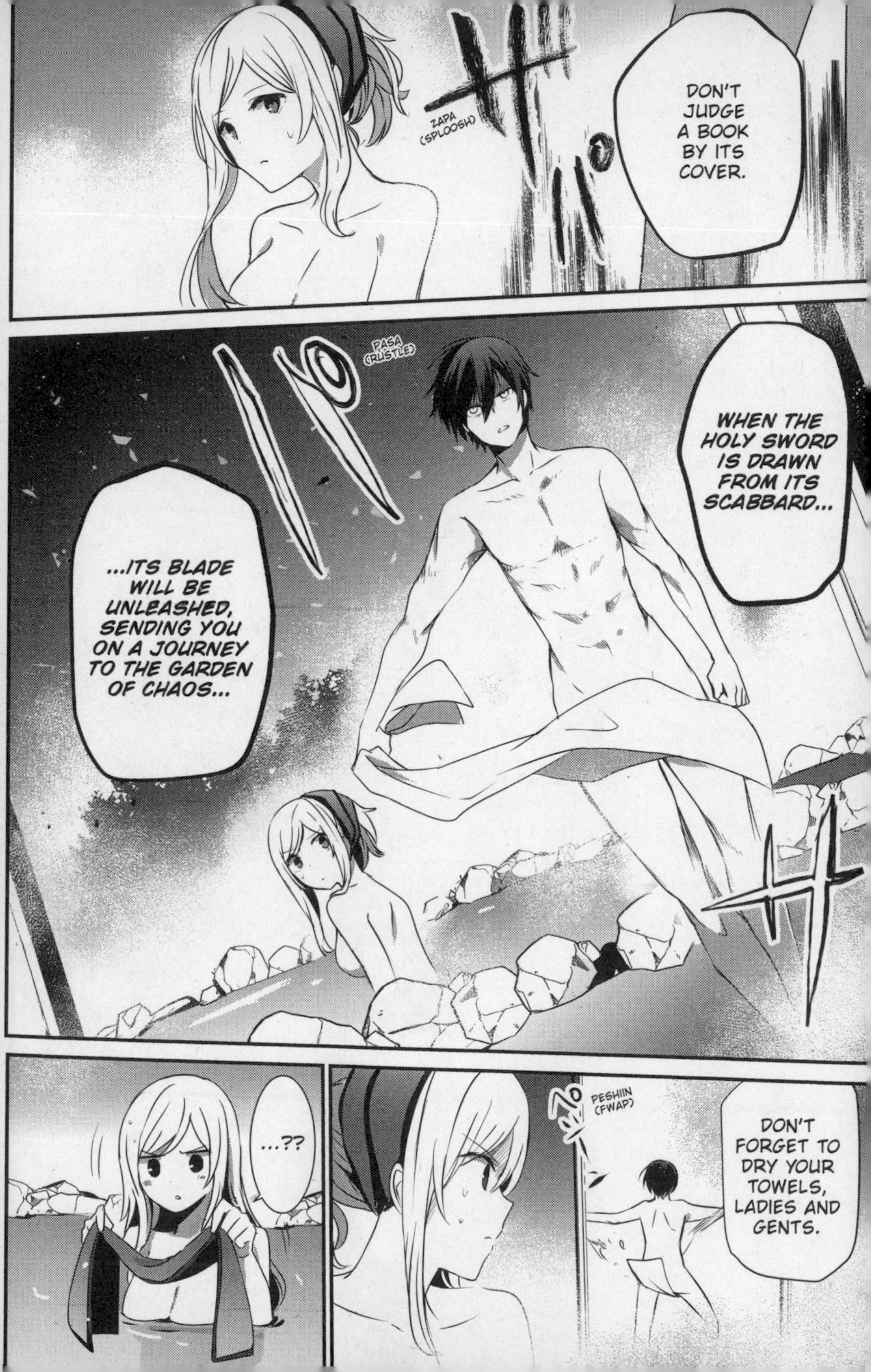
DON'T JUDGE A BOOK BY ITS COVER.
ZAPA (SPLOOSH)
WHEN THE HOLY SWORD IS DRAWN FROM ITS SCABBARD...
PASA (RUSTLE)
...ITS BLADE WILL BE UNLEASHED, SENDING YOU ON A JOURNEY TO THE GARDEN OF CHAOS...
DON'T FORGET TO DRY YOUR TOWELS, LADIES AND GENTS.
PESHIIN (FWAP)
...??

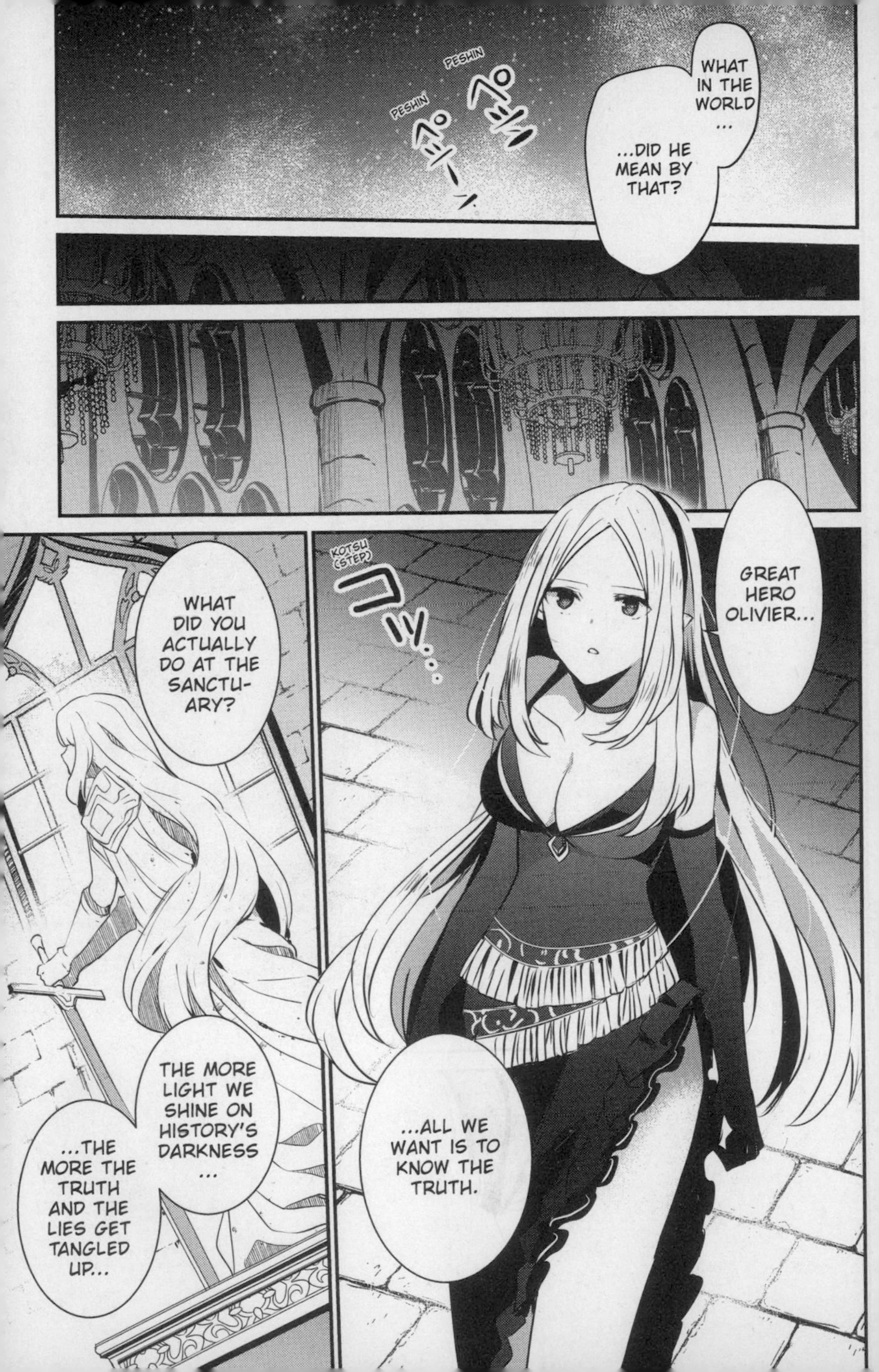
WHAT IN THE WORLD ...
...DID HE MEAN BY THAT?
PESHIN
PESHIN
GREAT HERO OLIVIER...
KOTSU (STEP)
...ALL WE WANT IS TO KNOW THE TRUTH.
WHAT DID YOU ACTUALLY DO AT THE SANCTU-ARY?
THE MORE LIGHT WE SHINE ON HISTORY'S DARKNESS ...
...THE MORE THE TRUTH AND THE LIES GET TANGLED UP...

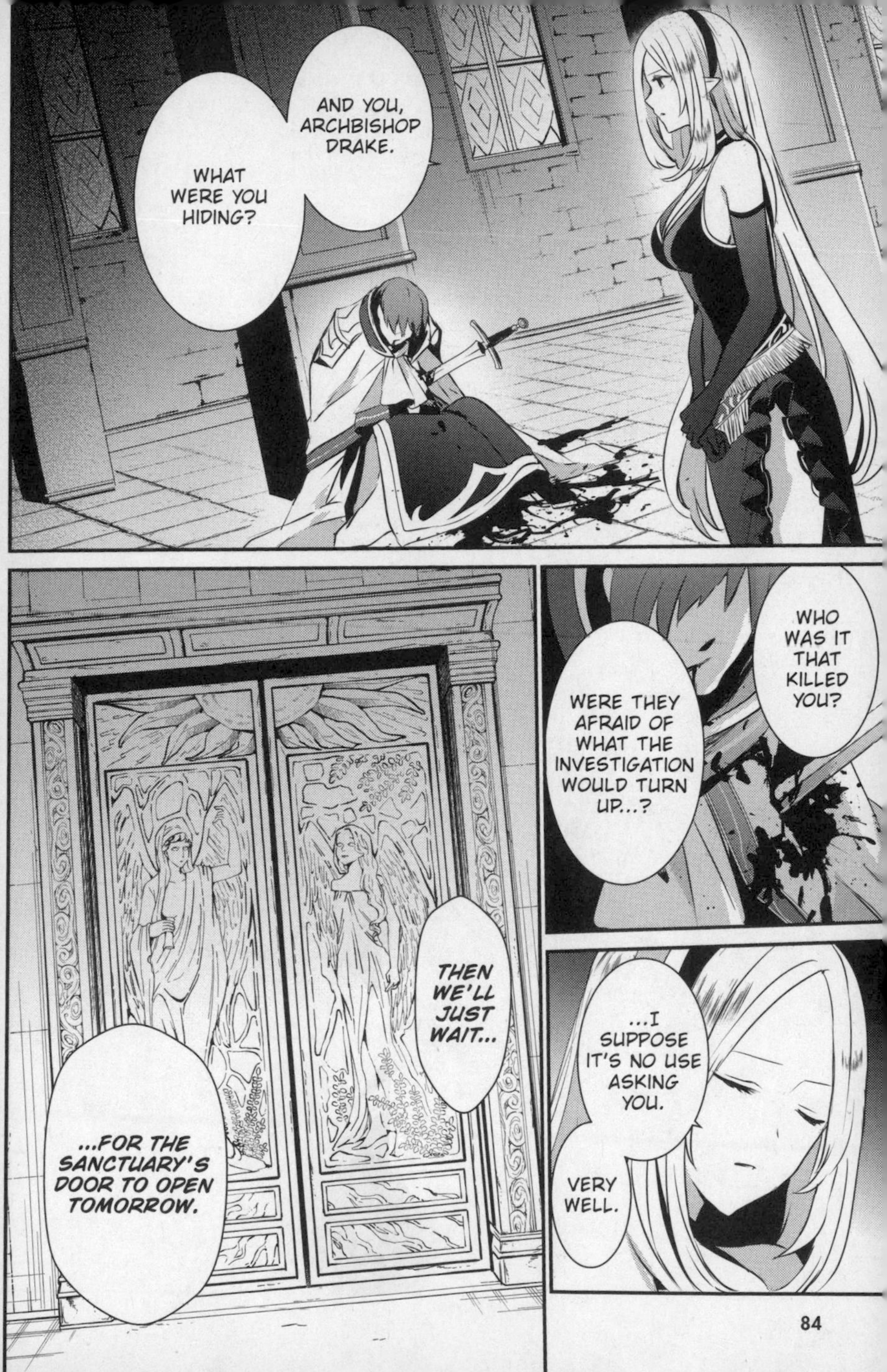
AND YOU, ARCHBISHOP DRAKE.
WHAT WERE YOU HIDING?
WHO WAS IT THAT KILLED YOU?
WERE THEY AFRAID OF WHAT THE INVESTIGATION WOULD TURN UP...?
...I SUPPOSE IT'S NO USE ASKING YOU.
VERY WELL.
THEN WE'LL JUST WAIT...
...FOR THE SANCTUARY'S DOOR TO OPEN TOMORROW.

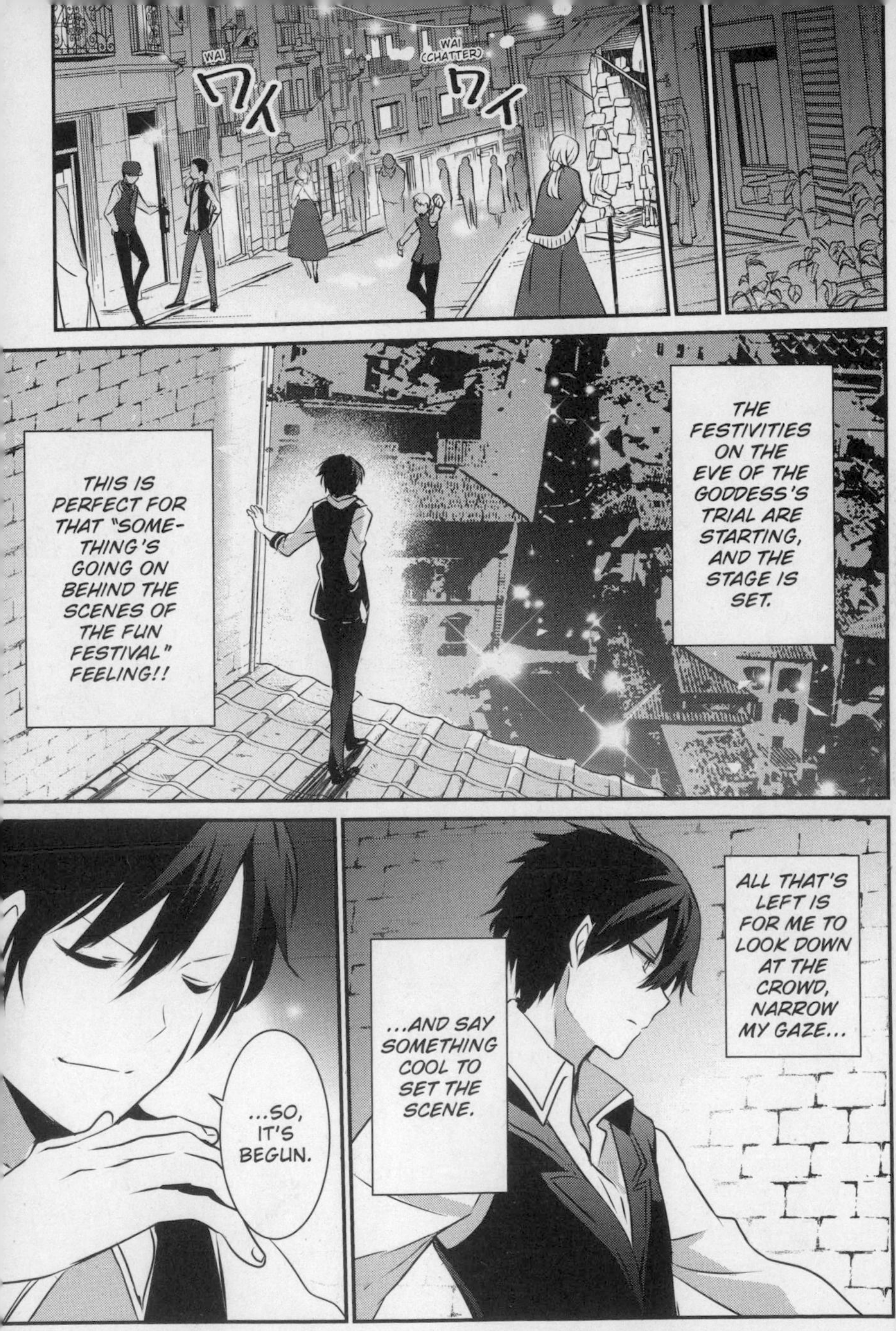
WAI (CHATTER)
ワイ
WAI
ワイ
THE FESTIVITIES ON THE EVE OF THE GODDESS'S TRIAL ARE STARTING, AND THE STAGE IS SET.
THIS IS PERFECT FOR THAT "SOMETHING'S GOING ON BEHIND THE SCENES OF THE FUN FESTIVAL" FEELING!!
ALL THAT'S LEFT IS FOR ME TO LOOK DOWN AT THE CROWD, NARROW MY GAZE...
...AND SAY SOMETHING COOL TO SET THE SCENE.
...SO, IT'S BEGUN.

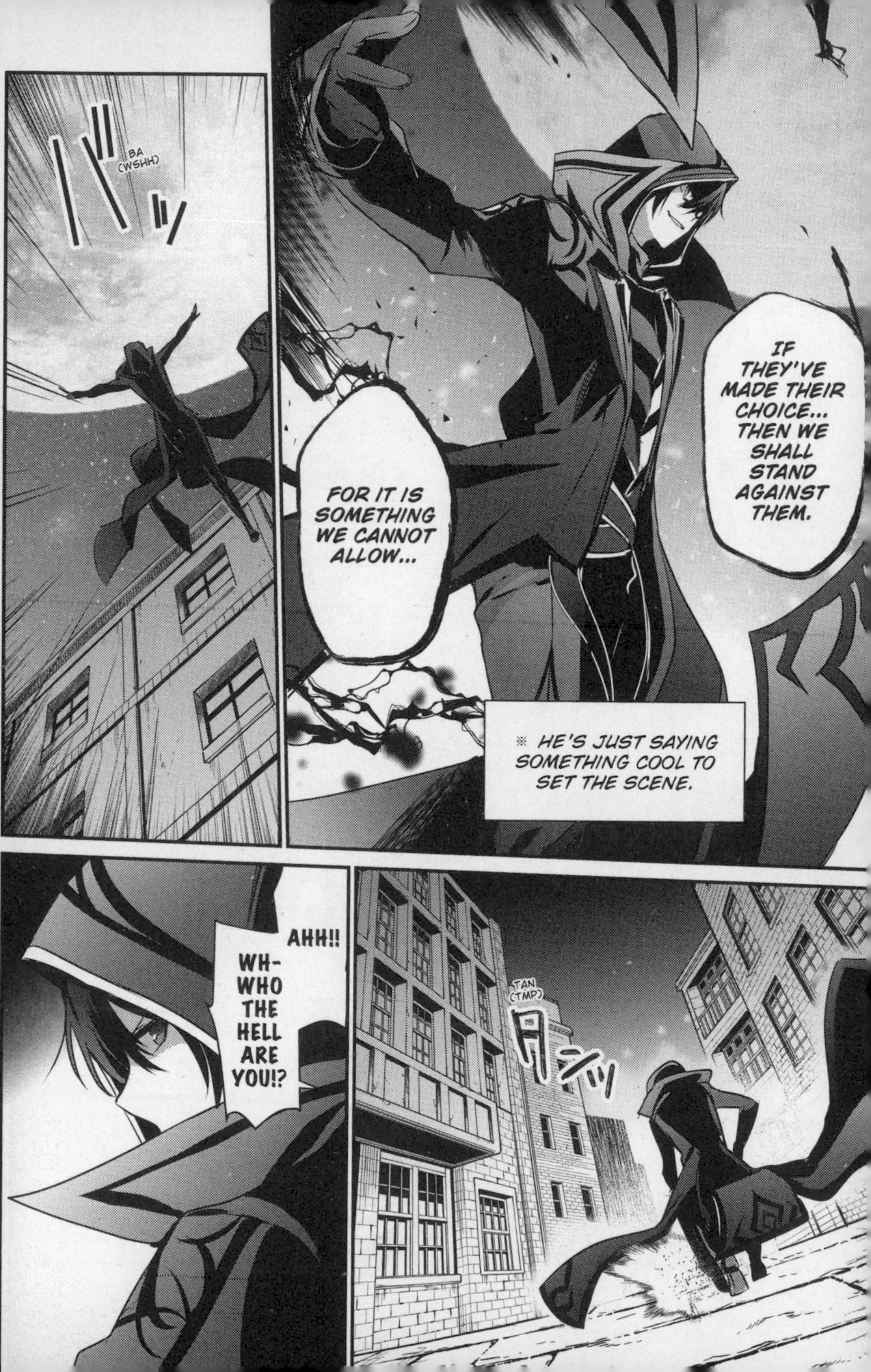
IF THEY'VE MADE THEIR CHOICE... THEN WE SHALL STAND AGAINST THEM.
FOR IT IS SOMETHING WE CANNOT ALLOW...
※ HE'S JUST SAYING SOMETHING COOL TO SET THE SCENE.
BA (WSHH)
TAN (TMP)
AHH!! WH-WHO THE HELL ARE YOU!?

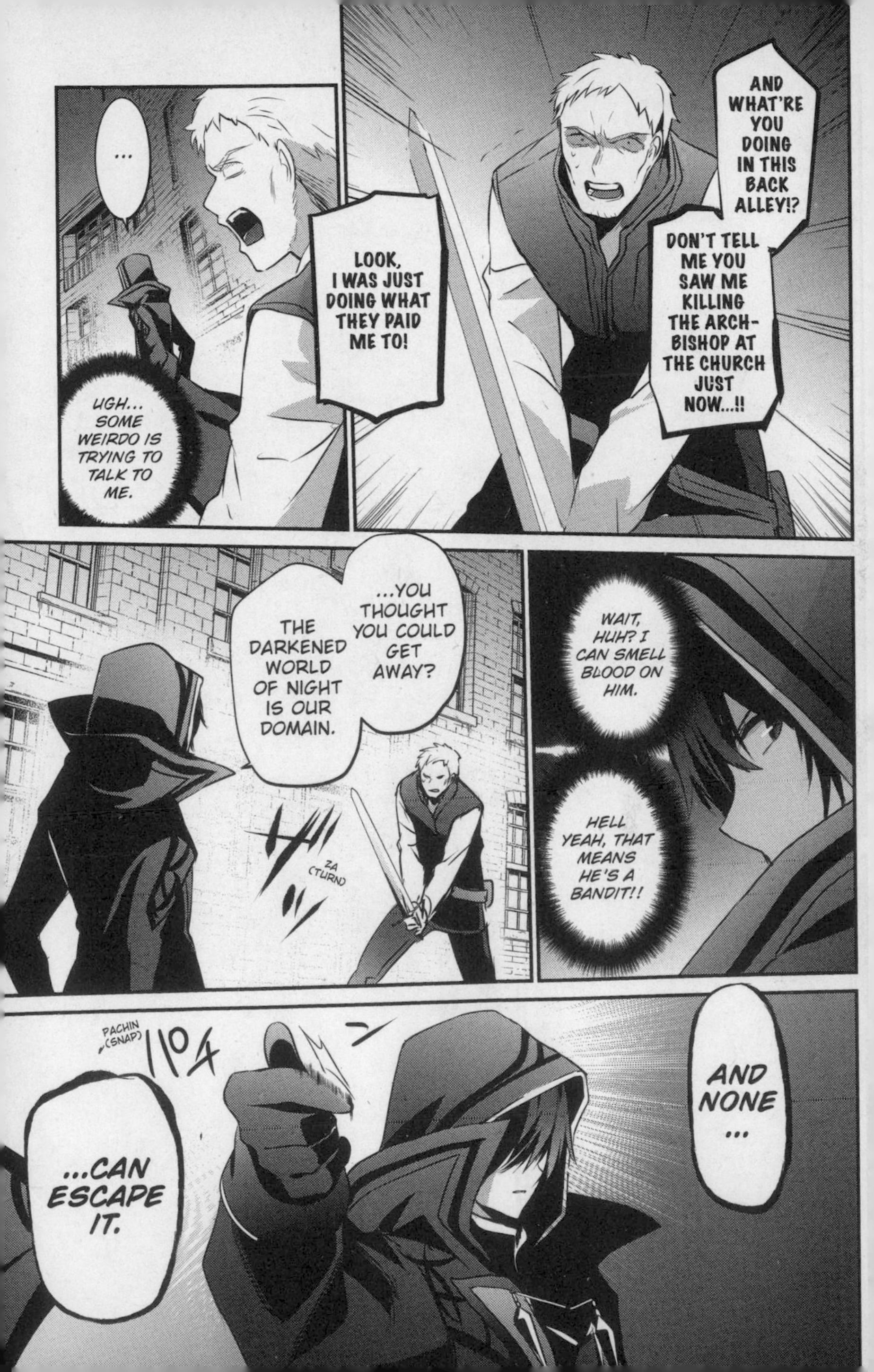
AND WHAT'RE YOU DOING IN THIS BACK ALLEY!?
DON'T TELL ME YOU SAW ME KILLING THE ARCH-BISHOP AT THE CHURCH JUST NOW...!!
LOOK, I WAS JUST DOING WHAT THEY PAID ME TO!
...
UGH... SOME WEIRDO IS TRYING TO TALK TO ME.
WAIT, HUH? I CAN SMELL BLOOD ON HIM.
HELL YEAH, THAT MEANS HE'S A BANDIT!!
...YOU THOUGHT YOU COULD GET AWAY?
THE DARKENED WORLD OF NIGHT IS OUR DOMAIN.
ZA (TURN)
AND NONE...
PACHIN (SNAP)
...CAN ESCAPE IT.

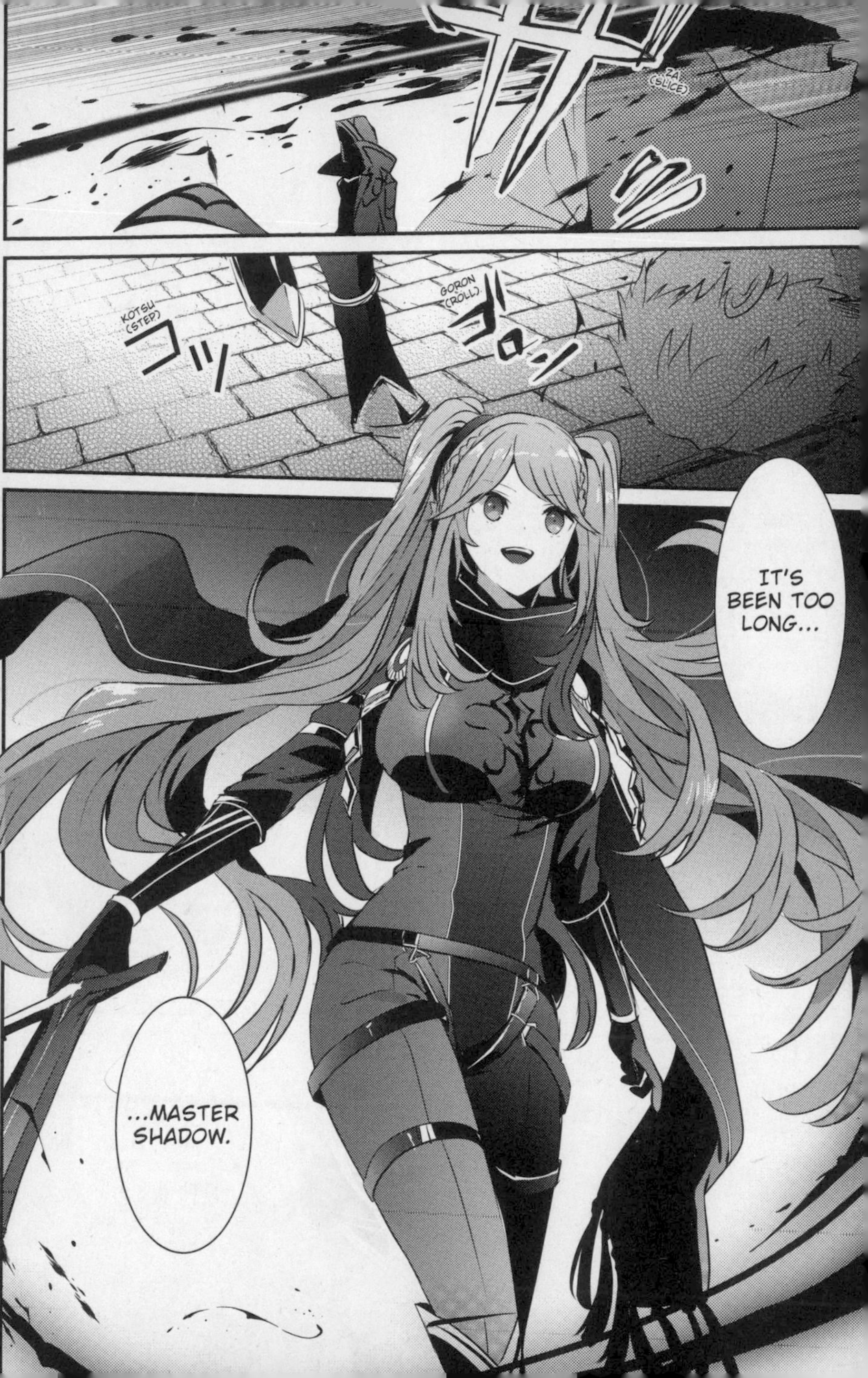
ZA (SLICE)
GORON (ROLL)
KOTSU (STEP)
IT'S BEEN TOO LONG...
...MASTER SHADOW.

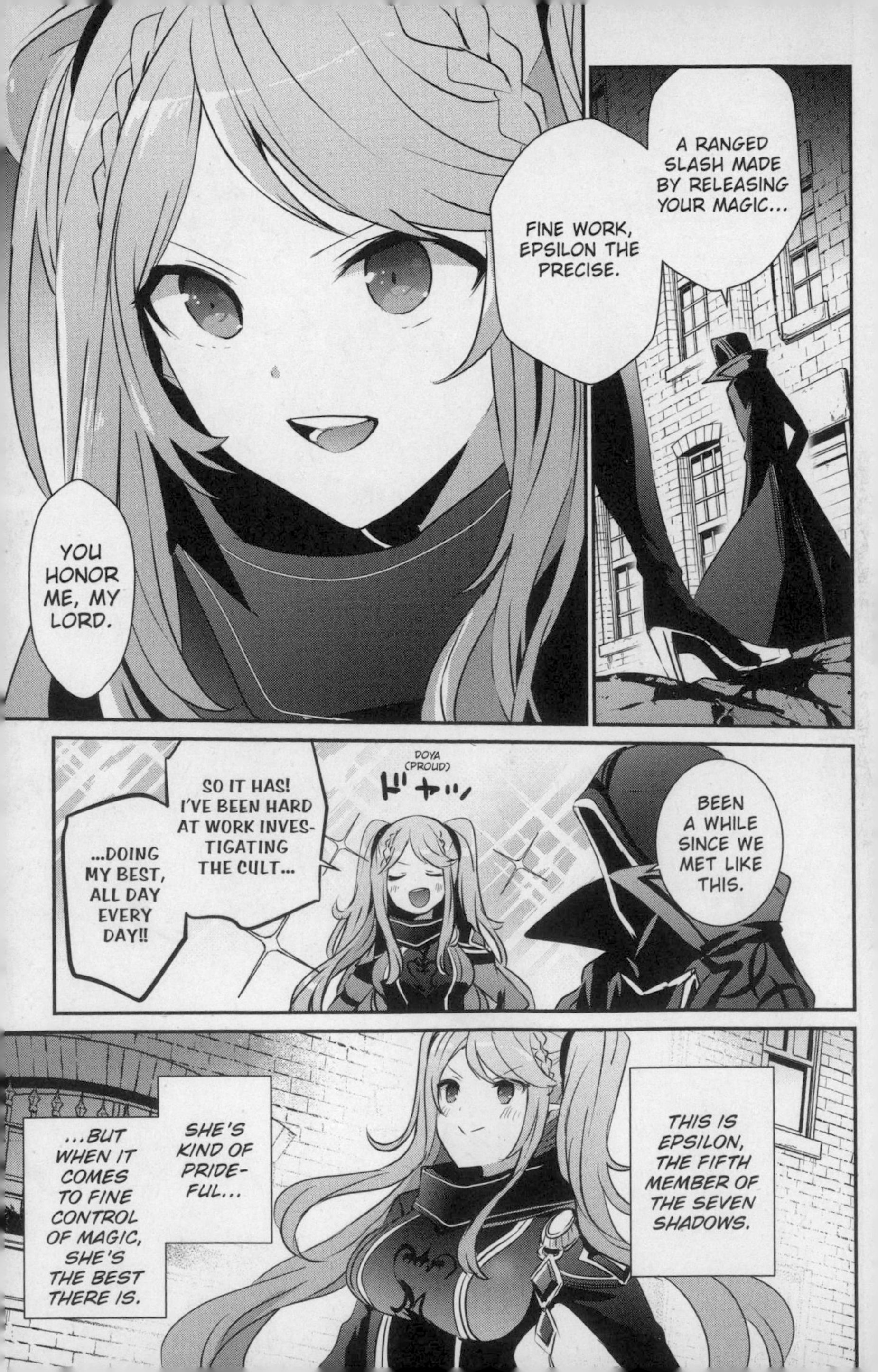
A RANGED SLASH MADE BY RELEASING YOUR MAGIC...
FINE WORK, EPSILON THE PRECISE.
YOU HONOR ME, MY LORD.
BEEN A WHILE SINCE WE MET LIKE THIS.
DOYA (PROUD)
ドヤッ
SO IT HAS! I'VE BEEN HARD AT WORK INVES-TIGATING THE CULT...
...DOING MY BEST, ALL DAY EVERY DAY!!
THIS IS EPSILON, THE FIFTH MEMBER OF THE SEVEN SHADOWS.
SHE'S KIND OF PRIDE-FUL...
...BUT WHEN IT COMES TO FINE CONTROL OF MAGIC, SHE'S THE BEST THERE IS.

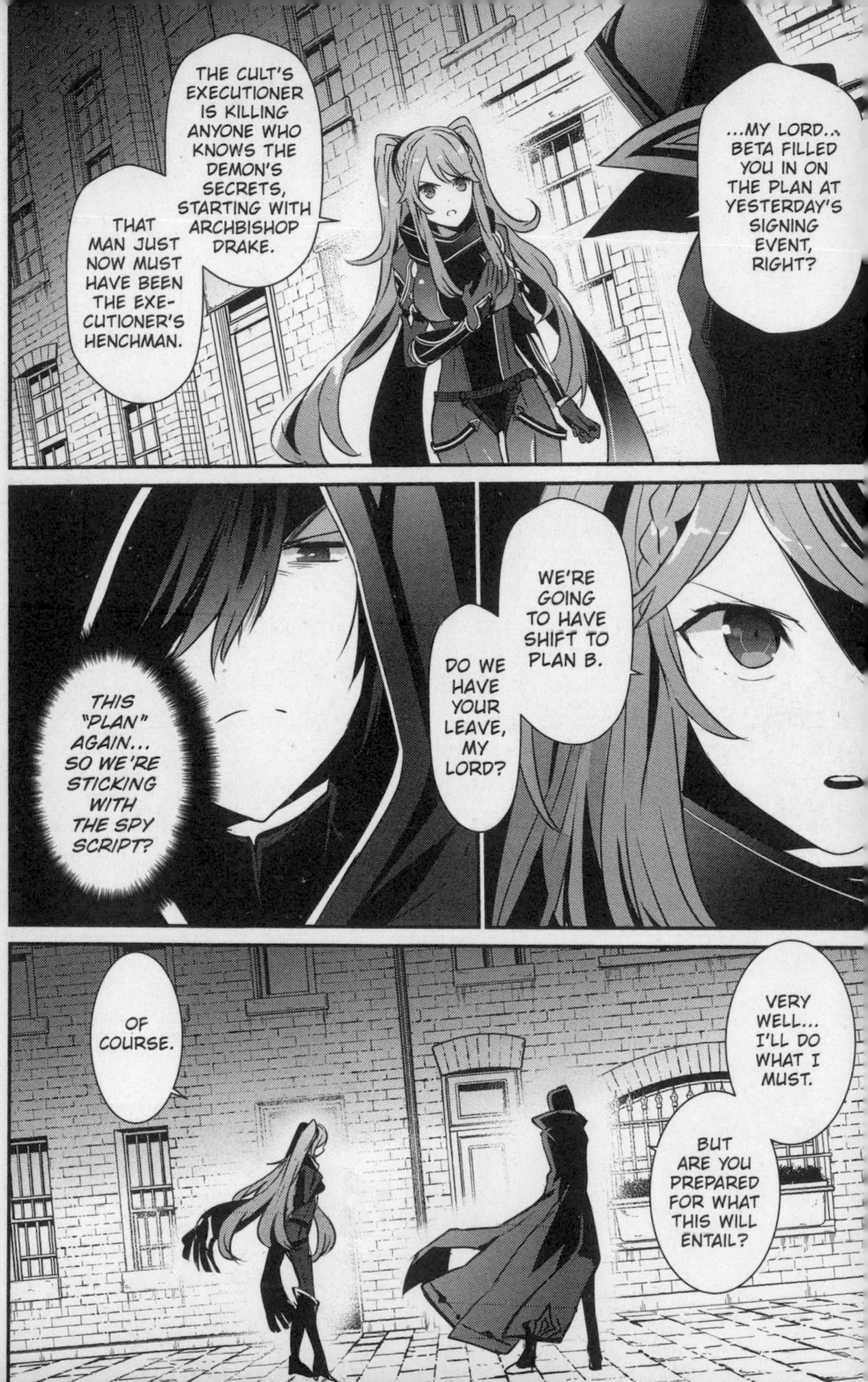
...MY LORD... BETA FILLED YOU IN ON THE PLAN AT YESTERDAY'S SIGNING EVENT, RIGHT?
THE CULT'S EXECUTIONER IS KILLING ANYONE WHO KNOWS THE DEMON'S SECRETS, STARTING WITH ARCHBISHOP DRAKE.
THAT MAN JUST NOW MUST HAVE BEEN THE EXE-CUTIONER'S HENCHMAN.
WE'RE GOING TO HAVE SHIFT TO PLAN B.
DO WE HAVE YOUR LEAVE, MY LORD?
THIS "PLAN" AGAIN... SO WE'RE STICKING WITH THE SPY SCRIPT?
VERY WELL... I'LL DO WHAT I MUST.
BUT ARE YOU PREPARED FOR WHAT THIS WILL ENTAIL?
OF COURSE.

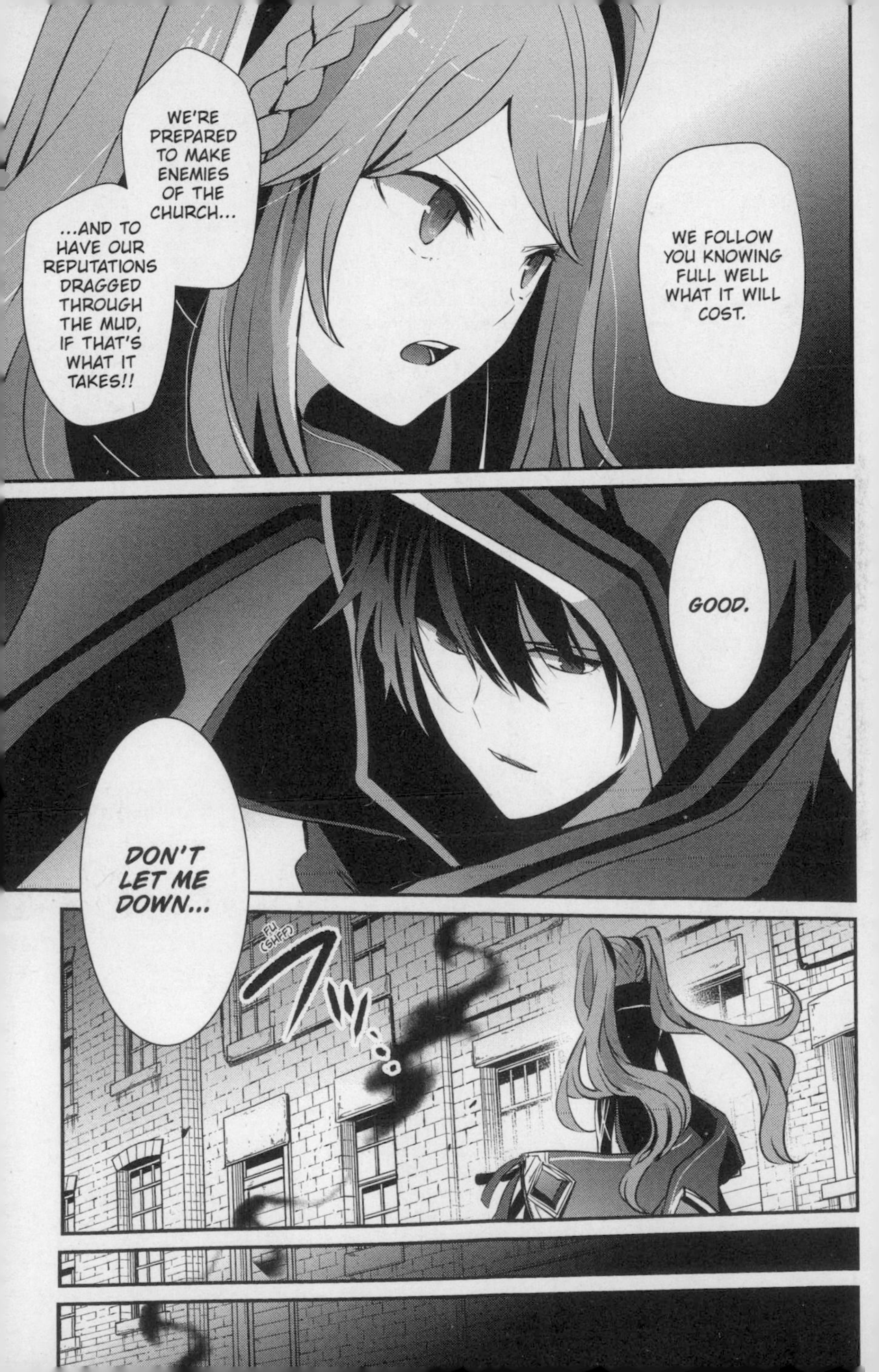

WE FOLLOW YOU KNOWING FULL WELL WHAT IT WILL COST.
WE'RE PREPARED TO MAKE ENEMIES OF THE CHURCH...
...AND TO HAVE OUR REPUTATIONS DRAGGED THROUGH THE MUD, IF THAT'S WHAT IT TAKES!!
GOOD.
DON'T LET ME DOWN...
FU (SNIFF)

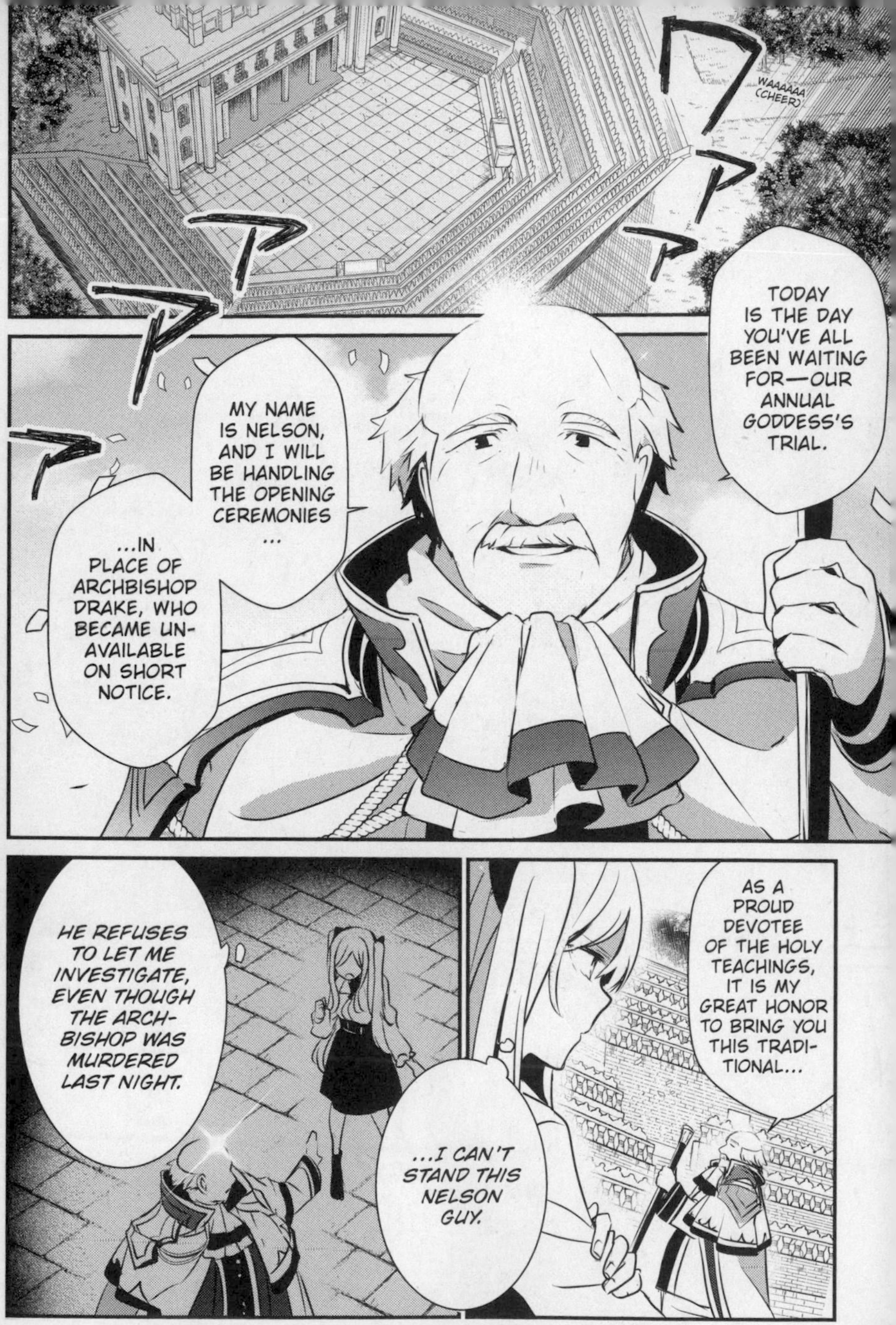
WAAAAAA (CHEER)
TODAY IS THE DAY YOU'VE ALL BEEN WAITING FOR—OUR ANNUAL GODDESS'S TRIAL.
MY NAME IS NELSON, AND I WILL BE HANDLING THE OPENING CEREMONIES...
...IN PLACE OF ARCHBISHOP DRAKE, WHO BECAME UN-AVAILABLE ON SHORT NOTICE.
AS A PROUD DEVOTEE OF THE HOLY TEACHINGS, IT IS MY GREAT HONOR TO BRING YOU THIS TRADI-TIONAL...
...I CAN'T STAND THIS NELSON GUY.
HE REFUSES TO LET ME INVESTIGATE, EVEN THOUGH THE ARCH-BISHOP WAS MURDERED LAST NIGHT.

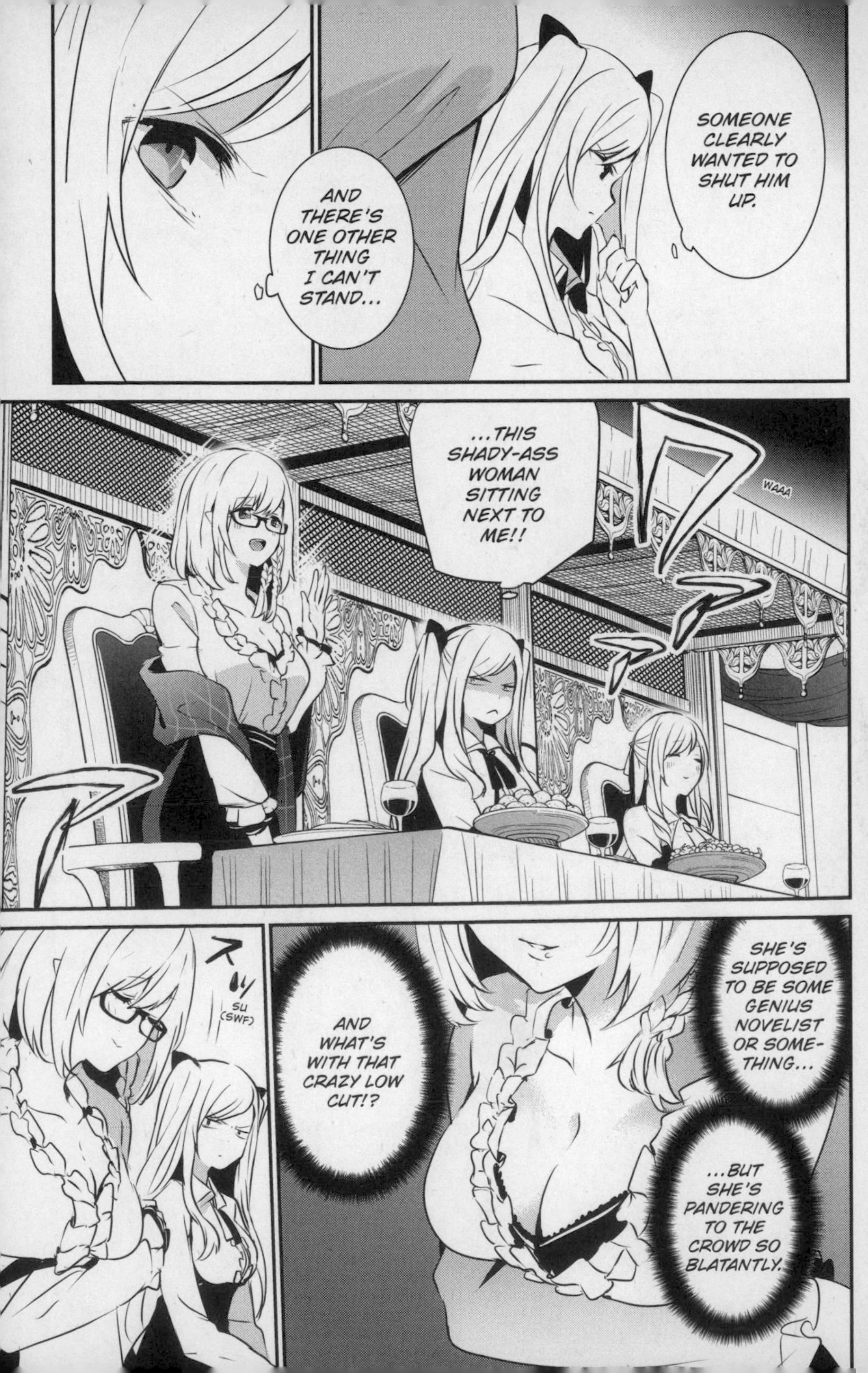
SOMEONE CLEARLY WANTED TO SHUT HIM UP.
AND THERE'S ONE OTHER THING I CAN'T STAND...
...THIS SHADY-ASS WOMAN SITTING NEXT TO ME!!
WAAA
SHE'S SUPPOSED TO BE SOME GENIUS NOVELIST OR SOME-THING...
...BUT SHE'S PANDERING TO THE CROWD SO BLATANTLY.
AND WHAT'S WITH THAT CRAZY LOW CUT!?
SU (SWF)

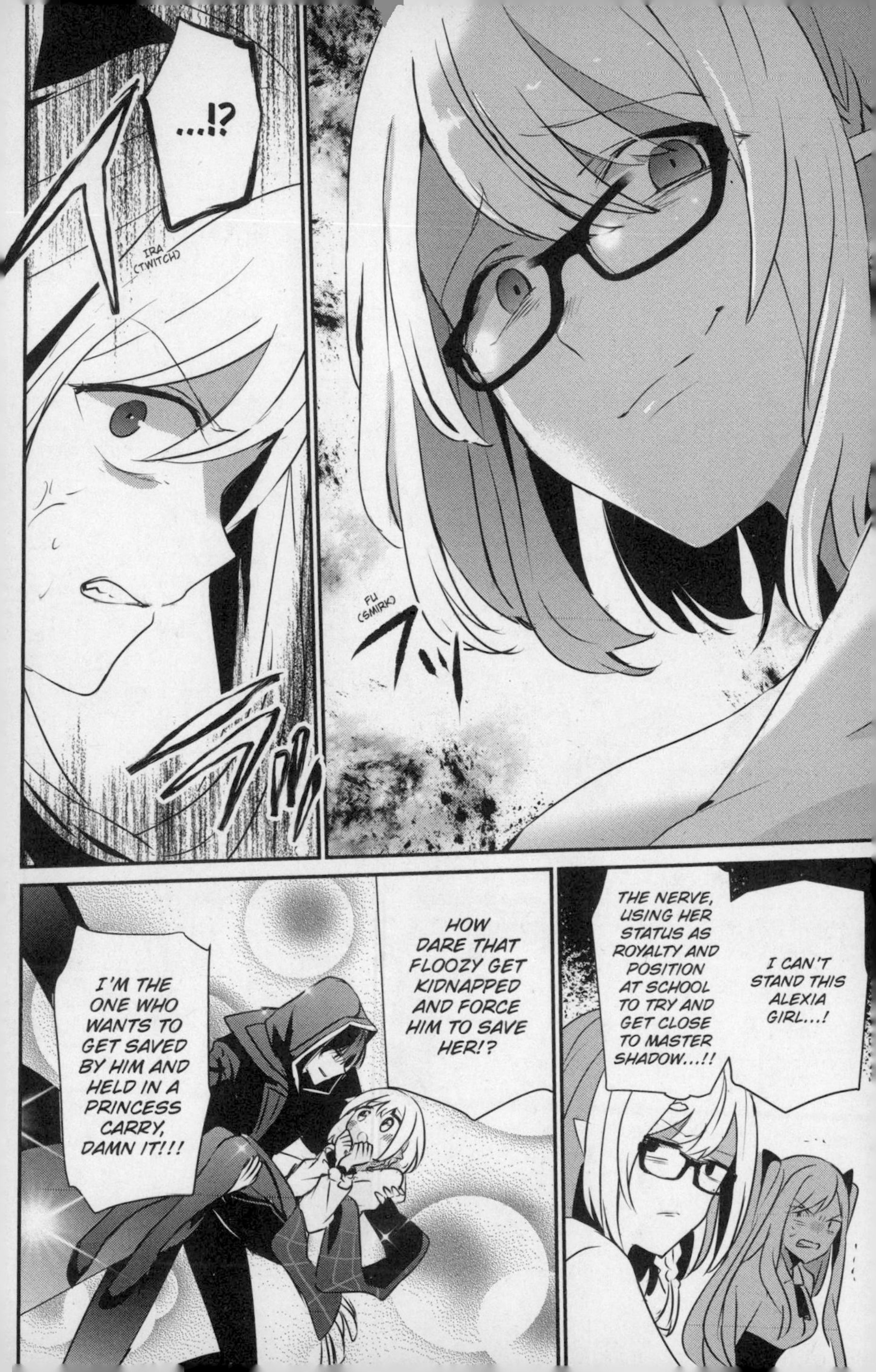
FU (SMIRK)
...!?
IRA (TWITCH)
I CAN'T STAND THIS ALEXIA GIRL...!
THE NERVE, USING HER STATUS AS ROYALTY AND POSITION AT SCHOOL TO TRY AND GET CLOSE TO MASTER SHADOW...!!
HOW DARE THAT FLOOZY GET KIDNAPPED AND FORCE HIM TO SAVE HER!?
I'M THE ONE WHO WANTS TO GET SAVED BY HIM AND HELD IN A PRINCESS CARRY, DAMN IT!!!

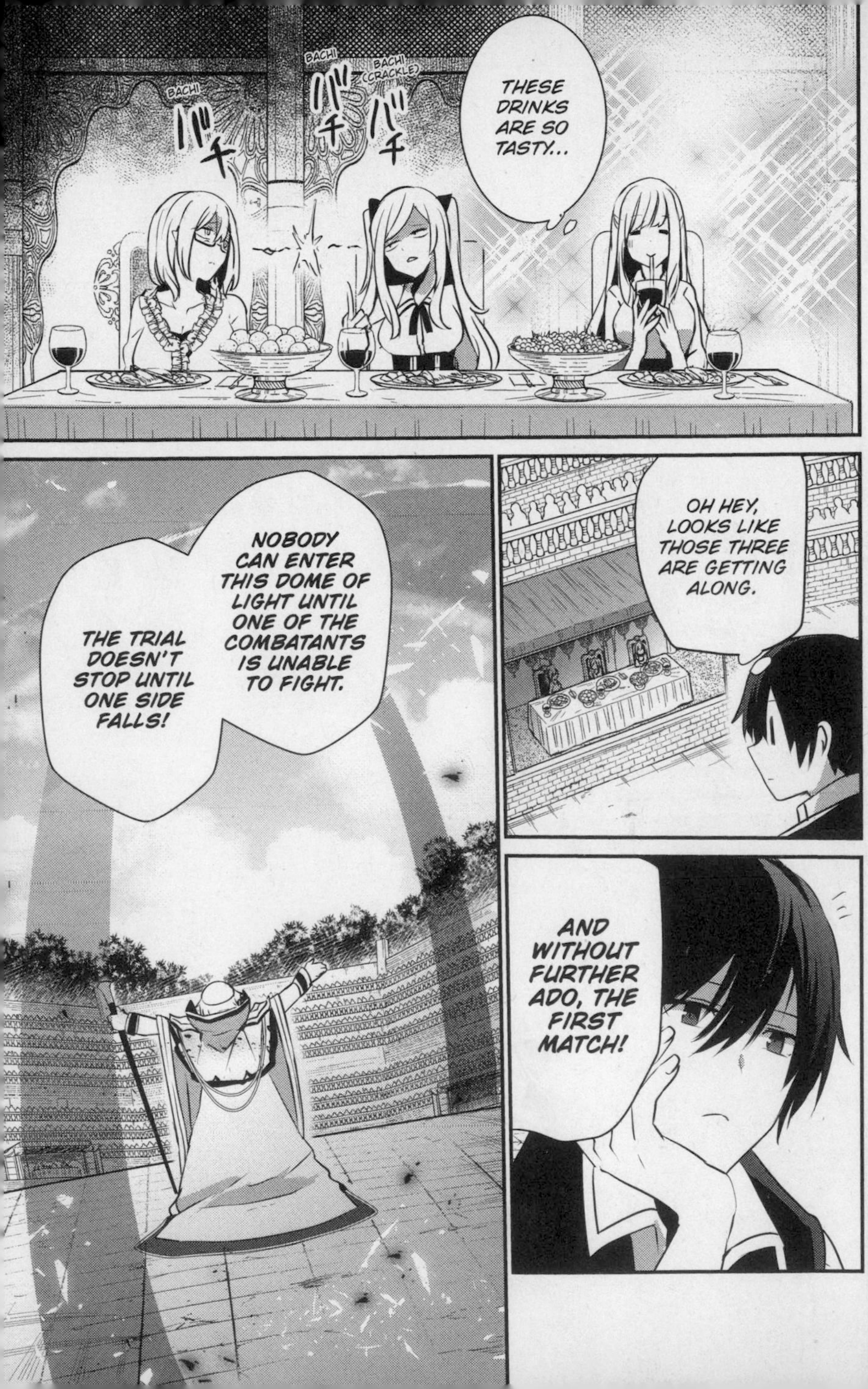
THESE DRINKS ARE SO TASTY...
BACHI (CRACKLE)
バチ
BACHI
バチ
BACHI
バチ
OH HEY, LOOKS LIKE THOSE THREE ARE GETTING ALONG.
AND WITHOUT FURTHER ADO, THE FIRST MATCH!
NOBODY CAN ENTER THIS DOME OF LIGHT UNTIL ONE OF THE COMBATANTS IS UNABLE TO FIGHT.
THE TRIAL DOESN'T STOP UNTIL ONE SIDE FALLS!

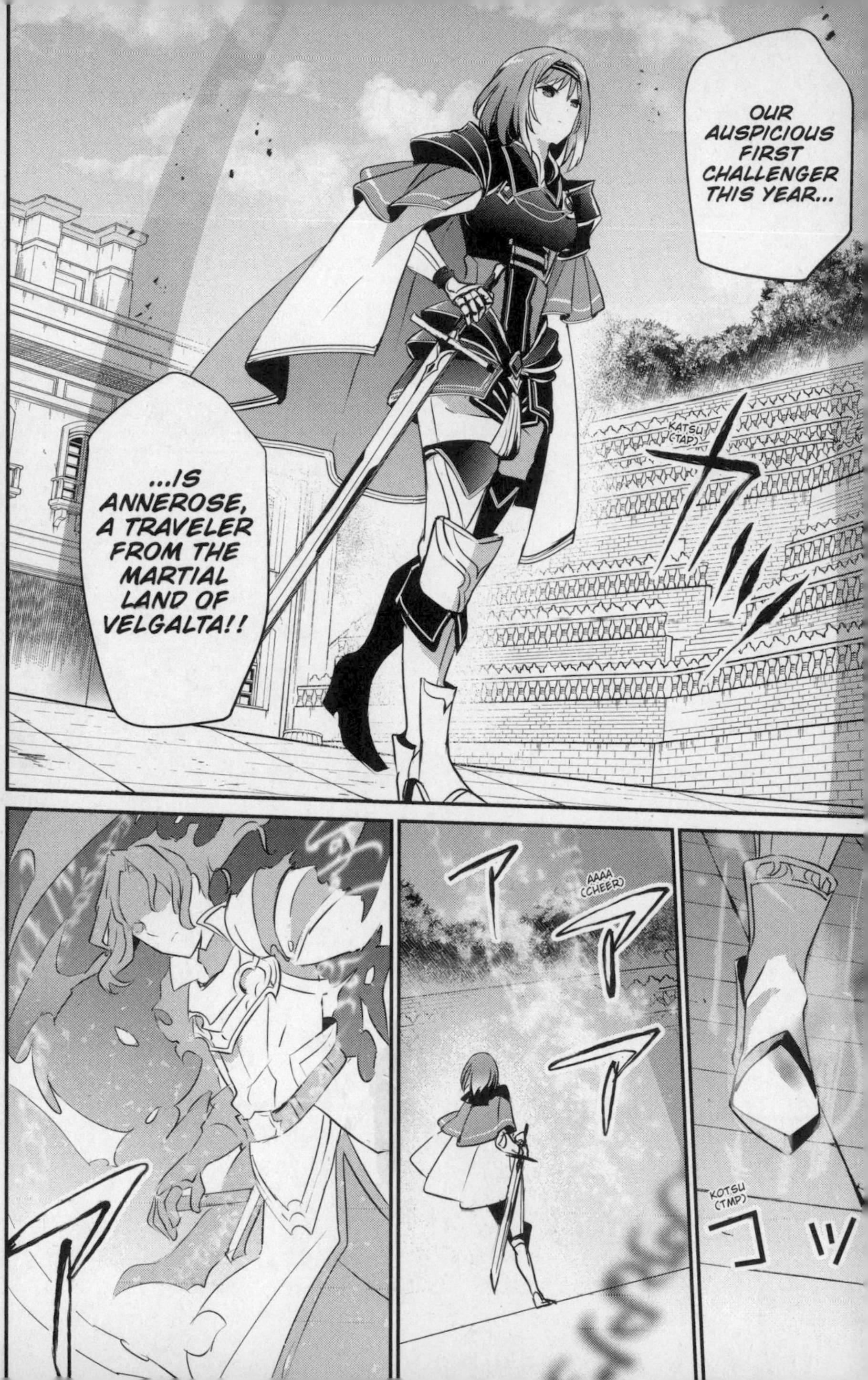
OUR AUSPICIOUS FIRST CHALLENGER THIS YEAR...
...IS ANNEROSE, A TRAVELER FROM THE MARTIAL LAND OF VELGALTA!!
KATSU (TAP)
KOTSU (TMP)
AAAA (CHEER)

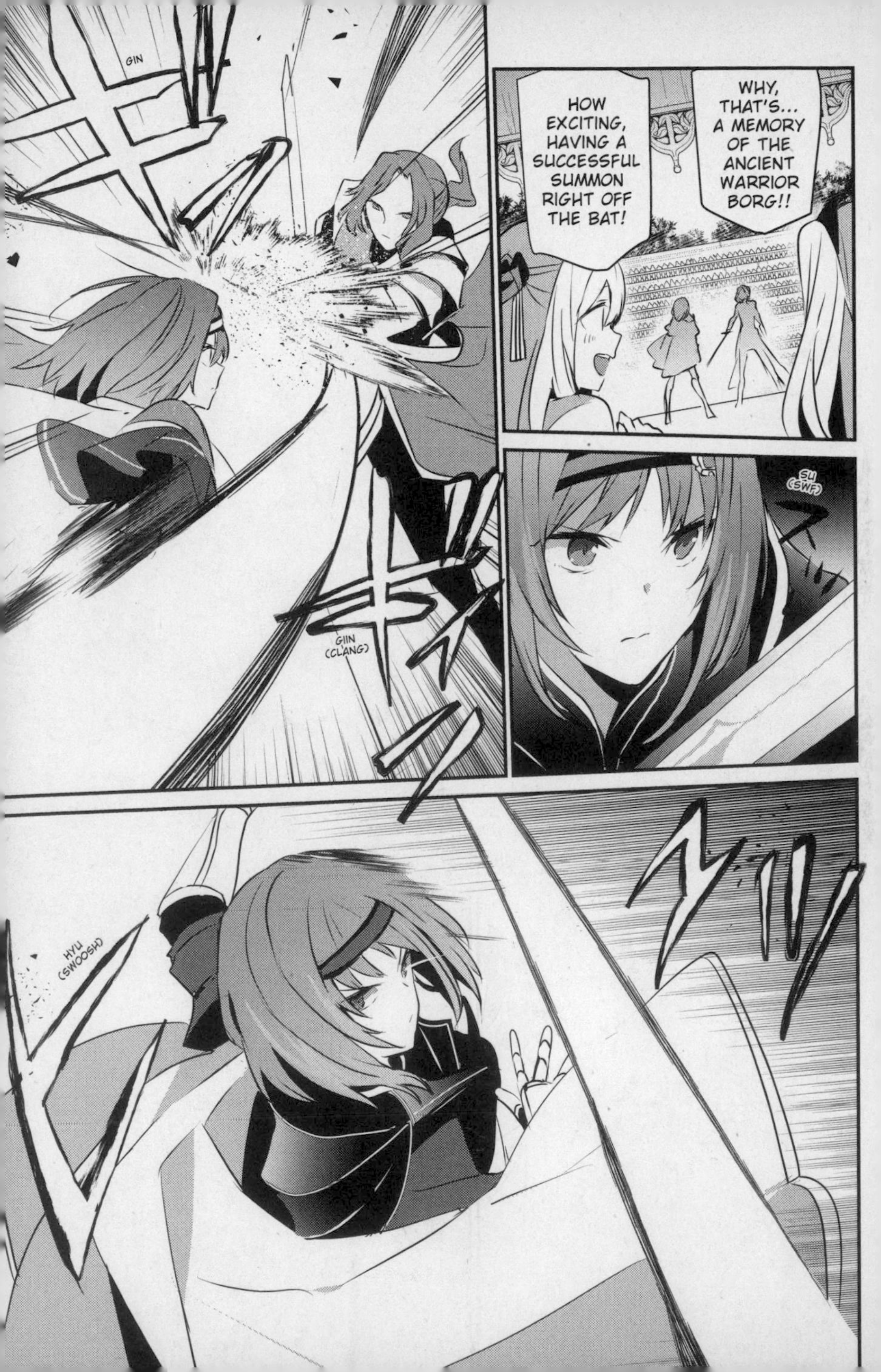
WHY, THAT'S... A MEMORY OF THE ANCIENT WARRIOR BORG!!
HOW EXCITING, HAVING A SUCCESSFUL SUMMON RIGHT OFF THE BAT!
SU (SWF)
GIN
GIIN (CLANG)
HYU (SWOOSH)

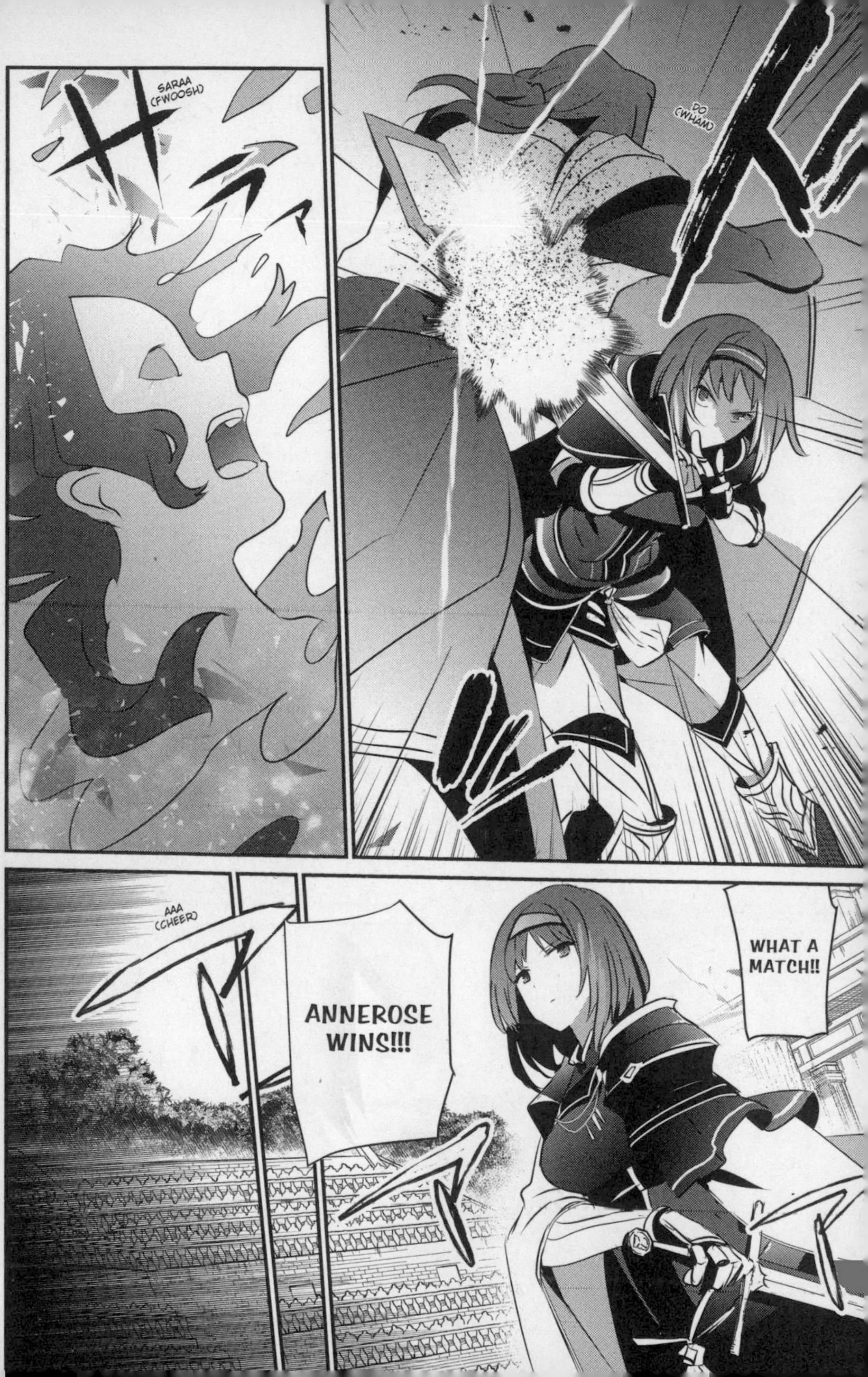
DO (WHAM)
SARAA (FWOOSH)
WHAT A MATCH!!
ANNEROSE WINS!!!
AAA (CHEER)

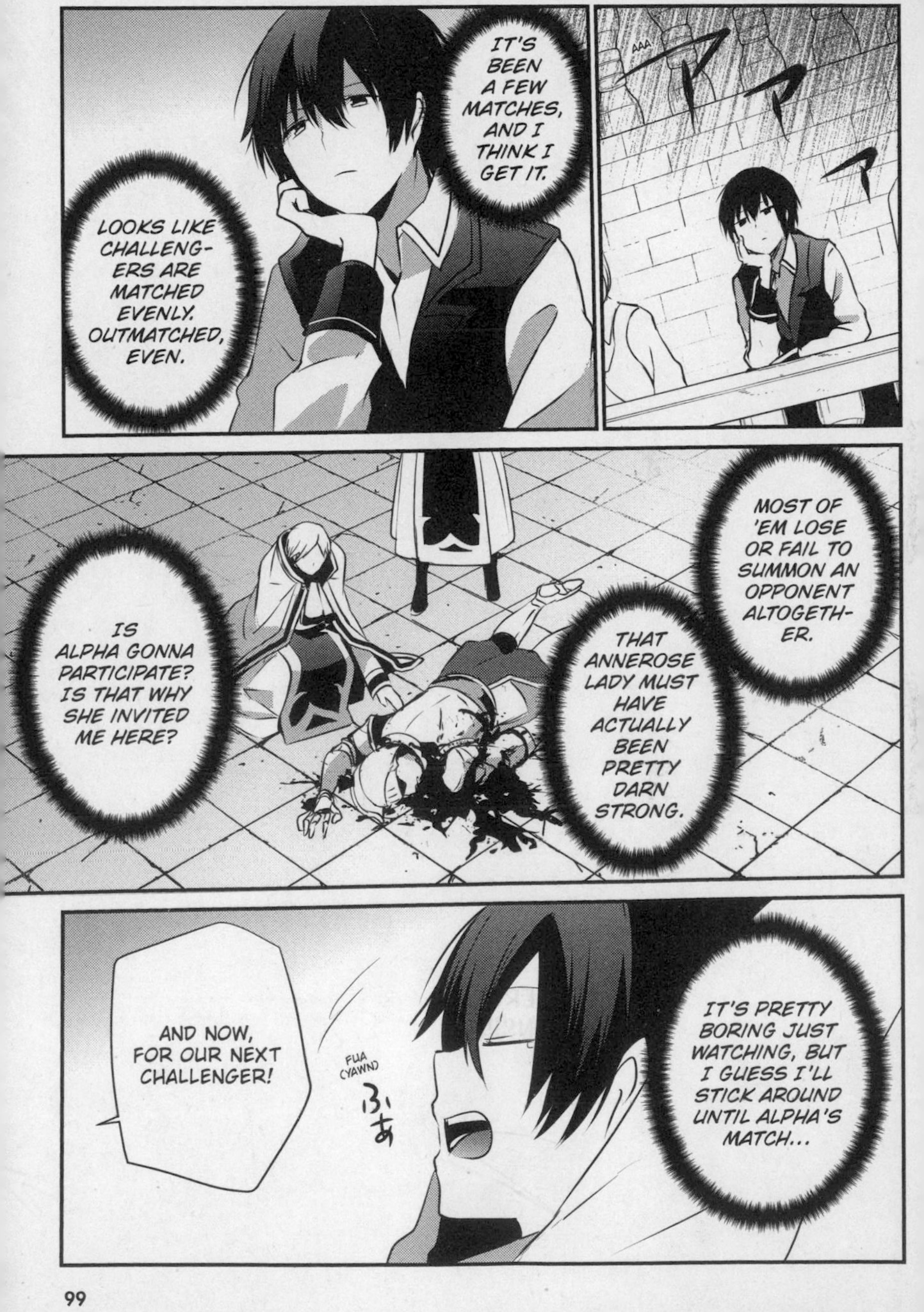
AAA
アアア
IT'S BEEN A FEW MATCHES, AND I THINK I GET IT.
LOOKS LIKE CHALLENGERS ARE MATCHED EVENLY. OUTMATCHED, EVEN.
MOST OF 'EM LOSE OR FAIL TO SUMMON AN OPPONENT ALTOGETHER.
THAT ANNEROSE LADY MUST HAVE ACTUALLY BEEN PRETTY DARN STRONG.
IS ALPHA GONNA PARTICIPATE? IS THAT WHY SHE INVITED ME HERE?
IT'S PRETTY BORING JUST WATCHING, BUT I GUESS I'LL STICK AROUND UNTIL ALPHA'S MATCH...
FUA (YAWN)
ふあ
AND NOW, FOR OUR NEXT CHALLENGER!

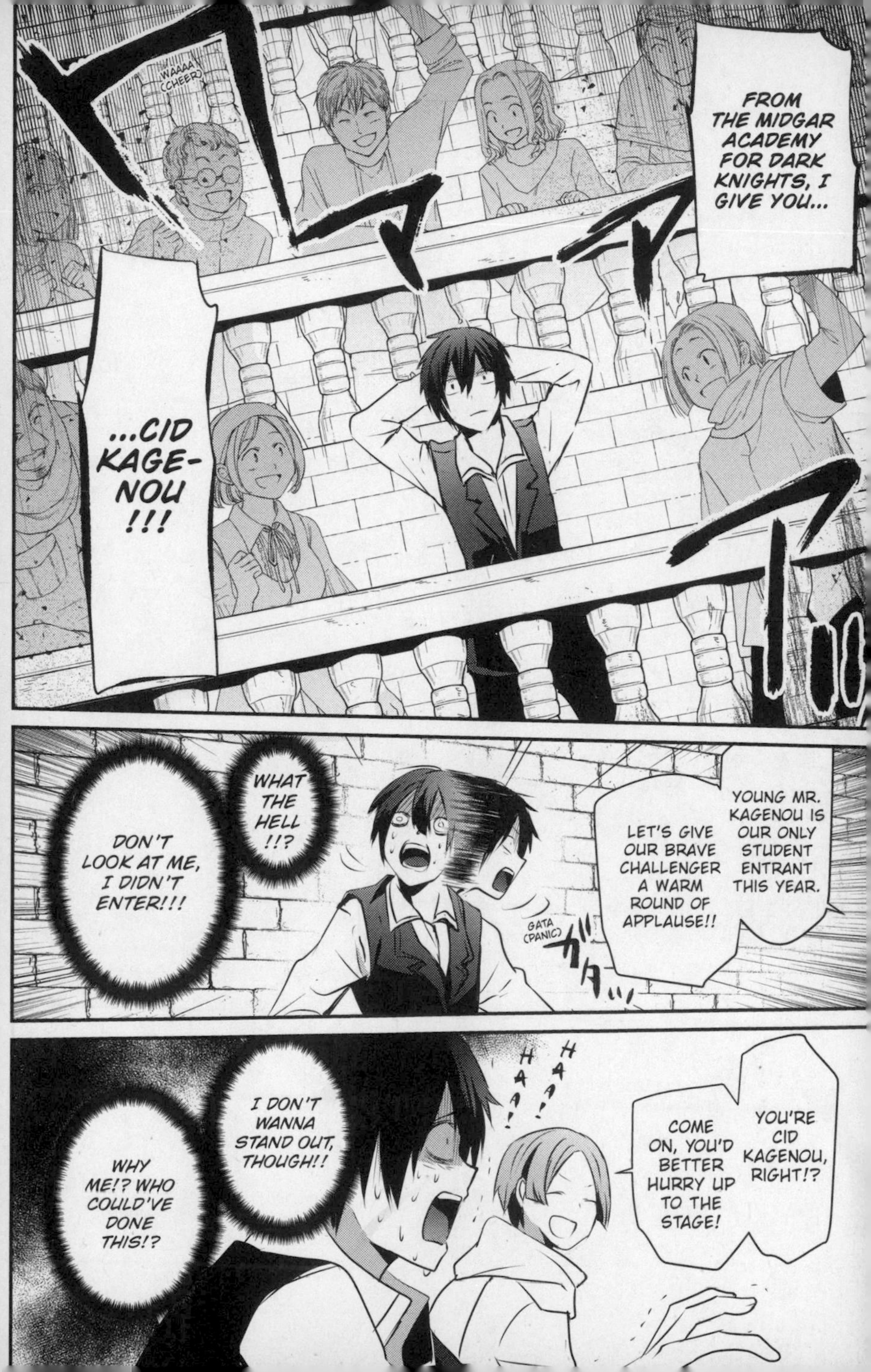
FROM THE MIDGAR ACADEMY FOR DARK KNIGHTS, I GIVE YOU...
WAAAA (CHEER)
...CID KAGENOU!!!
YOUNG MR. KAGENOU IS OUR ONLY STUDENT ENTRANT THIS YEAR.
LET'S GIVE OUR BRAVE CHALLENGER A WARM ROUND OF APPLAUSE!!
GATA (PANIC)
WHAT THE HELL!!?
DON'T LOOK AT ME, I DIDN'T ENTER!!!
YOU'RE CID KAGENOU, RIGHT!?
COME ON, YOU'D BETTER HURRY UP TO THE STAGE!
HAA! HAA!
I DON'T WANNA STAND OUT, THOUGH!!
WHY ME!? WHO COULD'VE DONE THIS!?

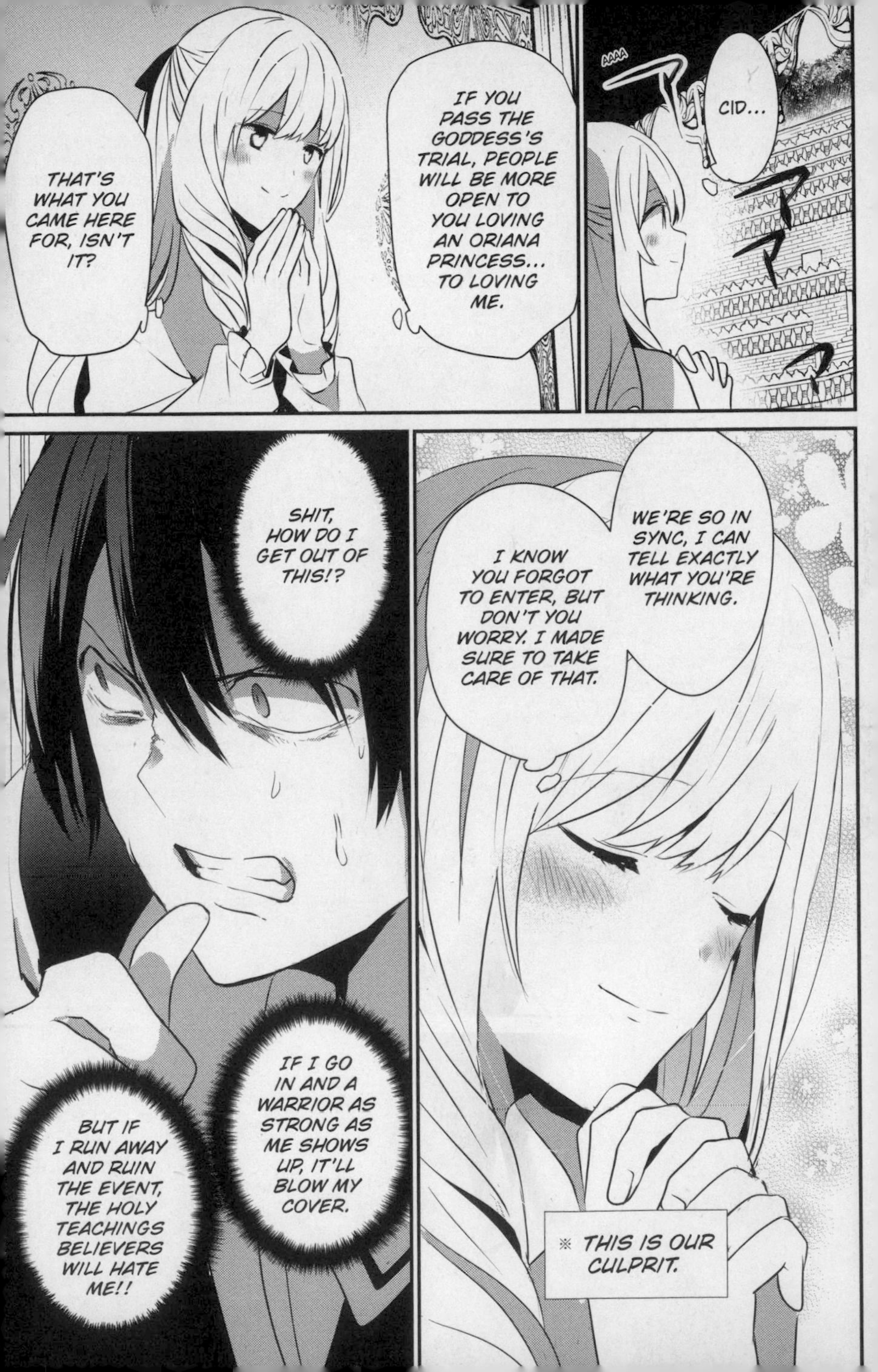
AAAA
CID...
IF YOU PASS THE GODDESS'S TRIAL, PEOPLE WILL BE MORE OPEN TO YOU LOVING AN ORIANA PRINCESS... TO LOVING ME.
THAT'S WHAT YOU CAME HERE FOR, ISN'T IT?
WE'RE SO IN SYNC, I CAN TELL EXACTLY WHAT YOU'RE THINKING.
I KNOW YOU FORGOT TO ENTER, BUT DON'T YOU WORRY. I MADE SURE TO TAKE CARE OF THAT.
※ THIS IS OUR CULPRIT.
SHIT, HOW DO I GET OUT OF THIS!?
IF I GO IN AND A WARRIOR AS STRONG AS ME SHOWS UP, IT'LL BLOW MY COVER.
BUT IF I RUN AWAY AND RUIN THE EVENT, THE HOLY TEACHINGS BELIEVERS WILL HATE ME!!

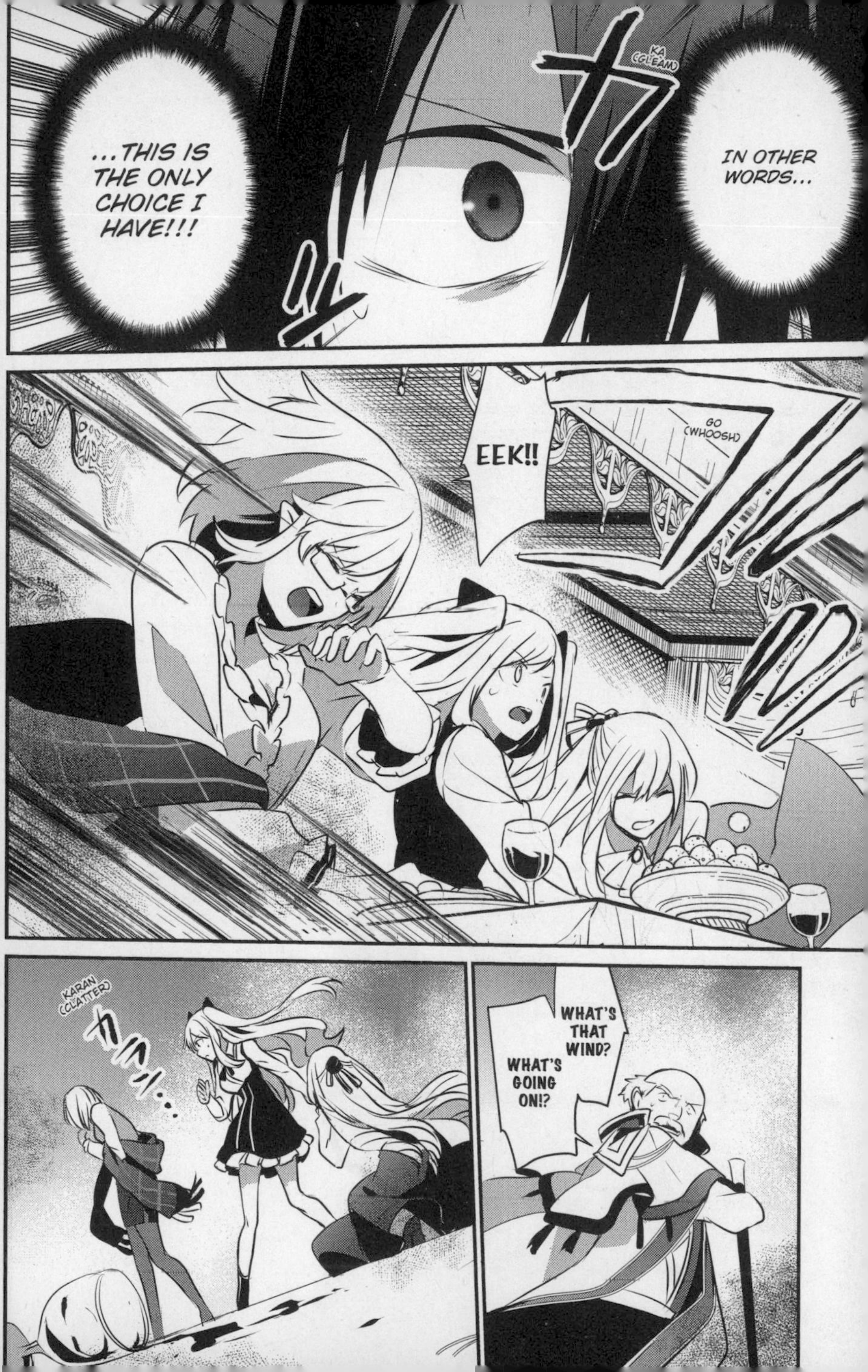
IN OTHER WORDS...
KA (GLEAM)
...THIS IS THE ONLY CHOICE I HAVE!!!
GO (WHOOSH)
EEK!!
WHAT'S THAT WIND?
WHAT'S GOING ON!?
KARAN (CLATTER)

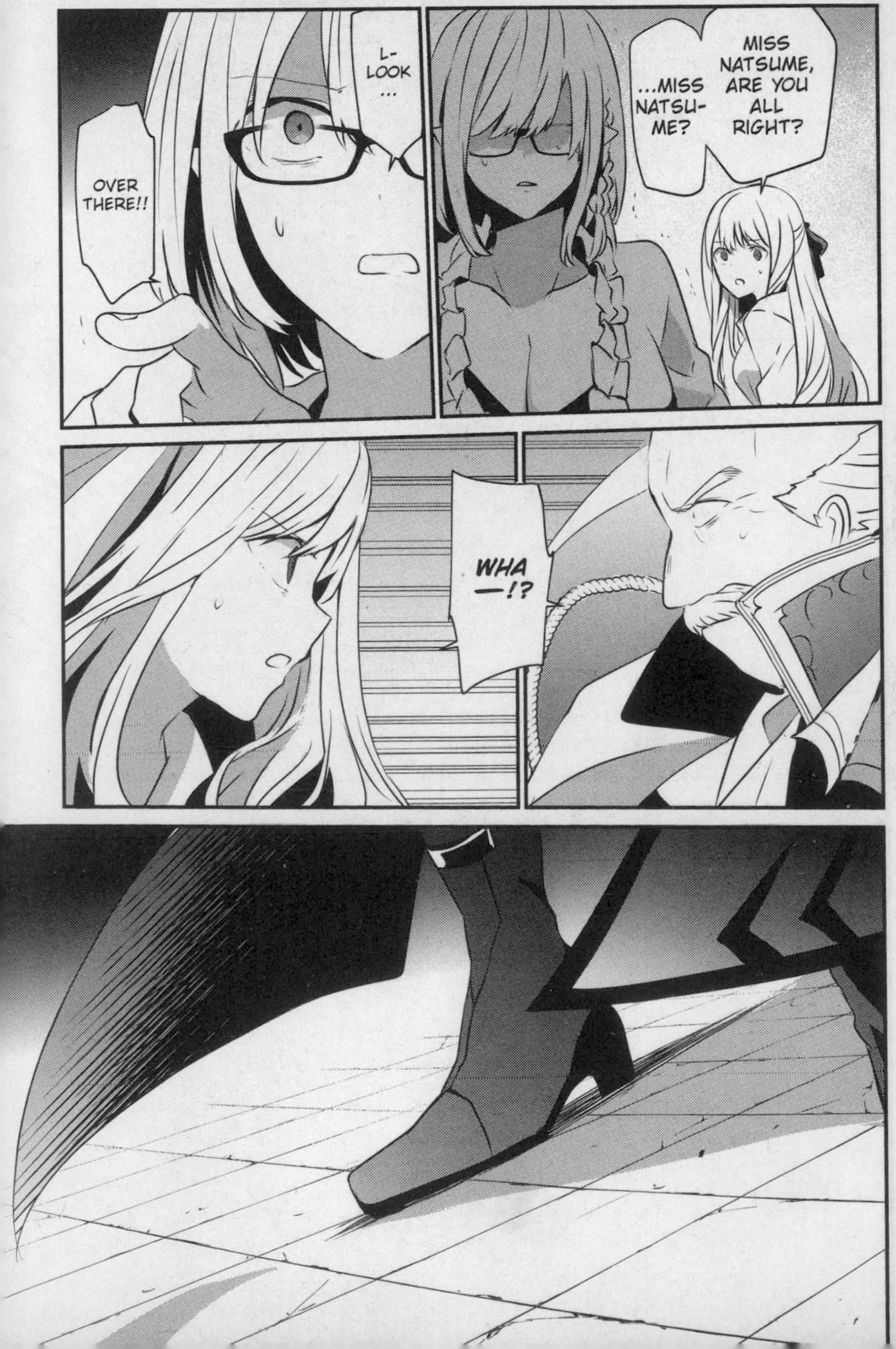
MISS NATSUME, ARE YOU ALL RIGHT?
...MISS NATSUME?
L-LOOK ...
OVER THERE!!
WHA—!?

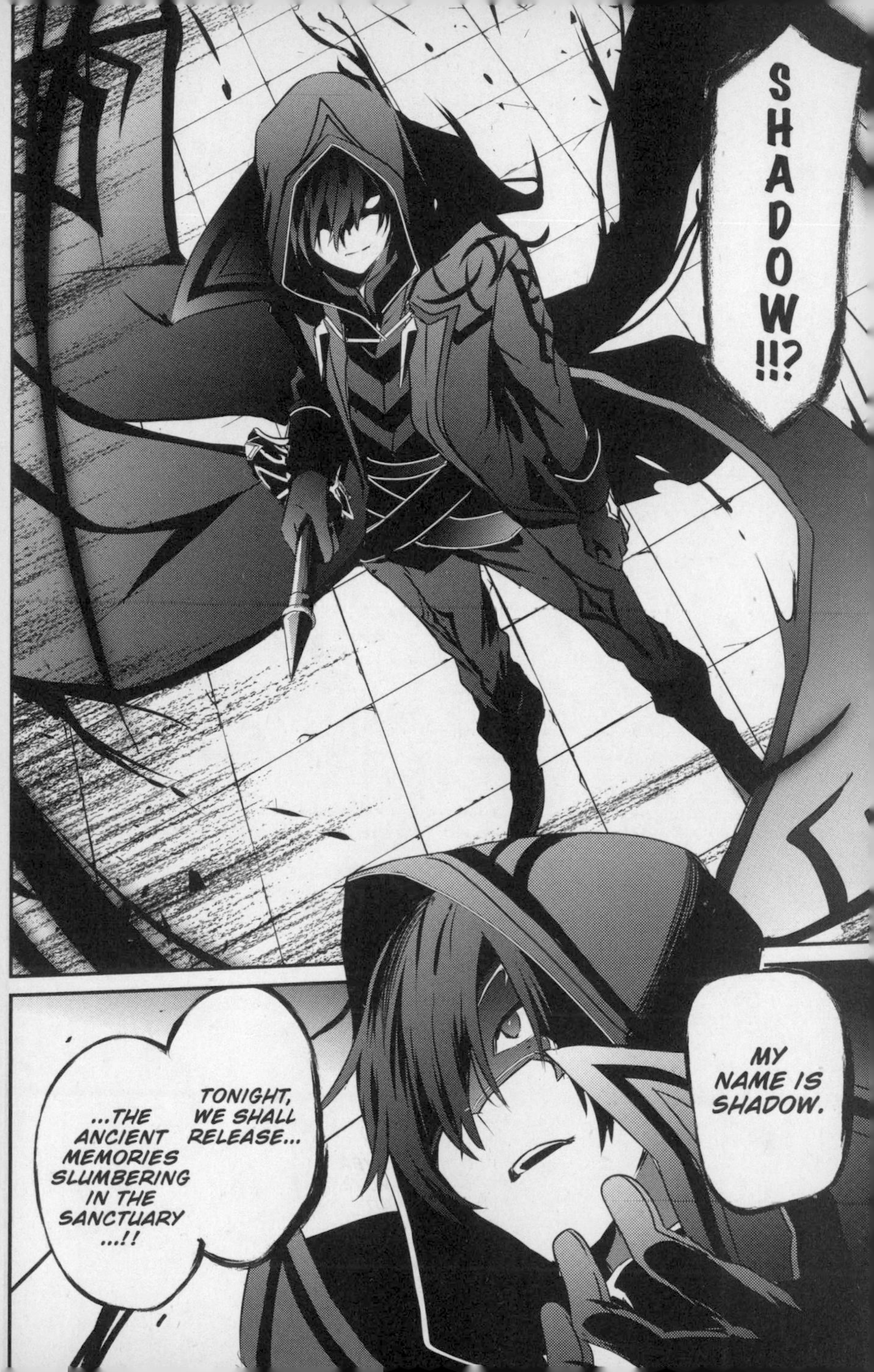
SHADOW!!?
MY NAME IS SHADOW.
TONIGHT, WE SHALL RELEASE...
...THE ANCIENT MEMORIES SLUMBERING IN THE SANCTUARY ...!!

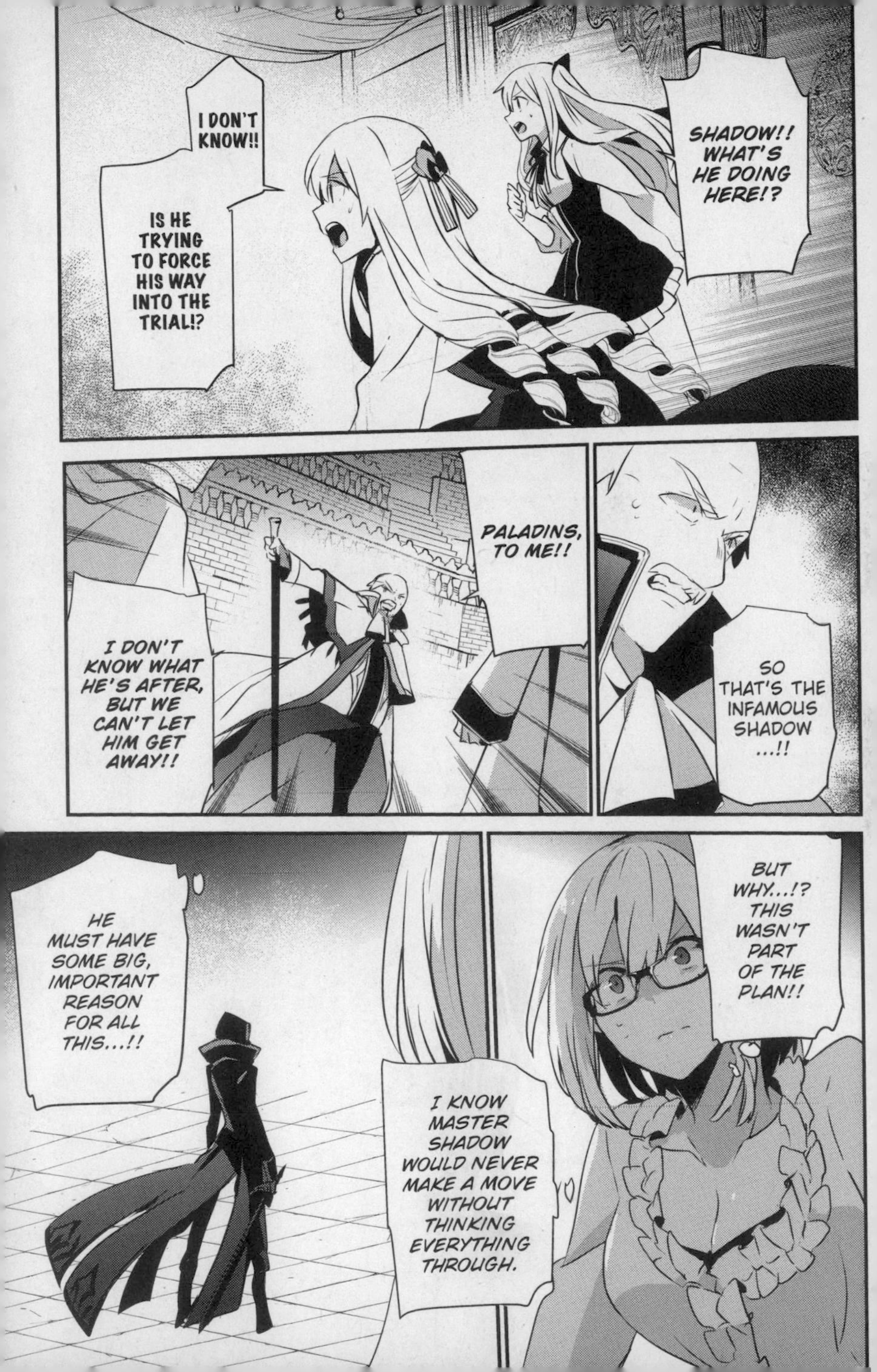
SHADOW!! WHAT'S HE DOING HERE!?
I DON'T KNOW!!
IS HE TRYING TO FORCE HIS WAY INTO THE TRIAL!?
SO THAT'S THE INFAMOUS SHADOW ...!!
PALADINS, TO ME!!
I DON'T KNOW WHAT HE'S AFTER, BUT WE CAN'T LET HIM GET AWAY!!
BUT WHY...!? THIS WASN'T PART OF THE PLAN!!
I KNOW MASTER SHADOW WOULD NEVER MAKE A MOVE WITHOUT THINKING EVERYTHING THROUGH.
HE MUST HAVE SOME BIG, IMPORTANT REASON FOR ALL THIS...!!

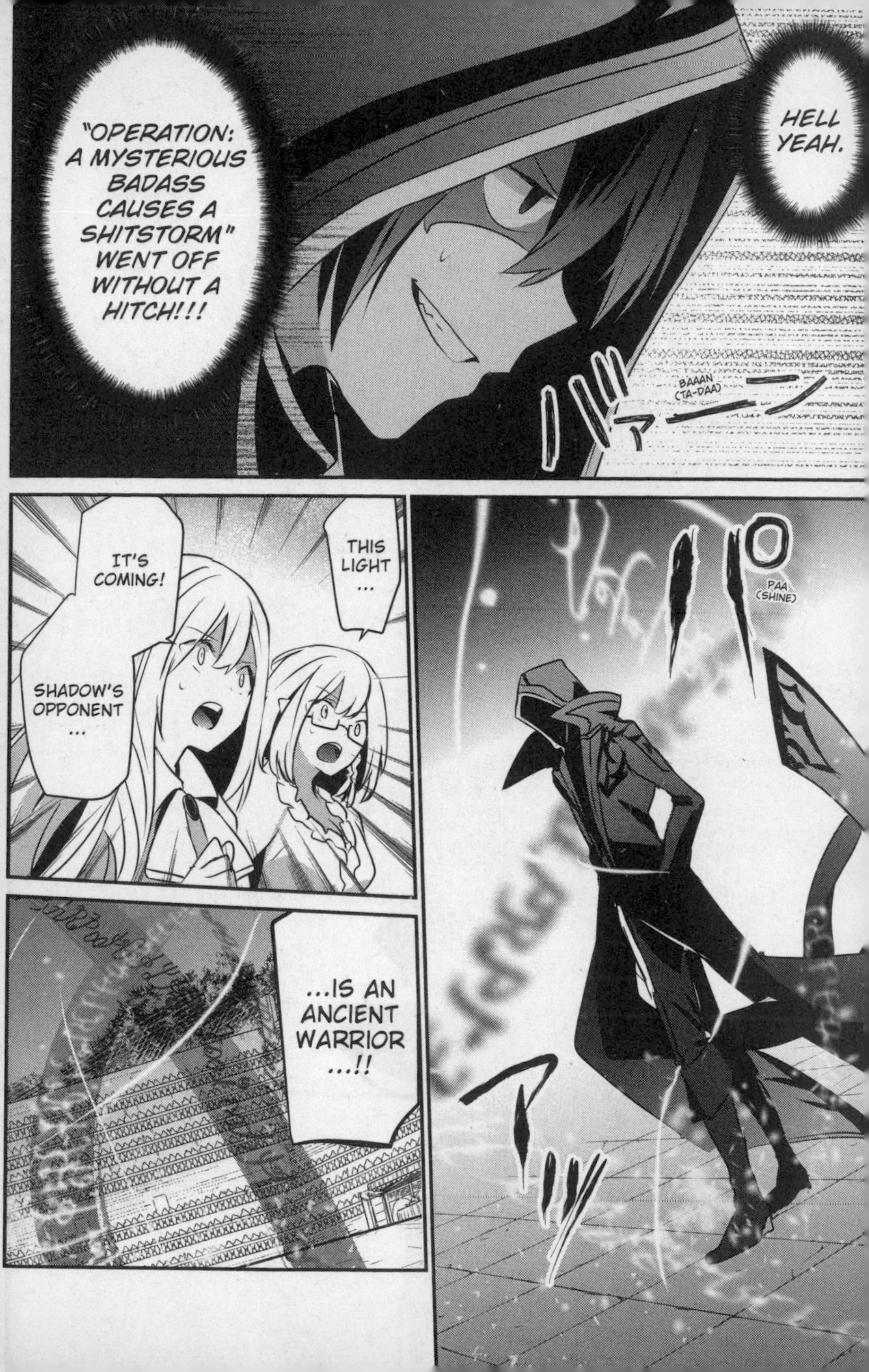
"OPERATION: A MYSTERIOUS BADASS CAUSES A SHITSTORM" WENT OFF WITHOUT A HITCH!!!
HELL YEAH.
BAAAN (TA-DAA)
PAA (SHINE)
THIS LIGHT ...
IT'S COMING!
SHADOW'S OPPONENT ...
...IS AN ANCIENT WARRIOR ...!!

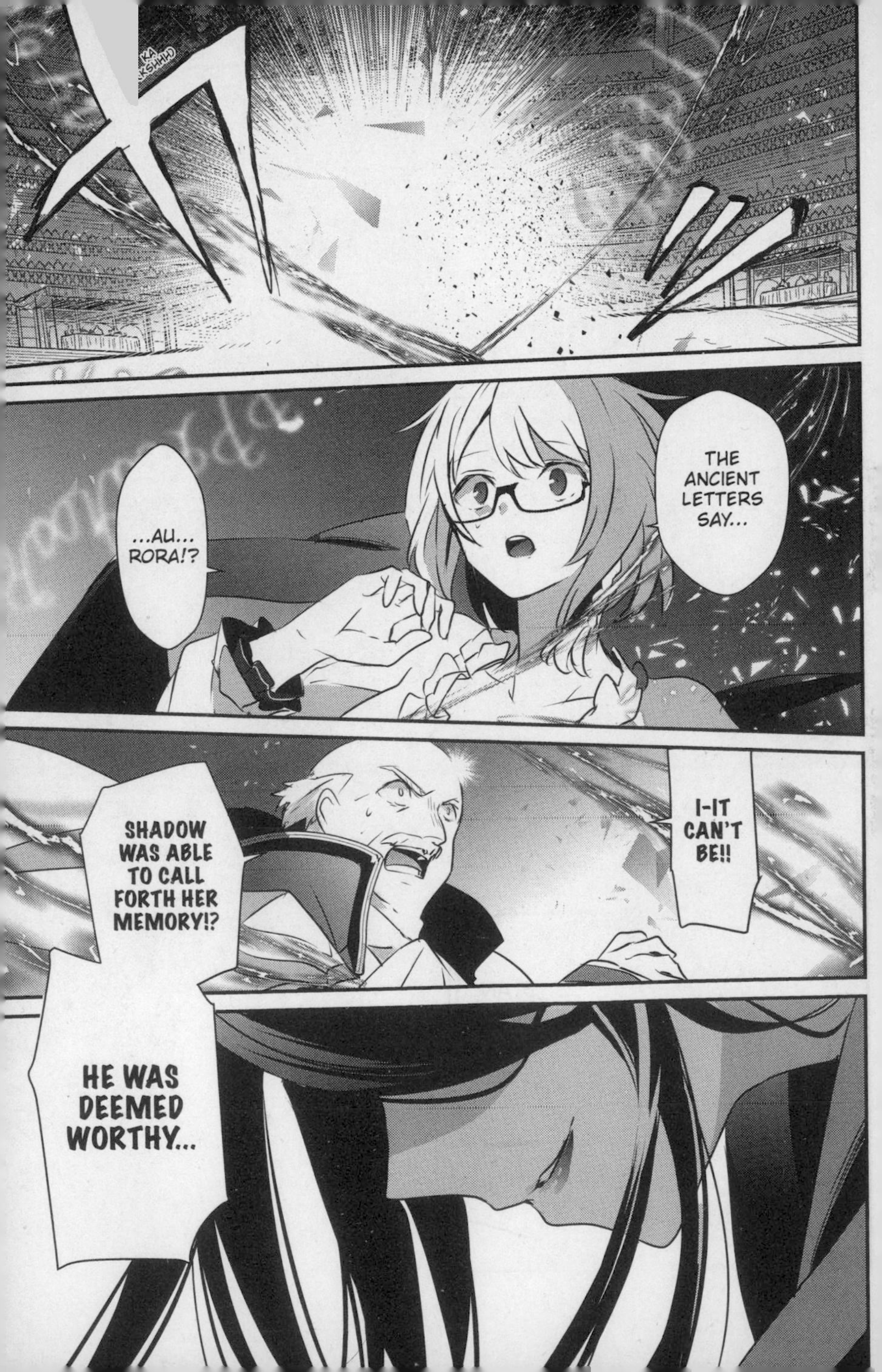
KA
THE ANCIENT LETTERS SAY...
...AU... RORA!?
I-IT CAN'T BE!!
SHADOW WAS ABLE TO CALL FORTH HER MEMORY!?
HE WAS DEEMED WORTHY...

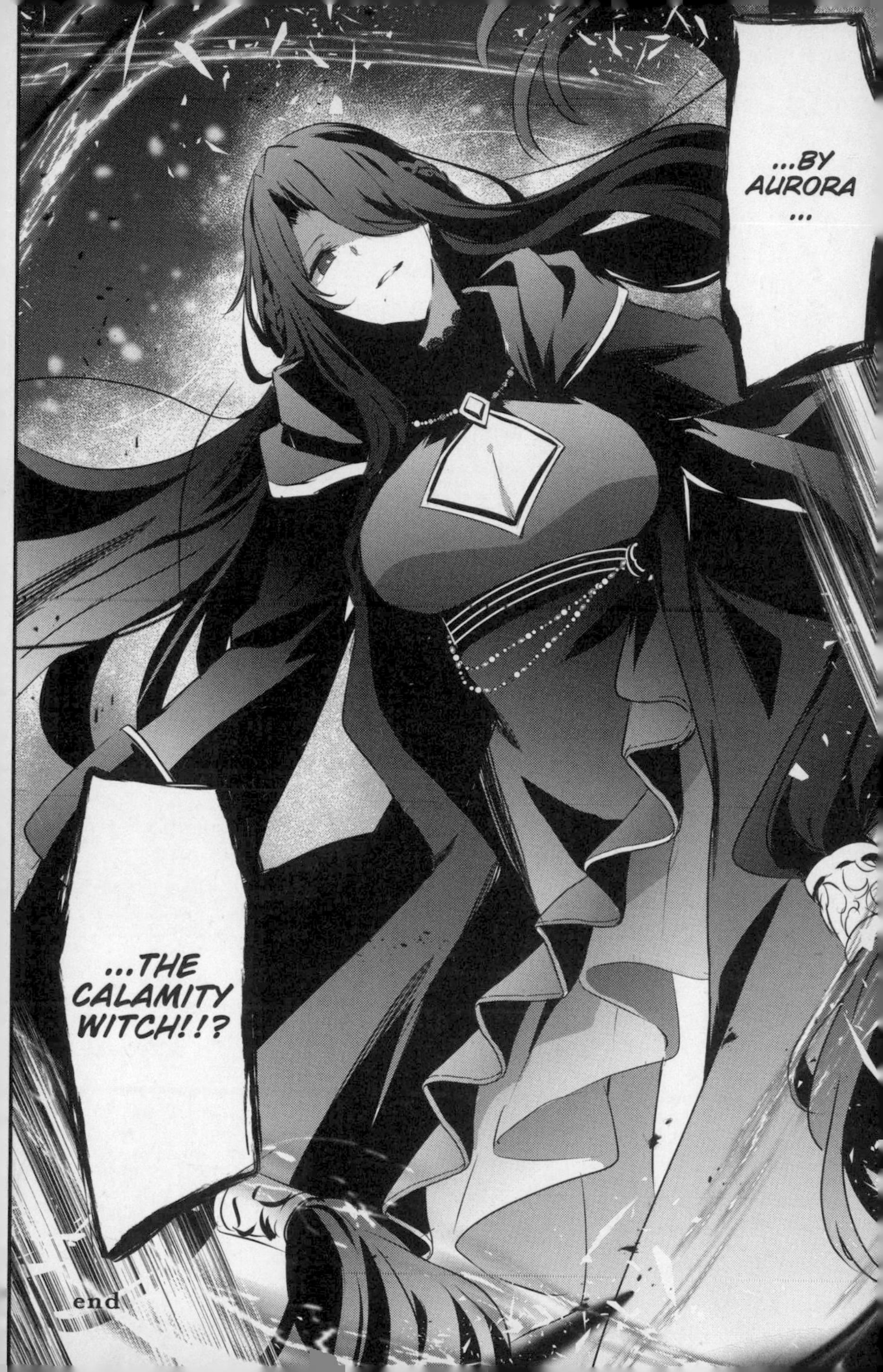
...BY AURORA ...
...THE CALAMITY WITCH!!?
end

Episode.16

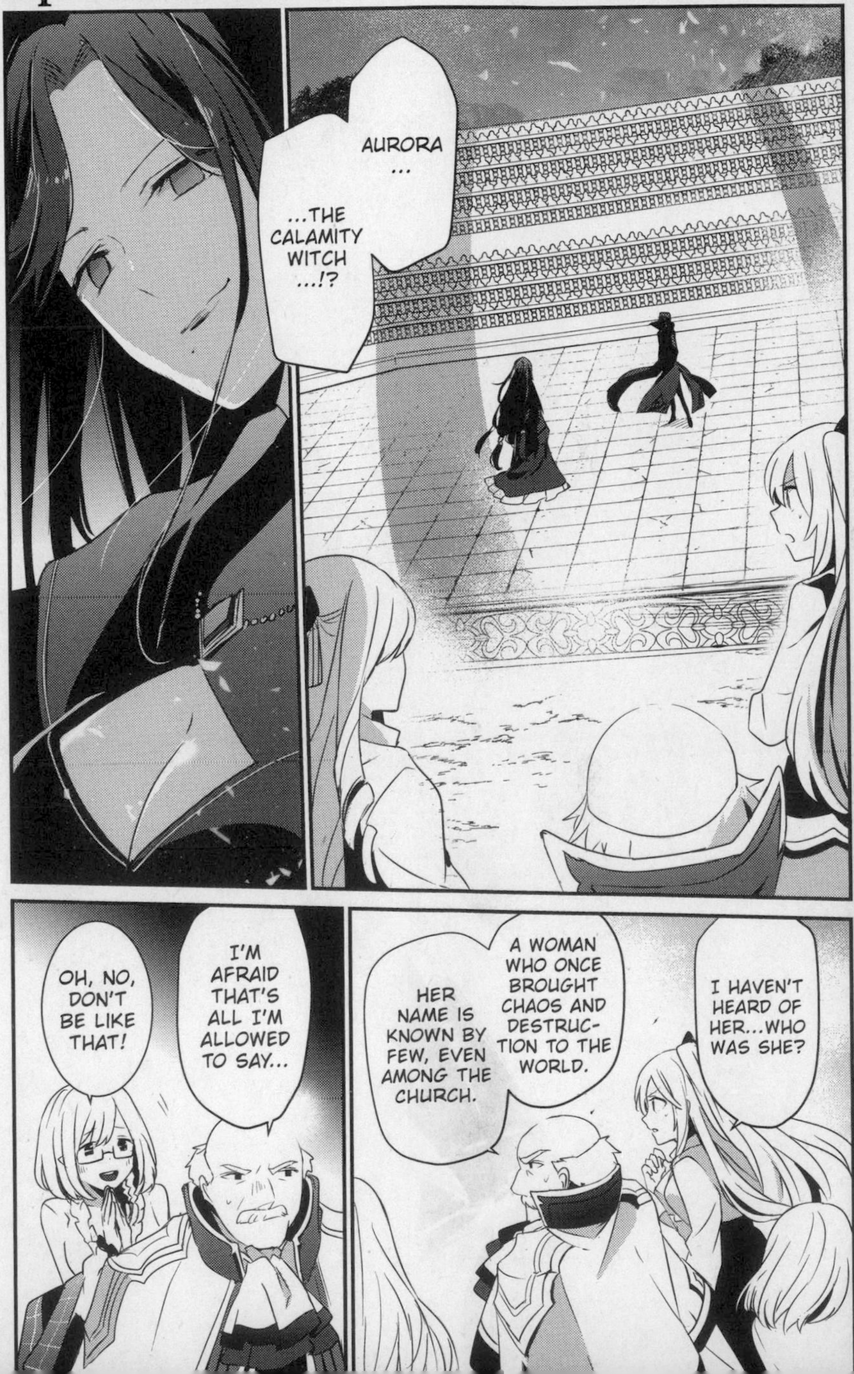
AURORA... ...THE CALAMITY WITCH...!?
I HAVEN'T HEARD OF HER...WHO WAS SHE?
A WOMAN WHO ONCE BROUGHT CHAOS AND DESTRUC-TION TO THE WORLD.
HER NAME IS KNOWN BY FEW, EVEN AMONG THE CHURCH.
I'M AFRAID THAT'S ALL I'M ALLOWED TO SAY...
OH, NO, DON'T BE LIKE THAT!

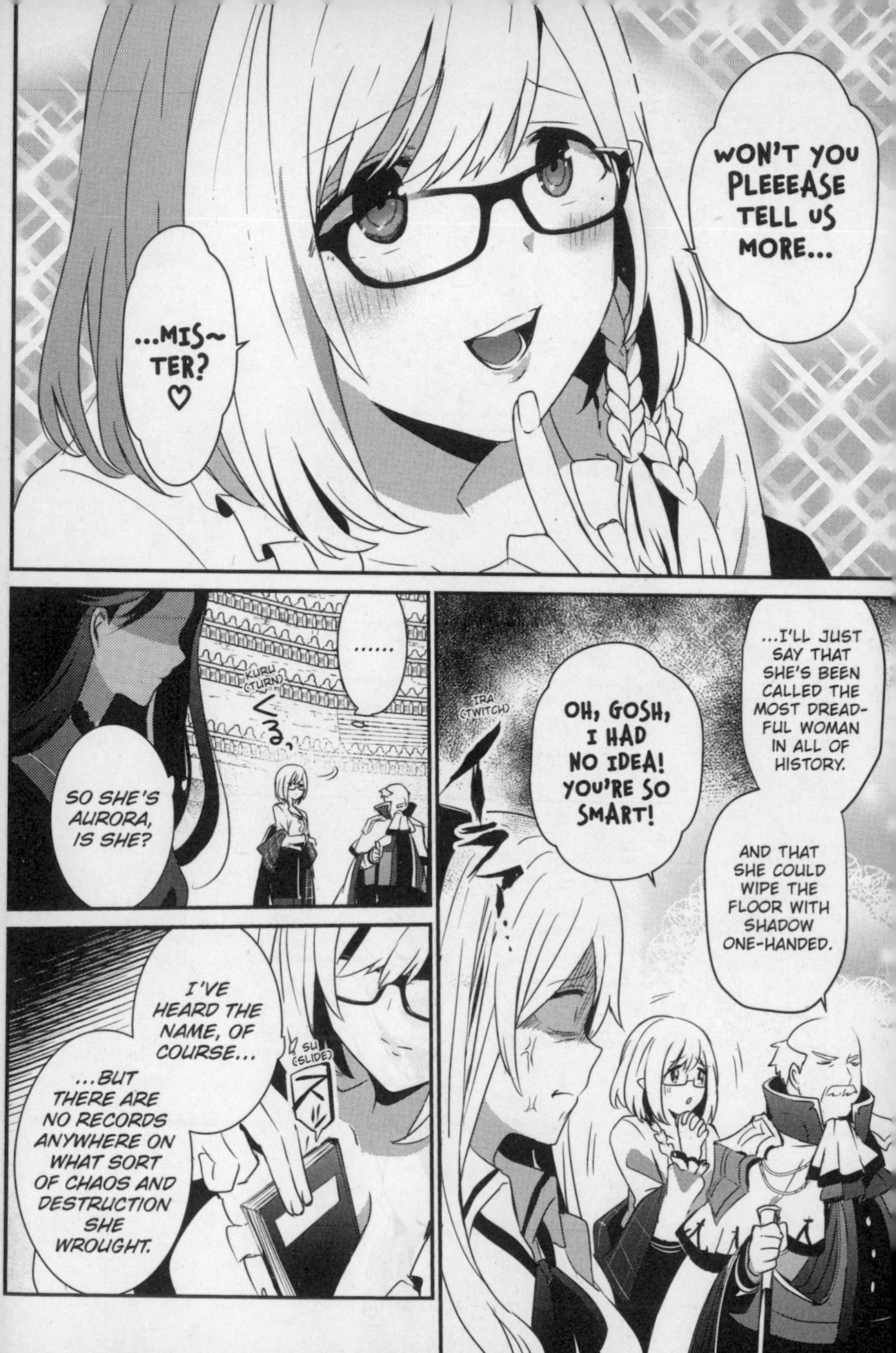

WON'T YOU PLEEEASE TELL US MORE...
...MIS~ TER? ♡
...I'LL JUST SAY THAT SHE'S BEEN CALLED THE MOST DREAD-FUL WOMAN IN ALL OF HISTORY.
AND THAT SHE COULD WIPE THE FLOOR WITH SHADOW ONE-HANDED.
OH, GOSH, I HAD NO IDEA! YOU'RE SO SMART!
IRA (TWITCH)
......
KURU (TURN)
SO SHE'S AURORA, IS SHE?
I'VE HEARD THE NAME, OF COURSE...
SU (SLIDE)
...BUT THERE ARE NO RECORDS ANYWHERE ON WHAT SORT OF CHAOS AND DESTRUCTION SHE WROUGHT.

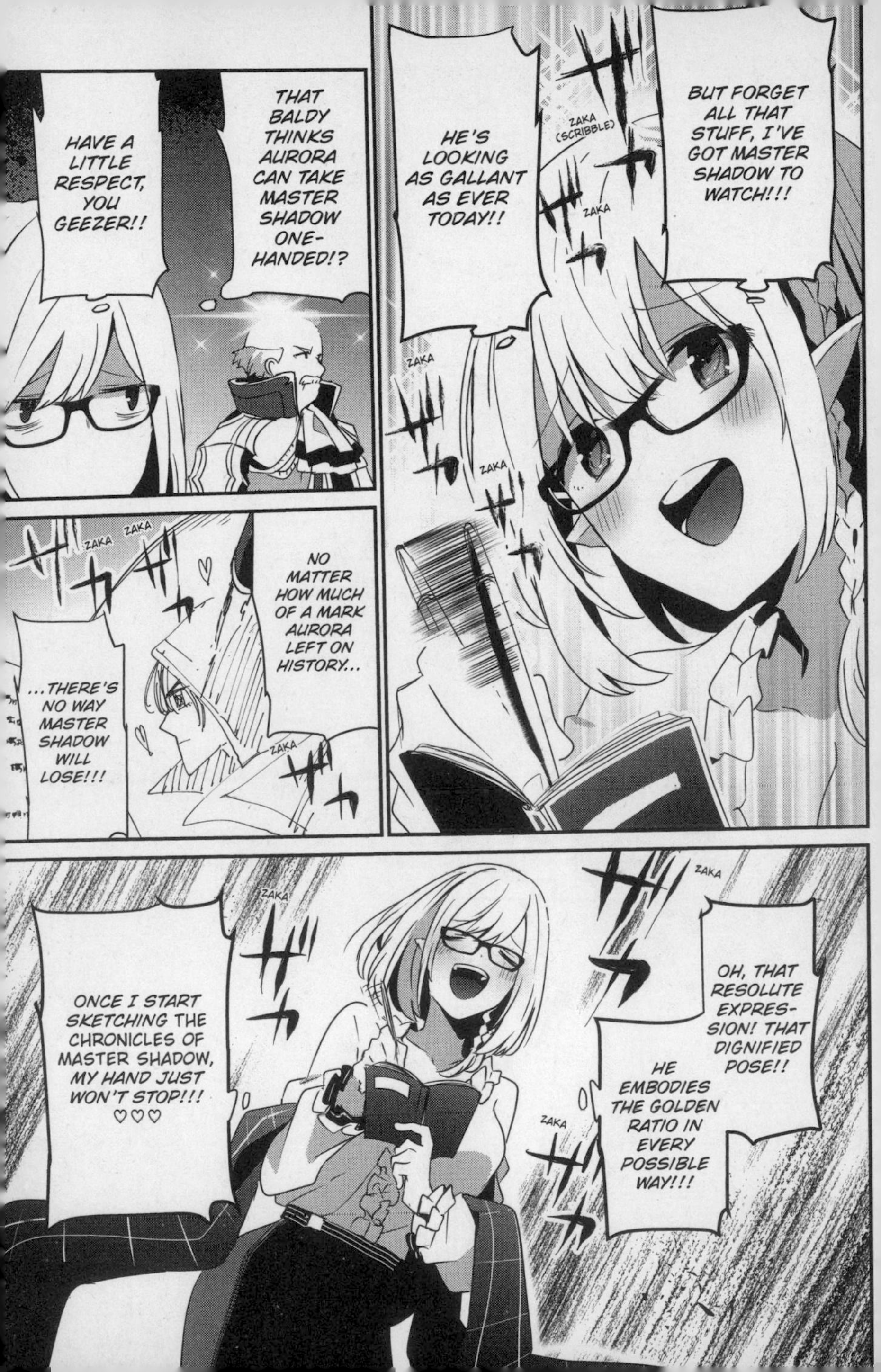
BUT FORGET ALL THAT STUFF, I'VE GOT MASTER SHADOW TO WATCH!!!
ZAKA (SCRIBBLE)
ZAKA
HE'S LOOKING AS GALLANT AS EVER TODAY!!
ZAKA
ZAKA
THAT BALDY THINKS AURORA CAN TAKE MASTER SHADOW ONE-HANDED!?
HAVE A LITTLE RESPECT, YOU GEEZER!!
NO MATTER HOW MUCH OF A MARK AURORA LEFT ON HISTORY...
ZAKA
ZAKA
...THERE'S NO WAY MASTER SHADOW WILL LOSE!!!
ZAKA
ZAKA
OH, THAT RESOLUTE EXPRES- SION! THAT DIGNIFIED POSE!!
HE EMBODIES THE GOLDEN RATIO IN EVERY POSSIBLE WAY!!!
ZAKA
ZAKA
ONCE I START SKETCHING THE CHRONICLES OF MASTER SHADOW, MY HAND JUST WON'T STOP!!! ♡♡♡

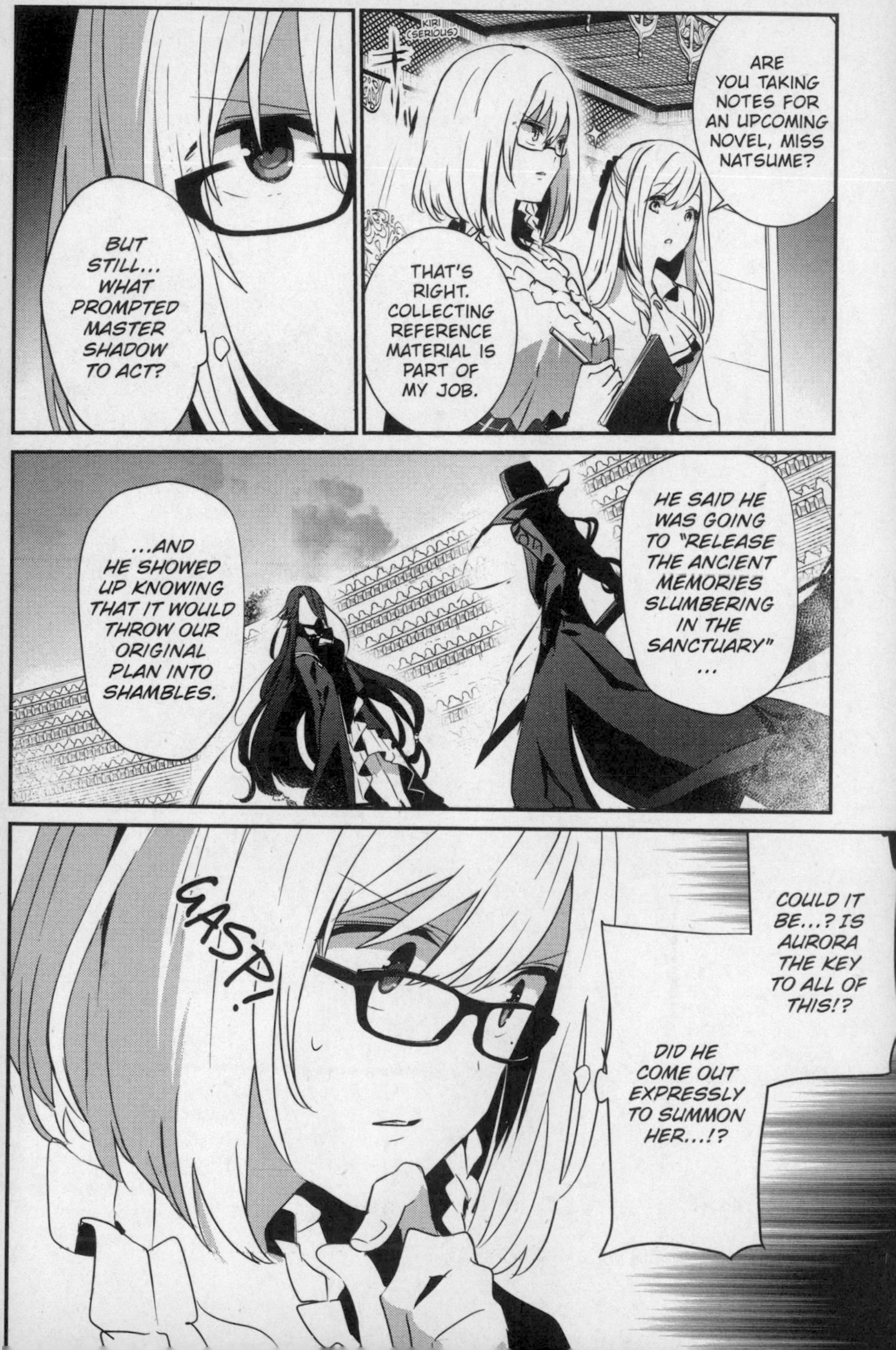
KIRI (SERIOUS)
ARE YOU TAKING NOTES FOR AN UPCOMING NOVEL, MISS NATSUME?
THAT'S RIGHT. COLLECTING REFERENCE MATERIAL IS PART OF MY JOB.
BUT STILL... WHAT PROMPTED MASTER SHADOW TO ACT?
HE SAID HE WAS GOING TO "RELEASE THE ANCIENT MEMORIES SLUMBERING IN THE SANCTUARY"...
...AND HE SHOWED UP KNOWING THAT IT WOULD THROW OUR ORIGINAL PLAN INTO SHAMBLES.
COULD IT BE...? IS AURORA THE KEY TO ALL OF THIS!?
DID HE COME OUT EXPRESSLY TO SUMMON HER...!?
GASP!

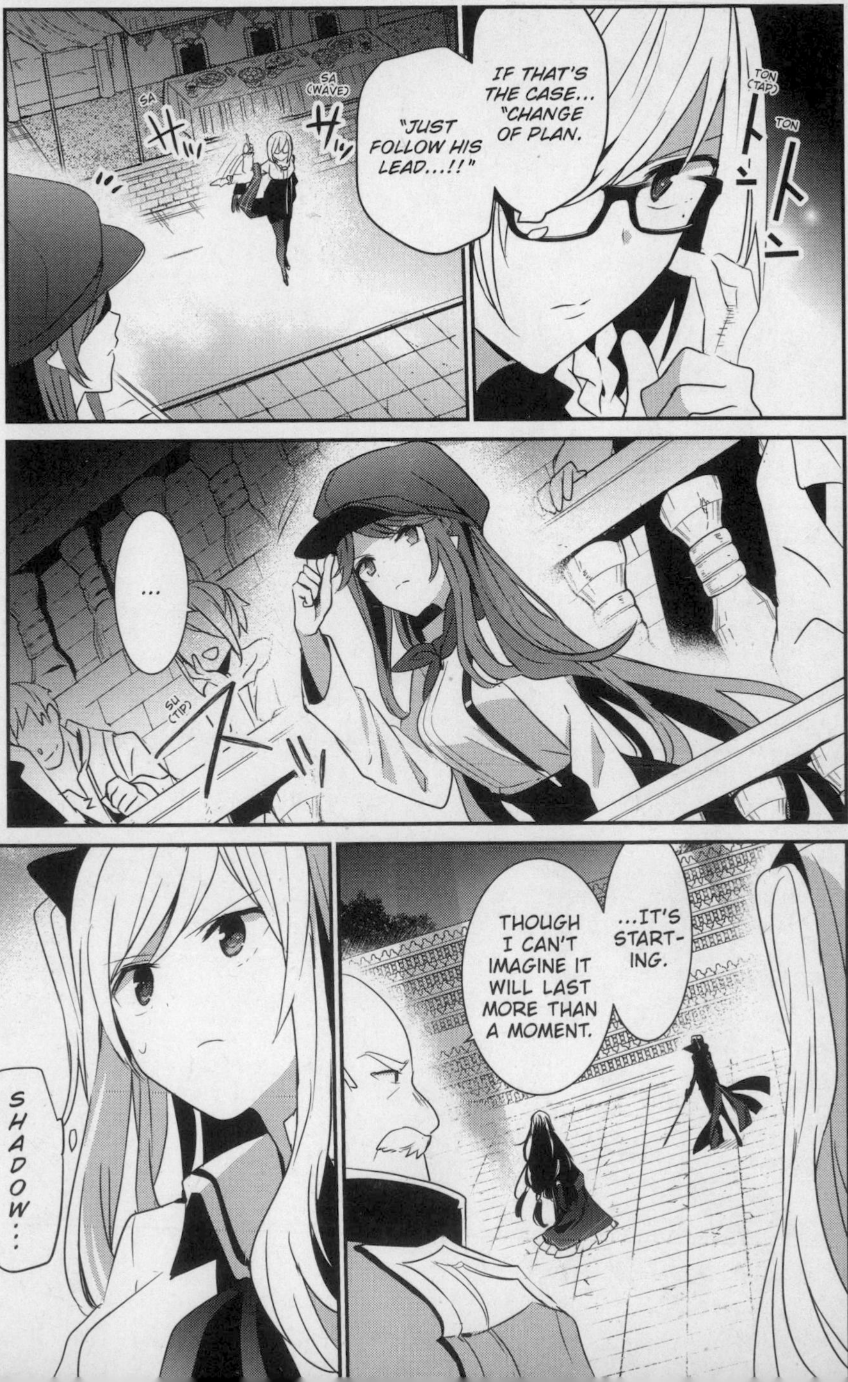
TON (TAP)
TON
IF THAT'S THE CASE... "CHANGE OF PLAN.
"JUST FOLLOW HIS LEAD...!!"
SA (WAVE)
SA
...
SU (TIP)
...IT'S START-ING.
THOUGH I CAN'T IMAGINE IT WILL LAST MORE THAN A MOMENT.
SHADOW...

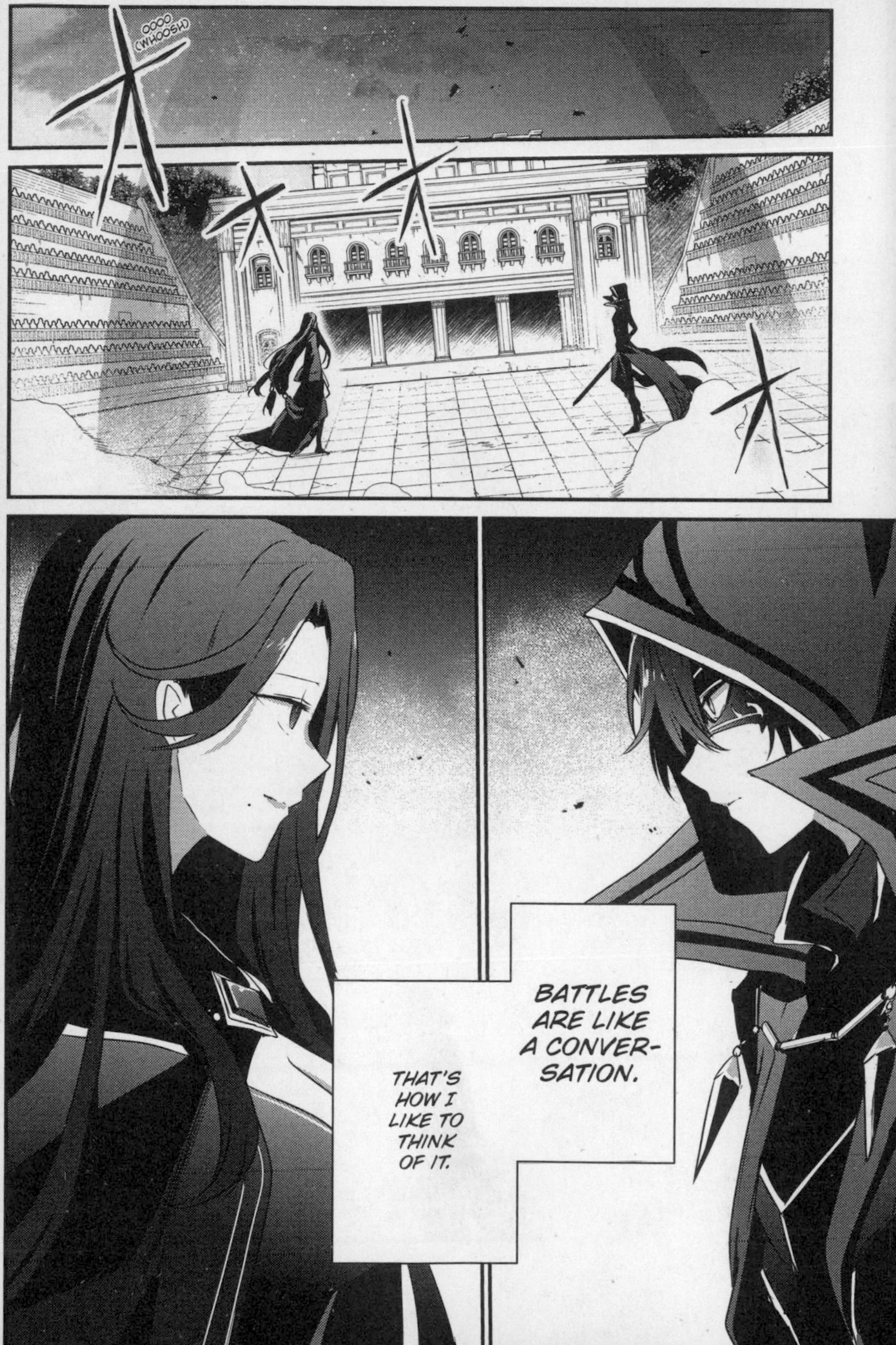
OOOO (WHOOSH)
BATTLES ARE LIKE A CONVER-SATION.
THAT'S HOW I LIKE TO THINK OF IT.

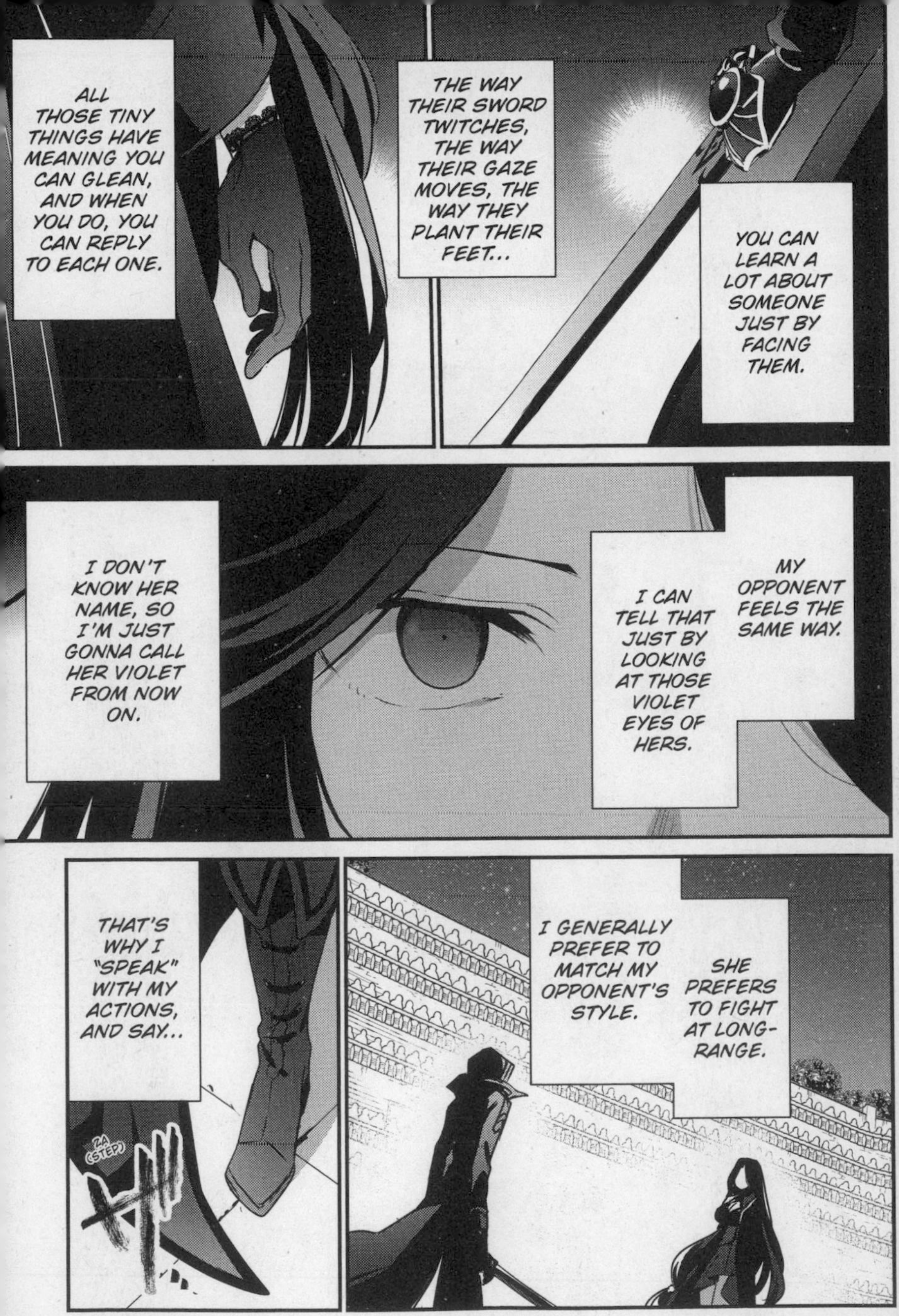
YOU CAN LEARN A LOT ABOUT SOMEONE JUST BY FACING THEM.
THE WAY THEIR SWORD TWITCHES, THE WAY THEIR GAZE MOVES, THE WAY THEY PLANT THEIR FEET...
ALL THOSE TINY THINGS HAVE MEANING YOU CAN GLEAN, AND WHEN YOU DO, YOU CAN REPLY TO EACH ONE.
MY OPPONENT FEELS THE SAME WAY.
I CAN TELL THAT JUST BY LOOKING AT THOSE VIOLET EYES OF HERS.
I DON'T KNOW HER NAME, SO I'M JUST GONNA CALL HER VIOLET FROM NOW ON.
SHE PREFERS TO FIGHT AT LONG-RANGE.
I GENERALLY PREFER TO MATCH MY OPPONENT'S STYLE.
THAT'S WHY I "SPEAK" WITH MY ACTIONS, AND SAY...
ZA (STEP)

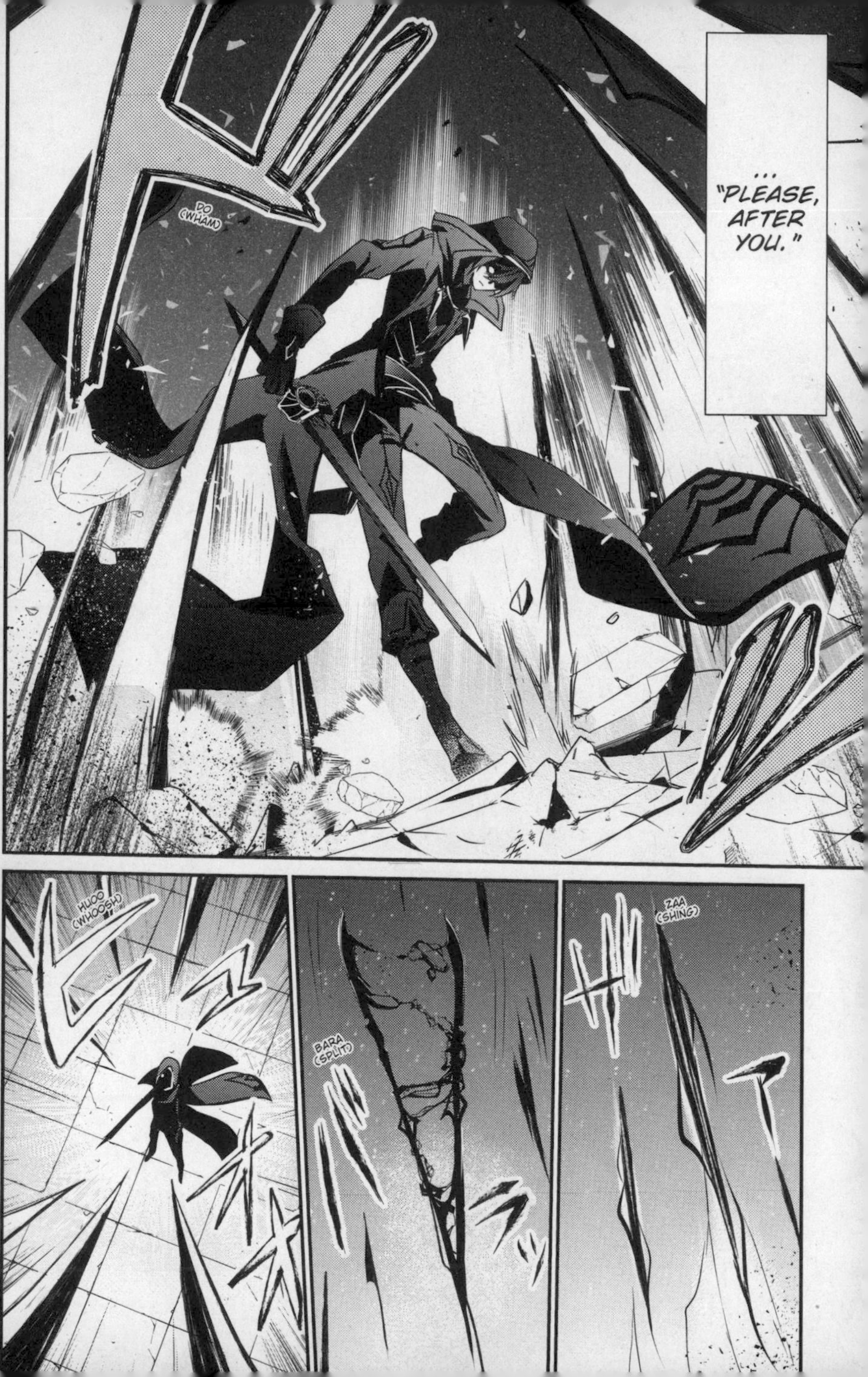
...
"PLEASE, AFTER YOU."
DO (WHAM)
ZAA (SHING)
BARA (SPLIT)
HUOO (WHOOSH)

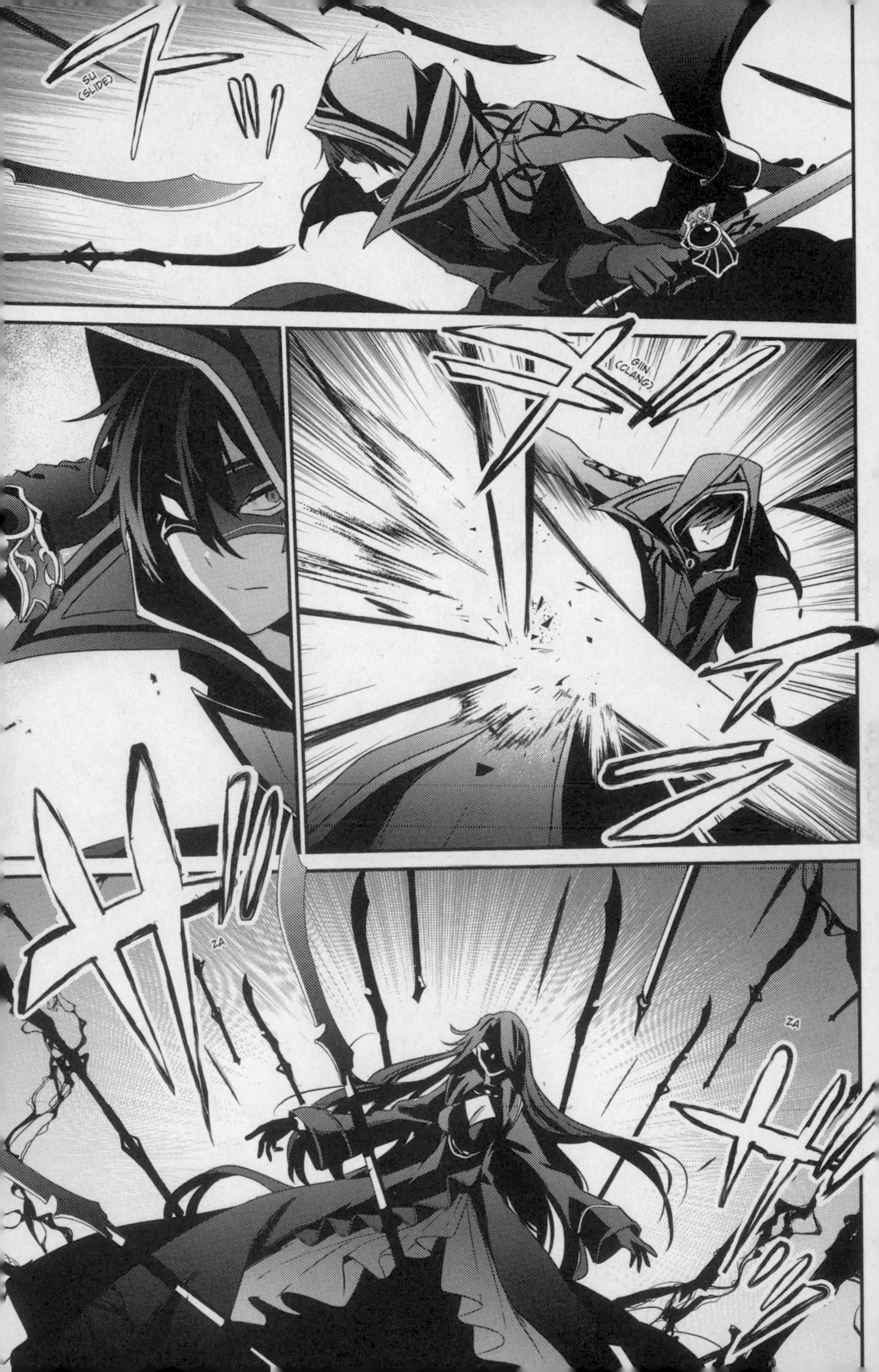
SU (SLIDE)
GIIN (CLANG)
ZA
ZA

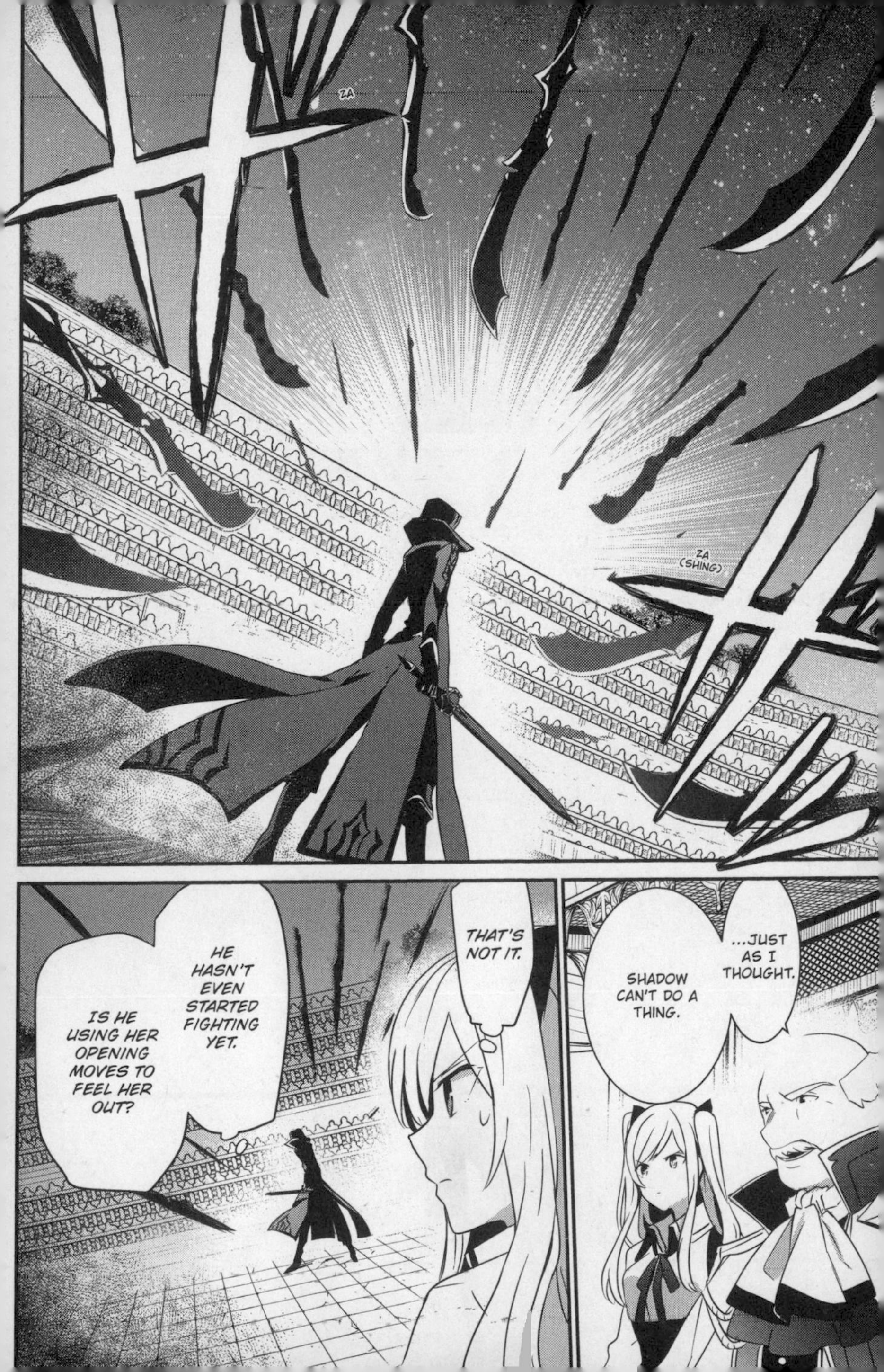
ZA
ZA (SHING)
...JUST AS I THOUGHT.
SHADOW CAN'T DO A THING.
THAT'S NOT IT.
HE HASN'T EVEN STARTED FIGHTING YET.
IS HE USING HER OPENING MOVES TO FEEL HER OUT?

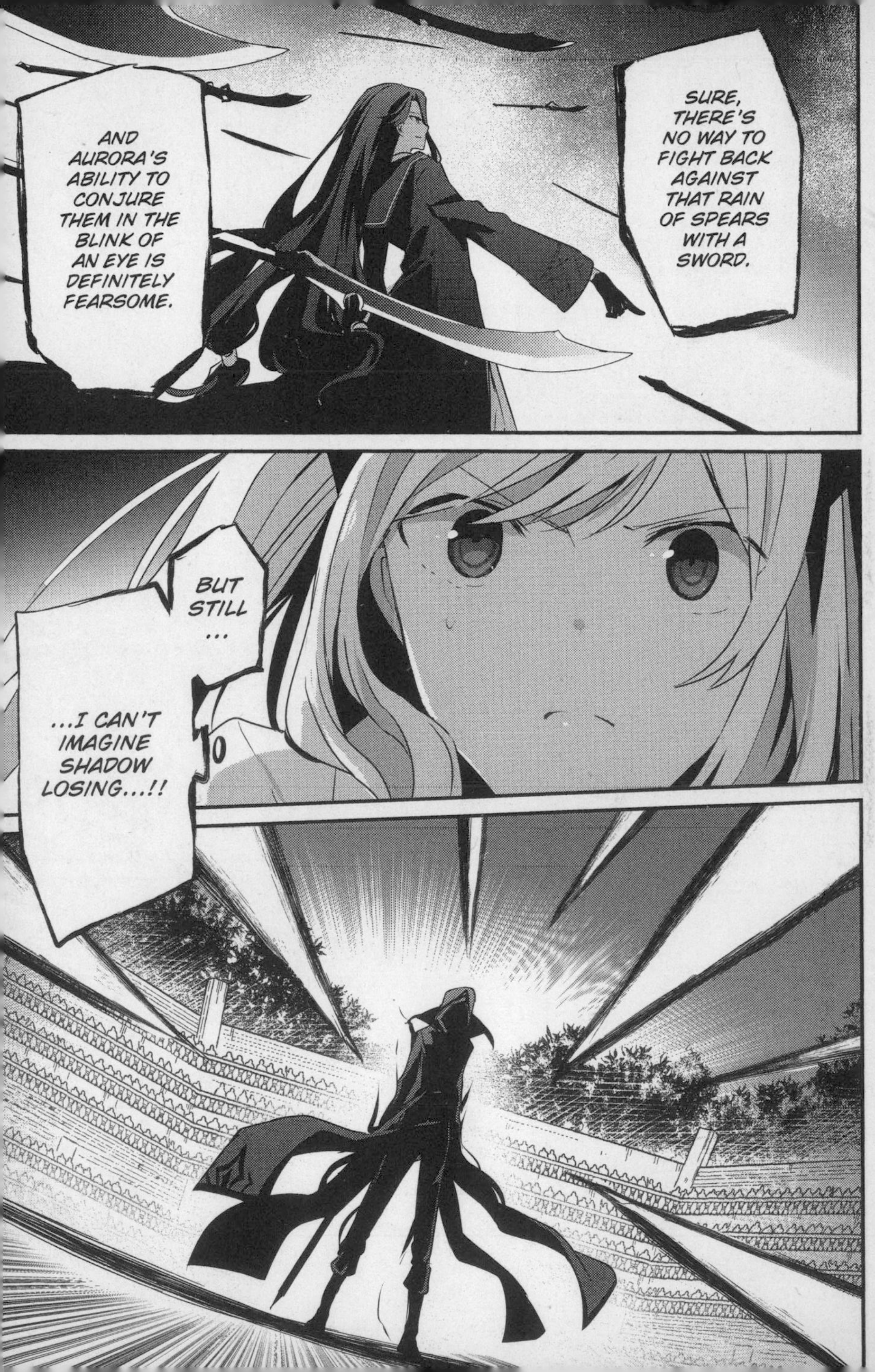
SURE, THERE'S NO WAY TO FIGHT BACK AGAINST THAT RAIN OF SPEARS WITH A SWORD.
AND AURORA'S ABILITY TO CONJURE THEM IN THE BLINK OF AN EYE IS DEFINITELY FEARSOME.
BUT STILL...
...I CAN'T IMAGINE SHADOW LOSING...!!

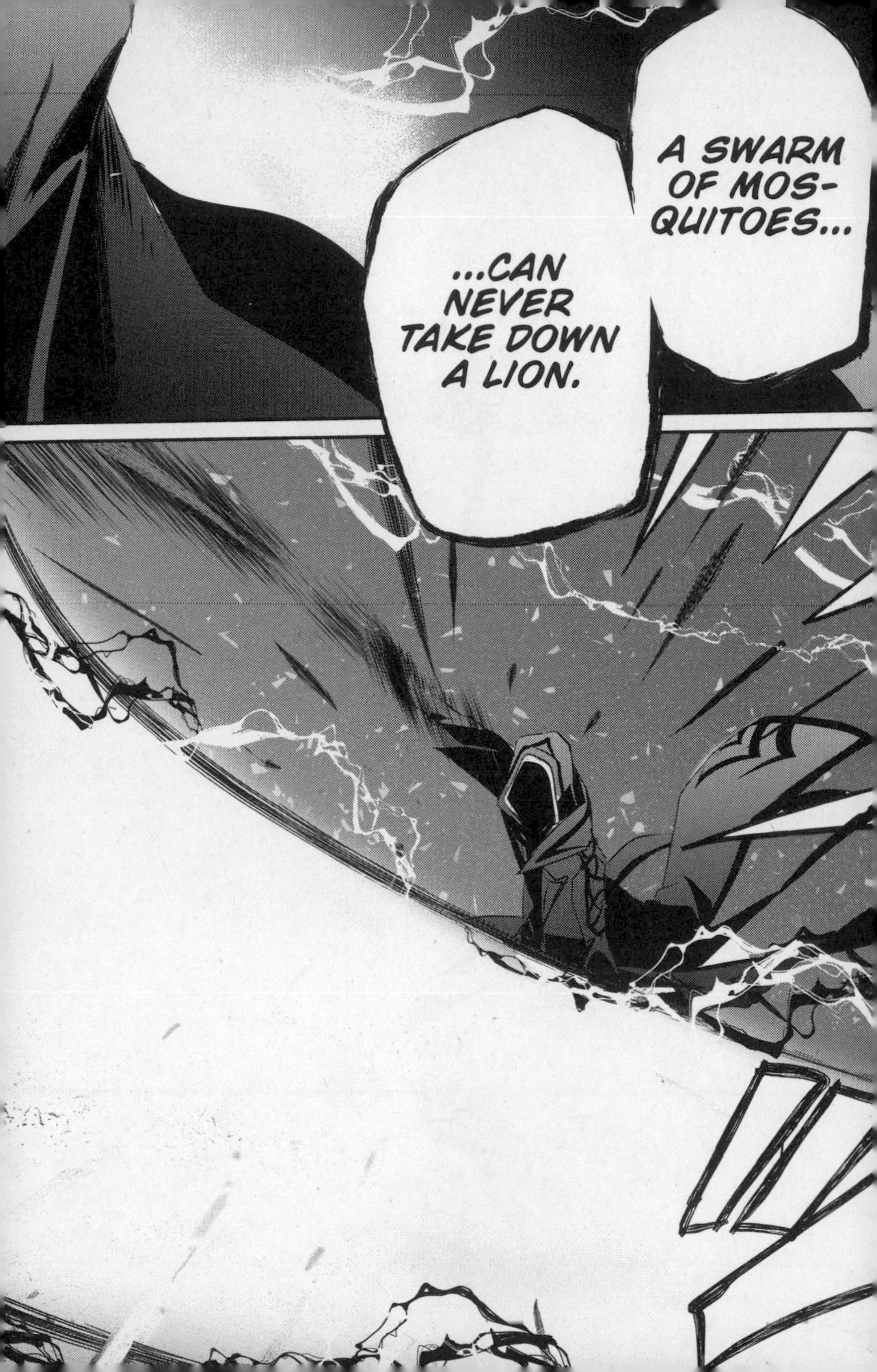
A SWARM OF MOS-QUITOES...
...CAN NEVER TAKE DOWN A LION.

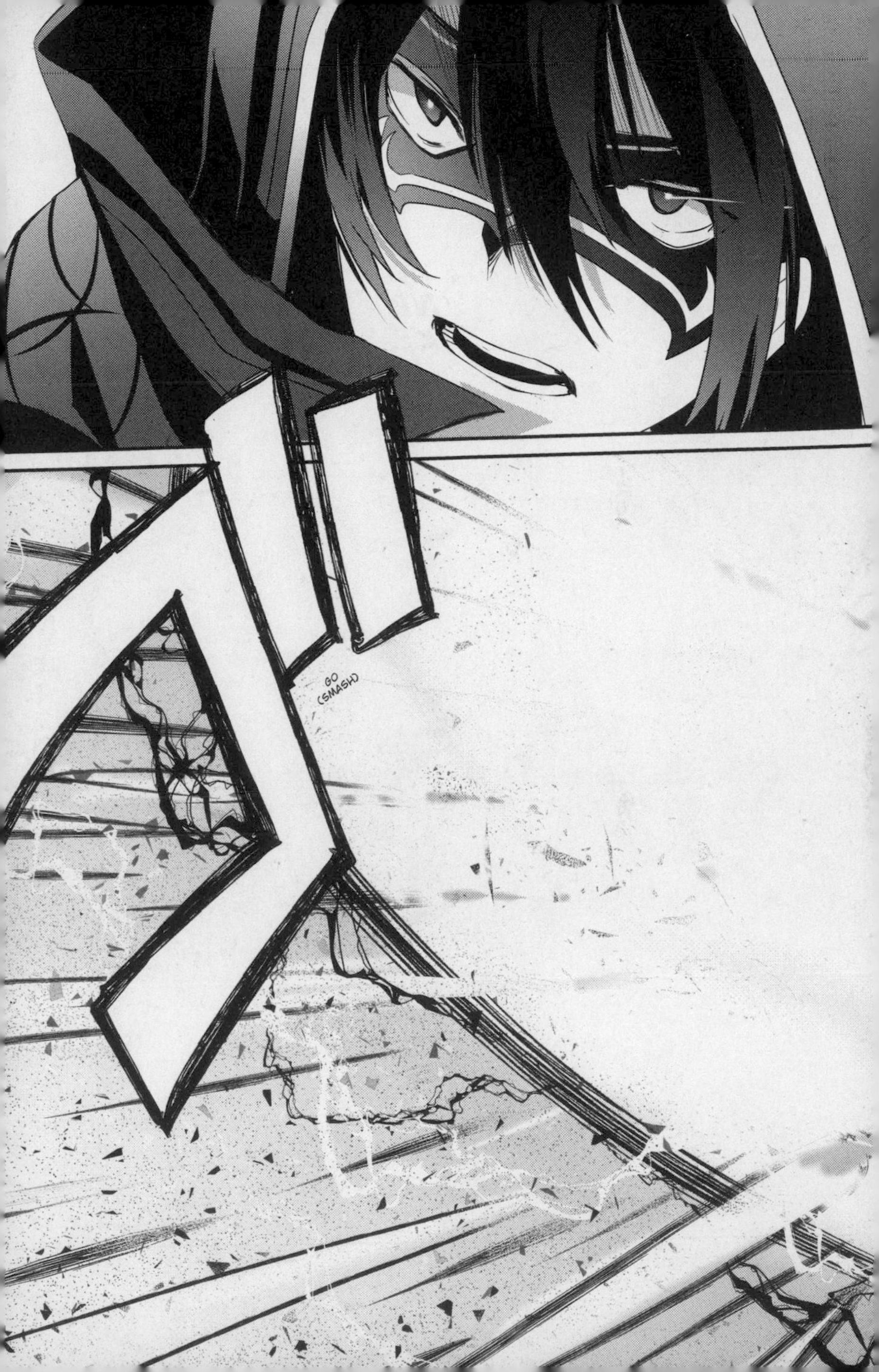
GO
(SMASH)

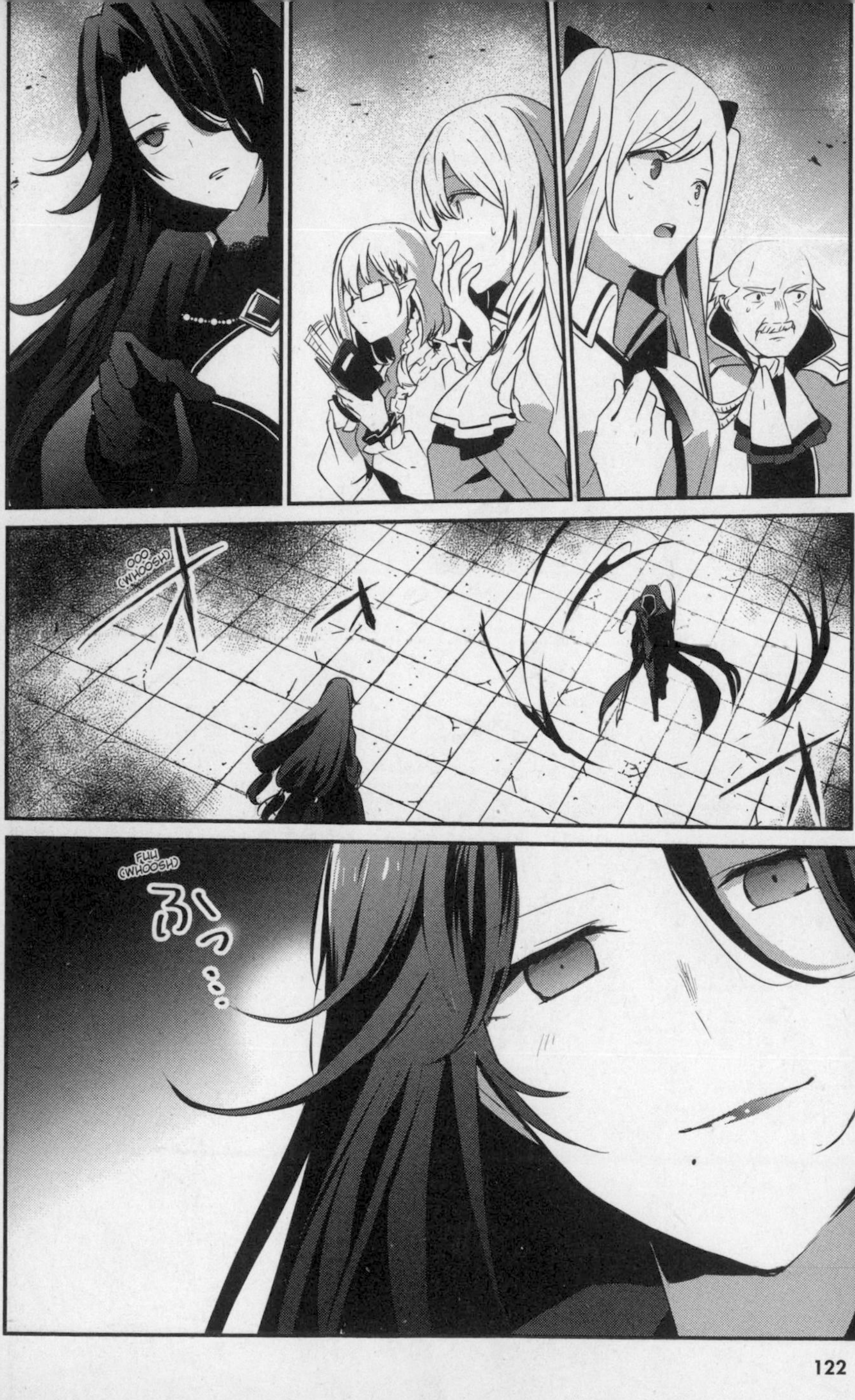
OOO
(WHOOSH)
FUU
(WHOOSH)
ふーっ…

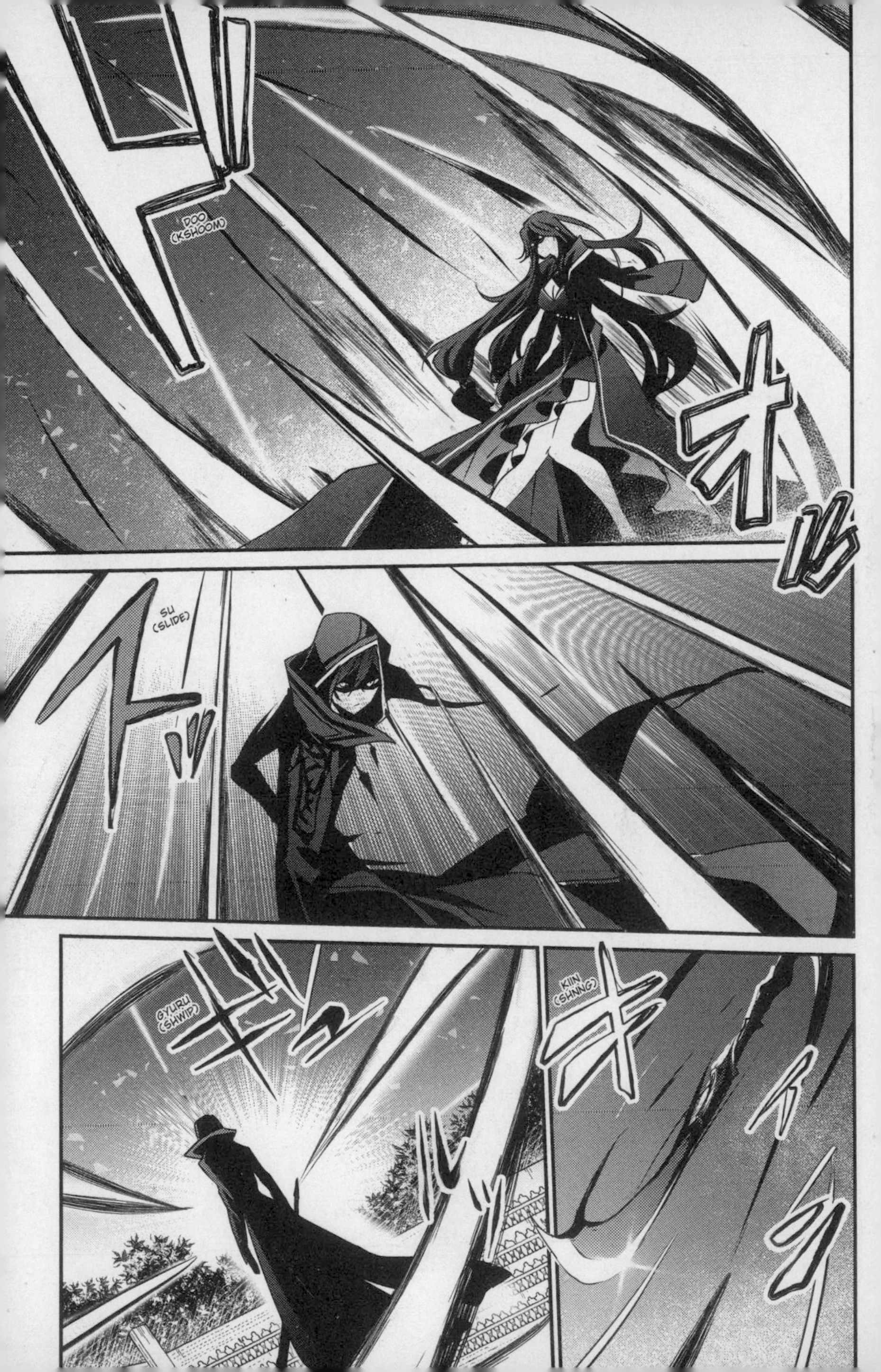
DOO (KSHOOM)
SU (SLIDE)
KIIN (SHNNG)
GYURU (SHWIP)

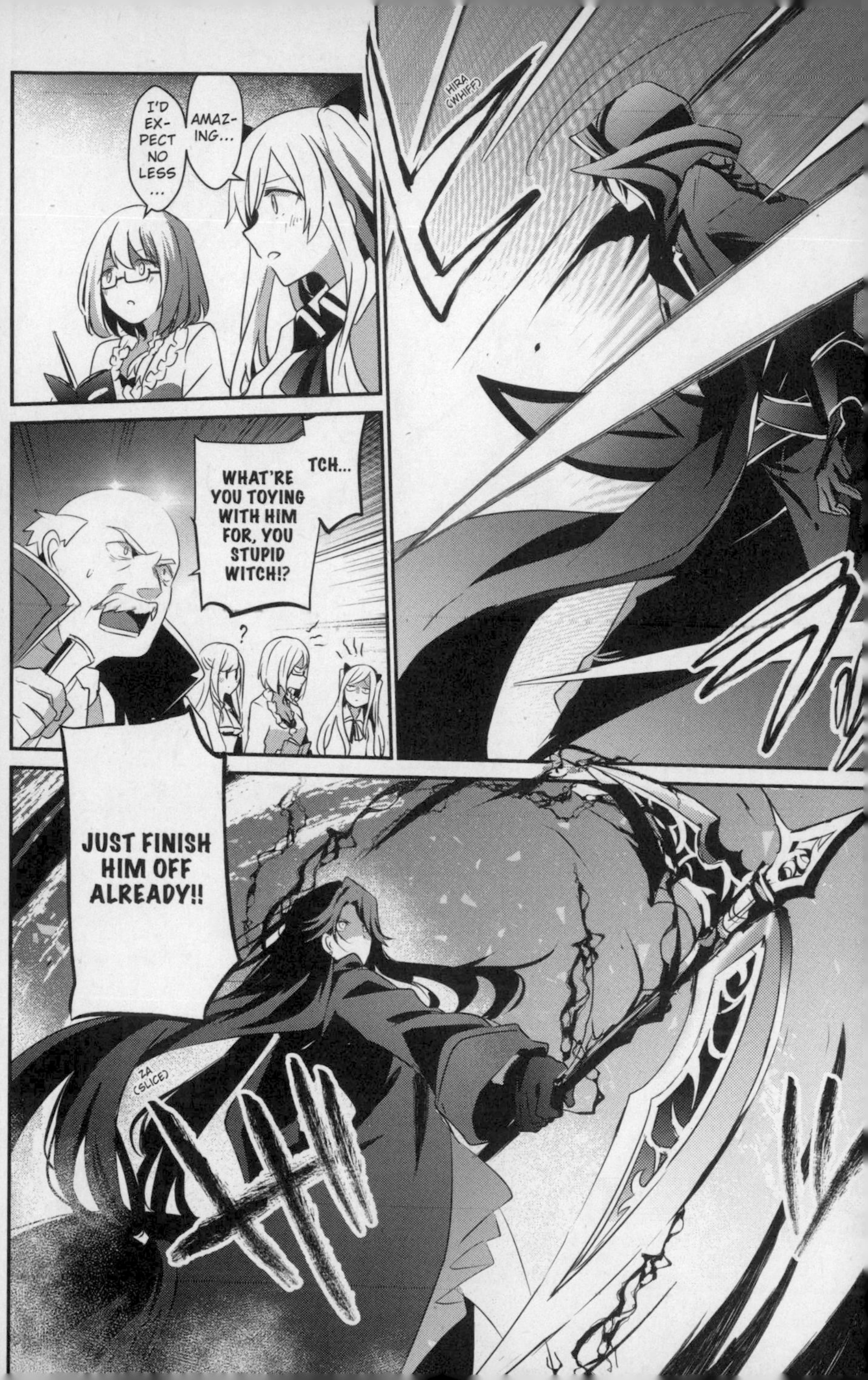
HIRA (WHIFF)
AMAZ-ING...
I'D EX-PECT NO LESS...
TCH...
WHAT'RE YOU TOYING WITH HIM FOR, YOU STUPID WITCH!?
?
JUST FINISH HIM OFF ALREADY!!
ZA (SLICE)

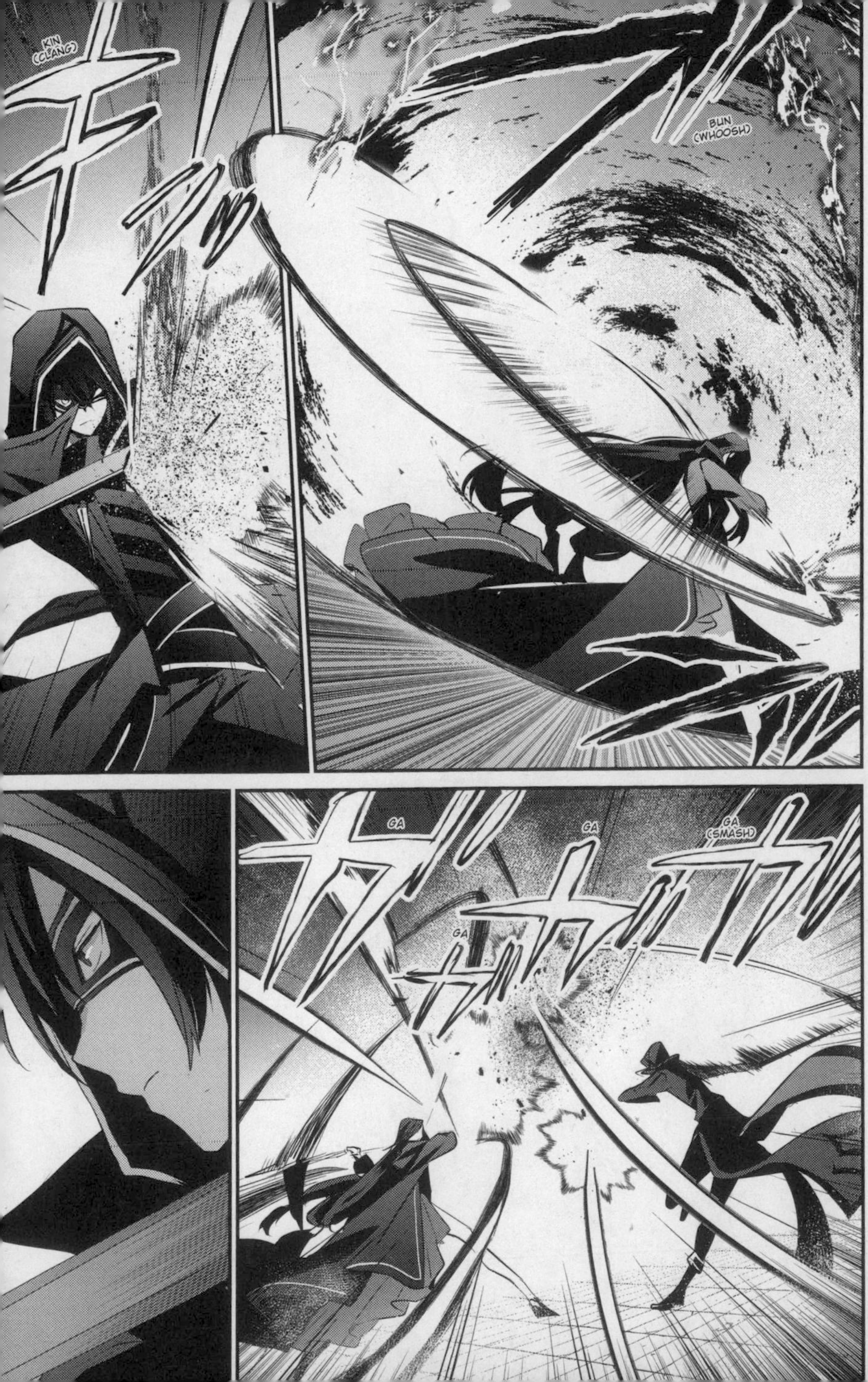
BUN (WHOOSH)
KIN (CLANG)
GA (SMASH)
GA
GA
GA

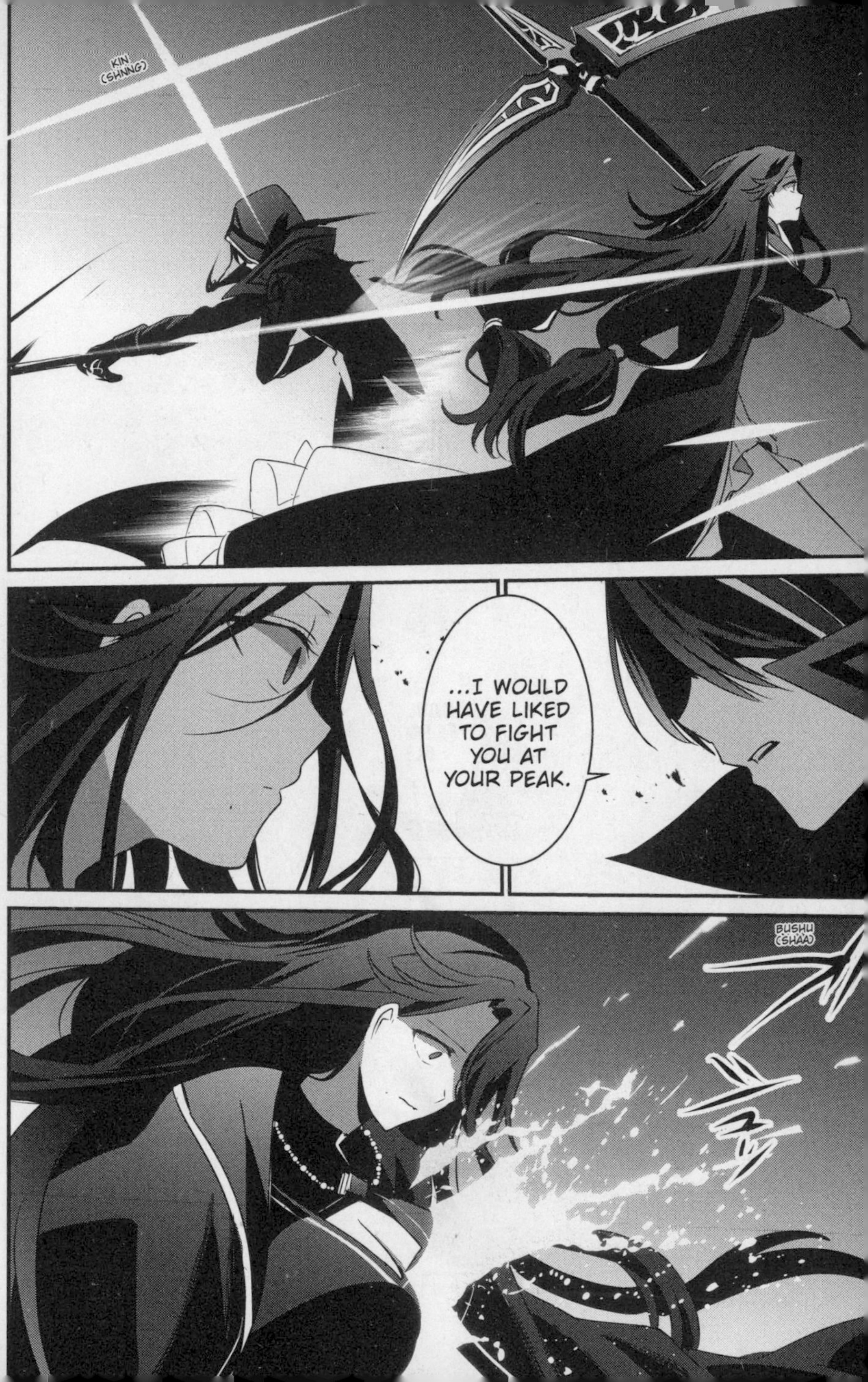
KIN (SHNNG)
...I WOULD HAVE LIKED TO FIGHT YOU AT YOUR PEAK.
BUSHU (SHAA)

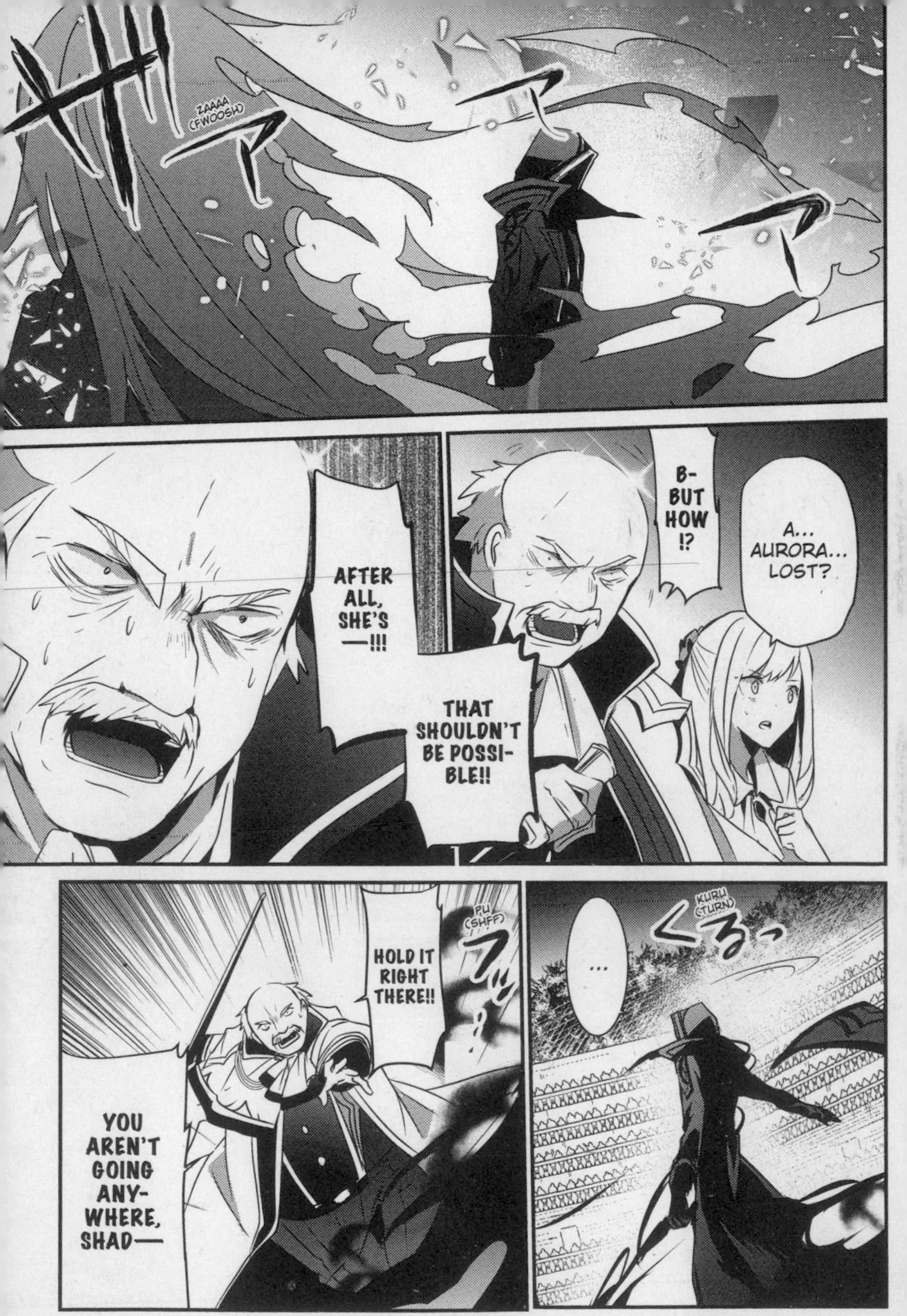
ZAAAA (FWOOSH)
A... AURORA... LOST?
B-BUT HOW!?
THAT SHOULDN'T BE POSSIBLE!!
AFTER ALL, SHE'S—!!!
KURU (TURN)
...
PU (SHFF)
HOLD IT RIGHT THERE!!
YOU AREN'T GOING ANYWHERE, SHAD—

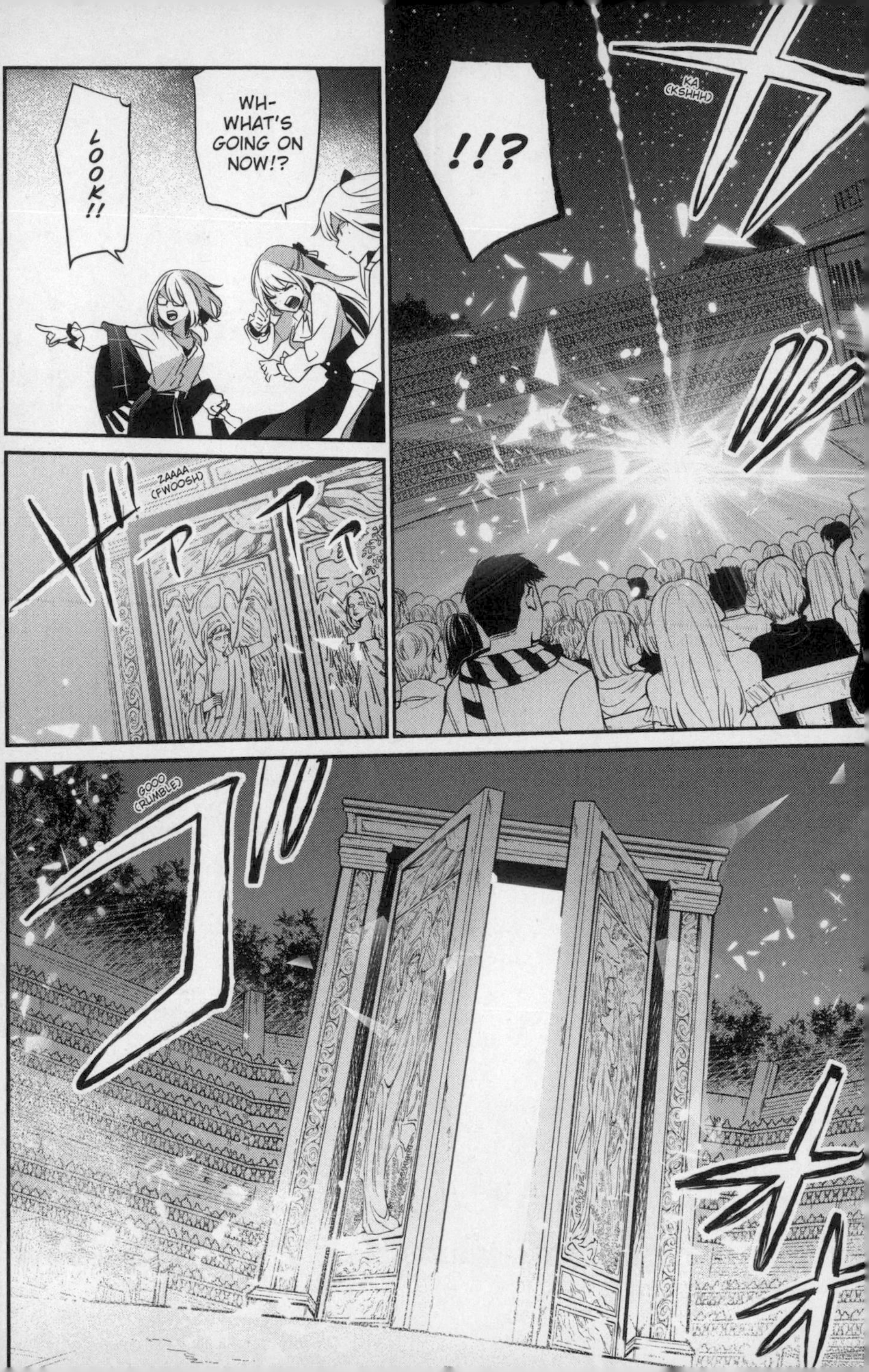
KA (KSHHH)
!!?
WH- WHAT'S GOING ON NOW!?
LOOK!!
ZAAAA (FWOOSH)
GOOO (RUMBLE)

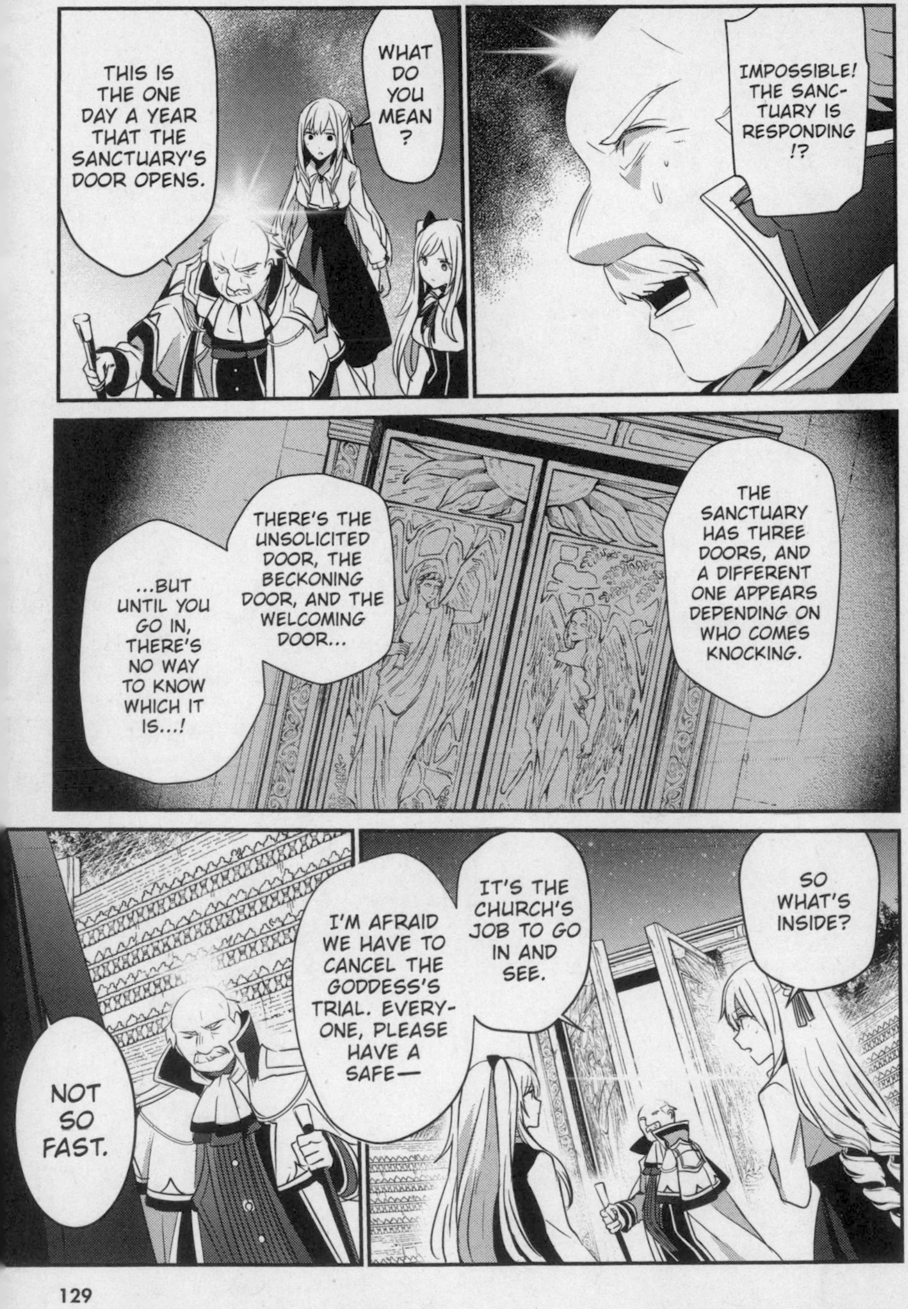
IMPOSSIBLE! THE SANCTUARY IS RESPONDING!?
WHAT DO YOU MEAN?
THIS IS THE ONE DAY A YEAR THAT THE SANCTUARY'S DOOR OPENS.
THE SANCTUARY HAS THREE DOORS, AND A DIFFERENT ONE APPEARS DEPENDING ON WHO COMES KNOCKING.
THERE'S THE UNSOLICITED DOOR, THE BECKONING DOOR, AND THE WELCOMING DOOR...
...BUT UNTIL YOU GO IN, THERE'S NO WAY TO KNOW WHICH IT IS...!
SO WHAT'S INSIDE?
IT'S THE CHURCH'S JOB TO GO IN AND SEE.
I'M AFRAID WE HAVE TO CANCEL THE GODDESS'S TRIAL. EVERYONE, PLEASE HAVE A SAFE—
NOT SO FAST.

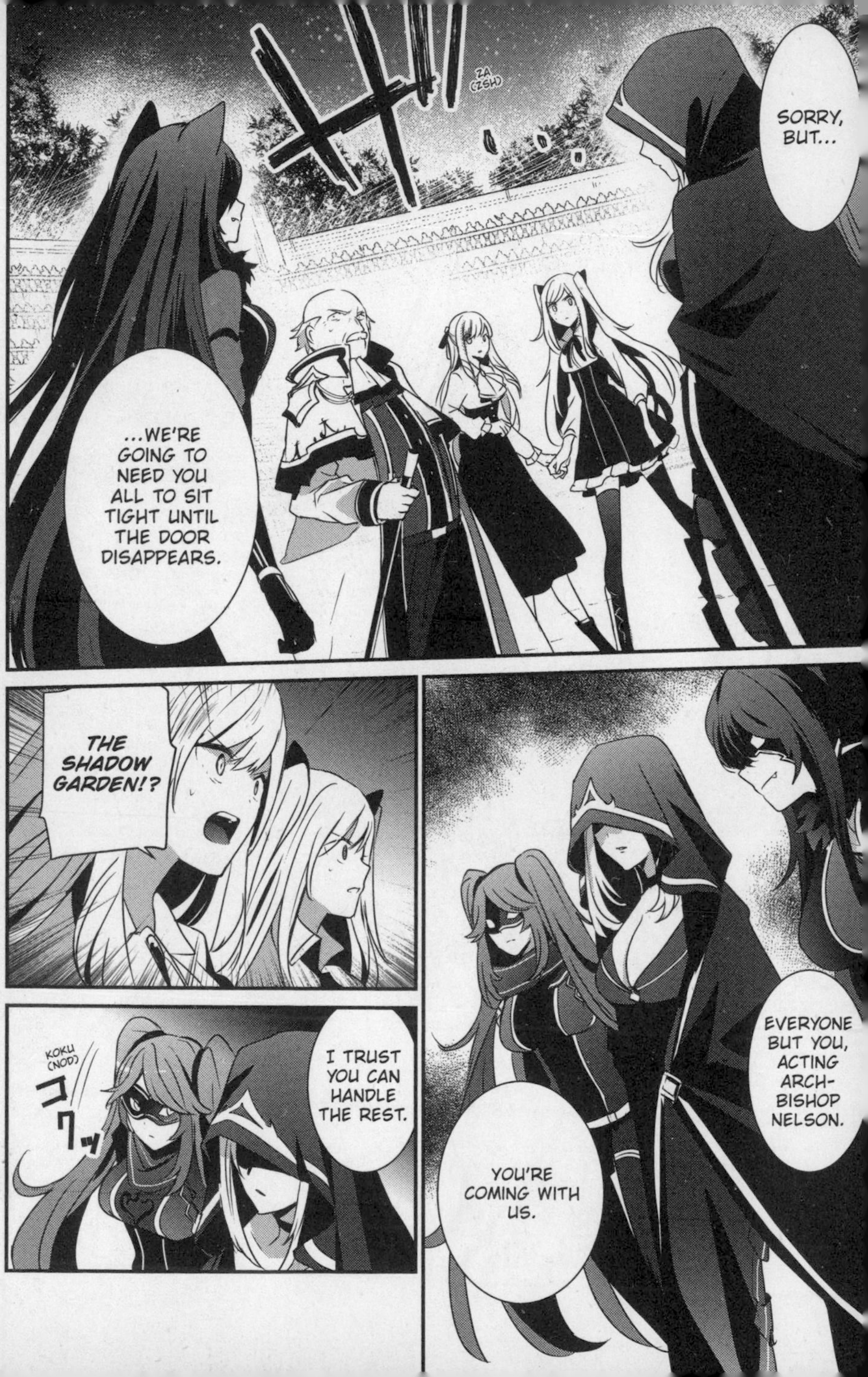
SORRY, BUT...
ZA (ZSH)
...WE'RE GOING TO NEED YOU ALL TO SIT TIGHT UNTIL THE DOOR DISAPPEARS.
EVERYONE BUT YOU, ACTING ARCH-BISHOP NELSON.
YOU'RE COMING WITH US.
THE SHADOW GARDEN!?
I TRUST YOU CAN HANDLE THE REST.
KOKU (NOD)

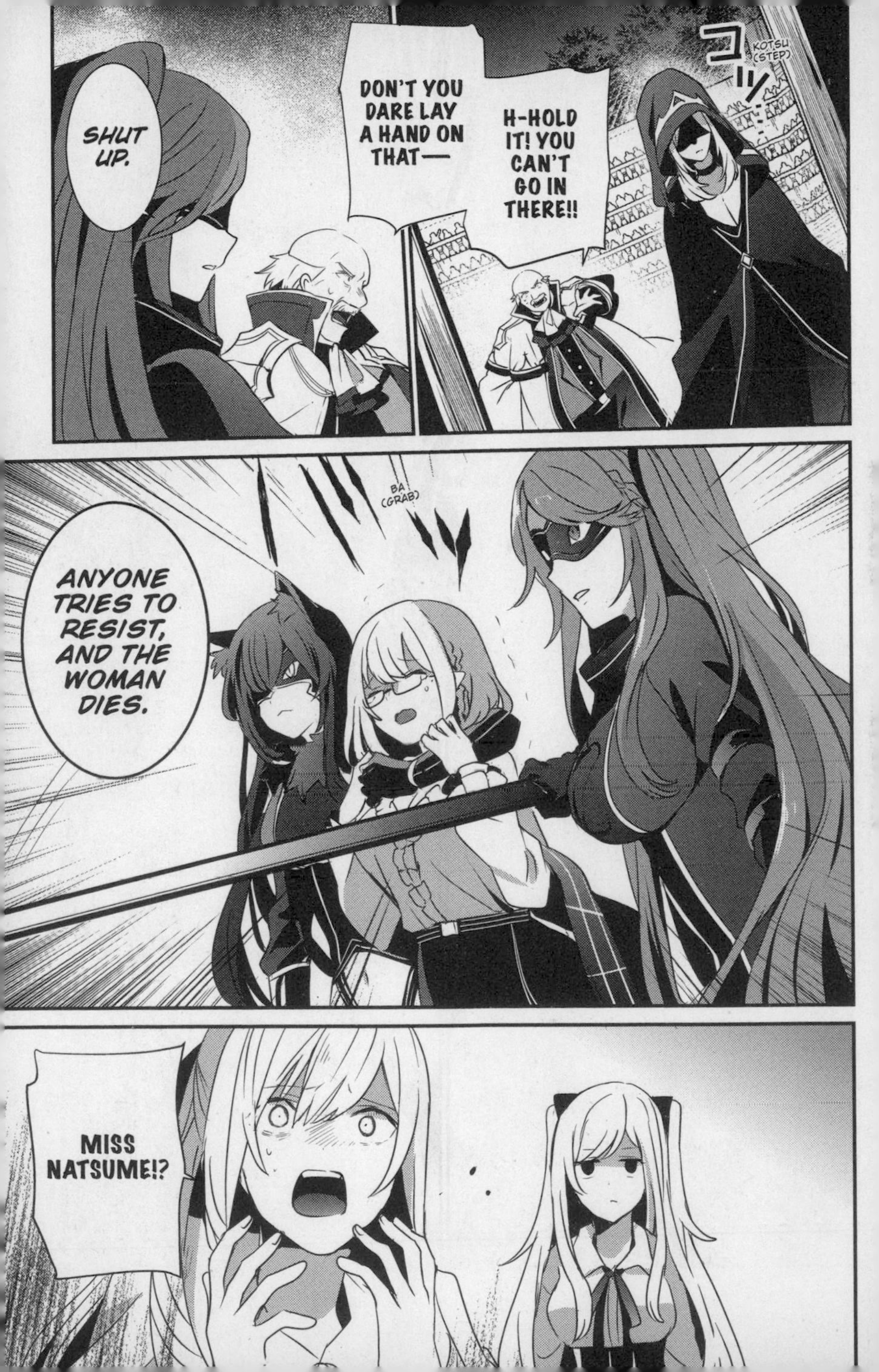
KOTSU (STEP)
H-HOLD IT! YOU CAN'T GO IN THERE!!
DON'T YOU DARE LAY A HAND ON THAT—
SHUT UP.
BA (GRAB)
ANYONE TRIES TO RESIST, AND THE WOMAN DIES.
MISS NATSUME!?

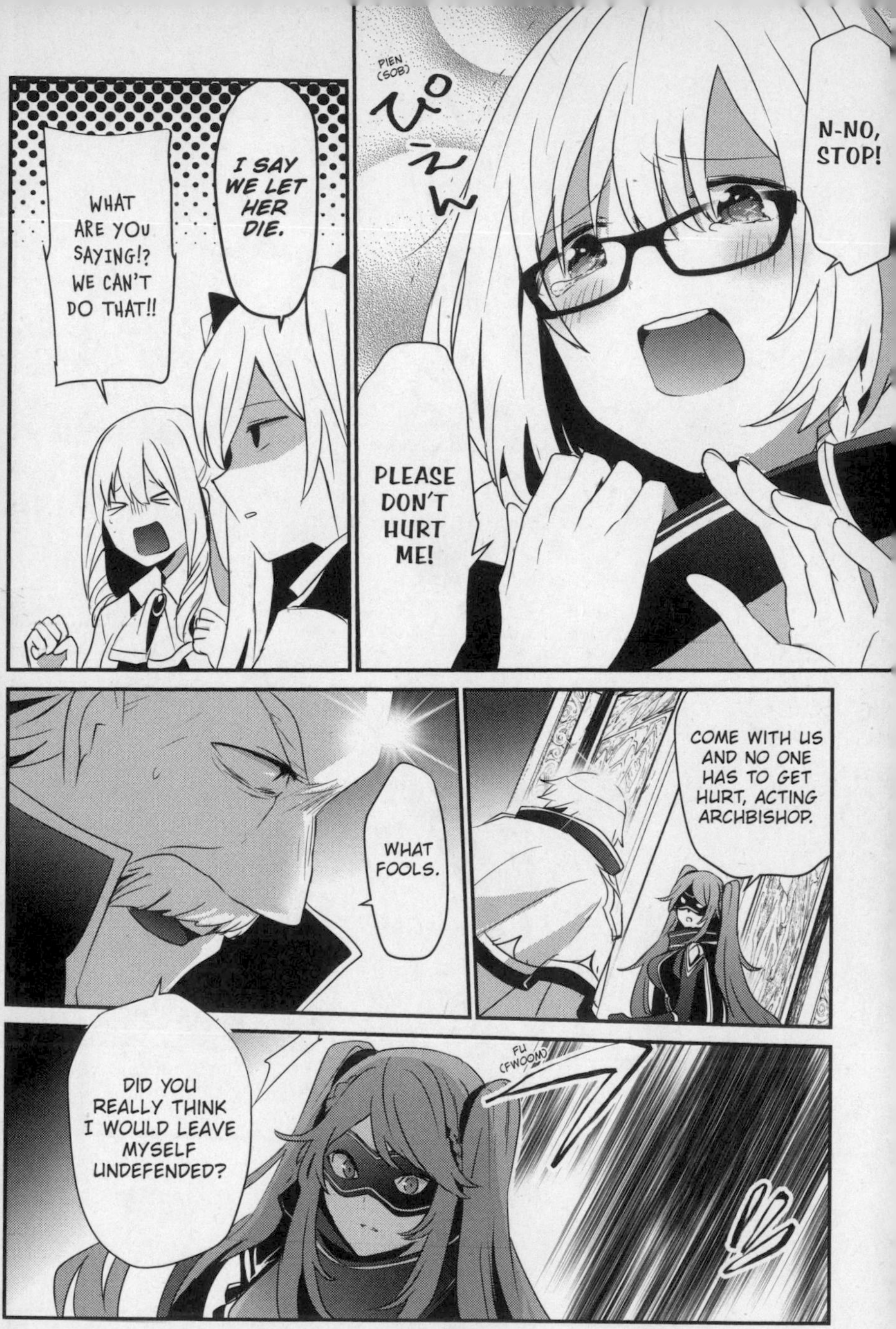
N-NO, STOP!
PIEN (SOB)
PLEASE DON'T HURT ME!
I SAY WE LET HER DIE.
WHAT ARE YOU SAYING!? WE CAN'T DO THAT!!
COME WITH US AND NO ONE HAS TO GET HURT, ACTING ARCHBISHOP.
WHAT FOOLS.
FU (FWOOM)
DID YOU REALLY THINK I WOULD LEAVE MYSELF UNDEFENDED?

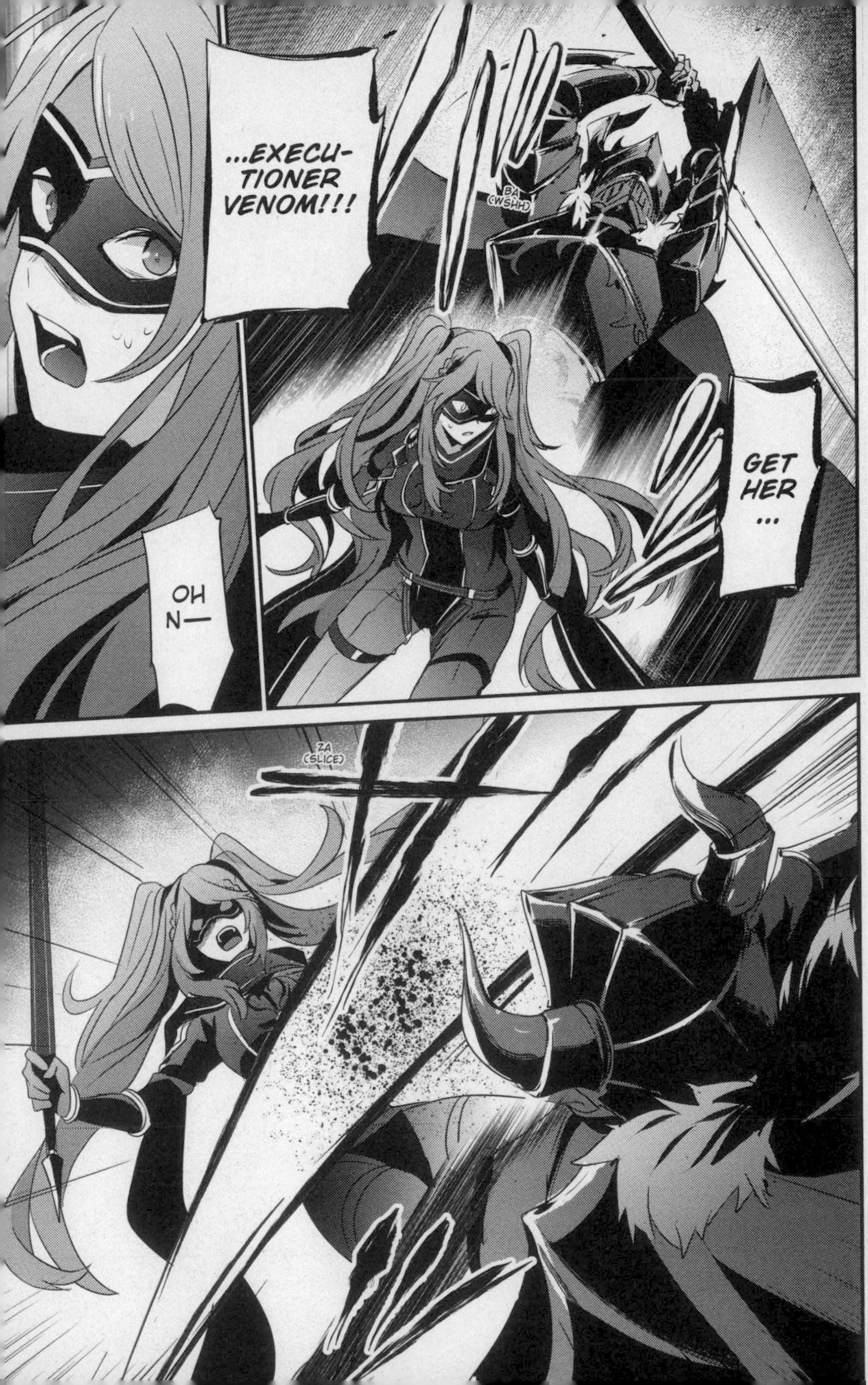
BA (WSHH)
GET HER...
...EXECUTIONER VENOM!!!
OH N—
ZA (SLICE)

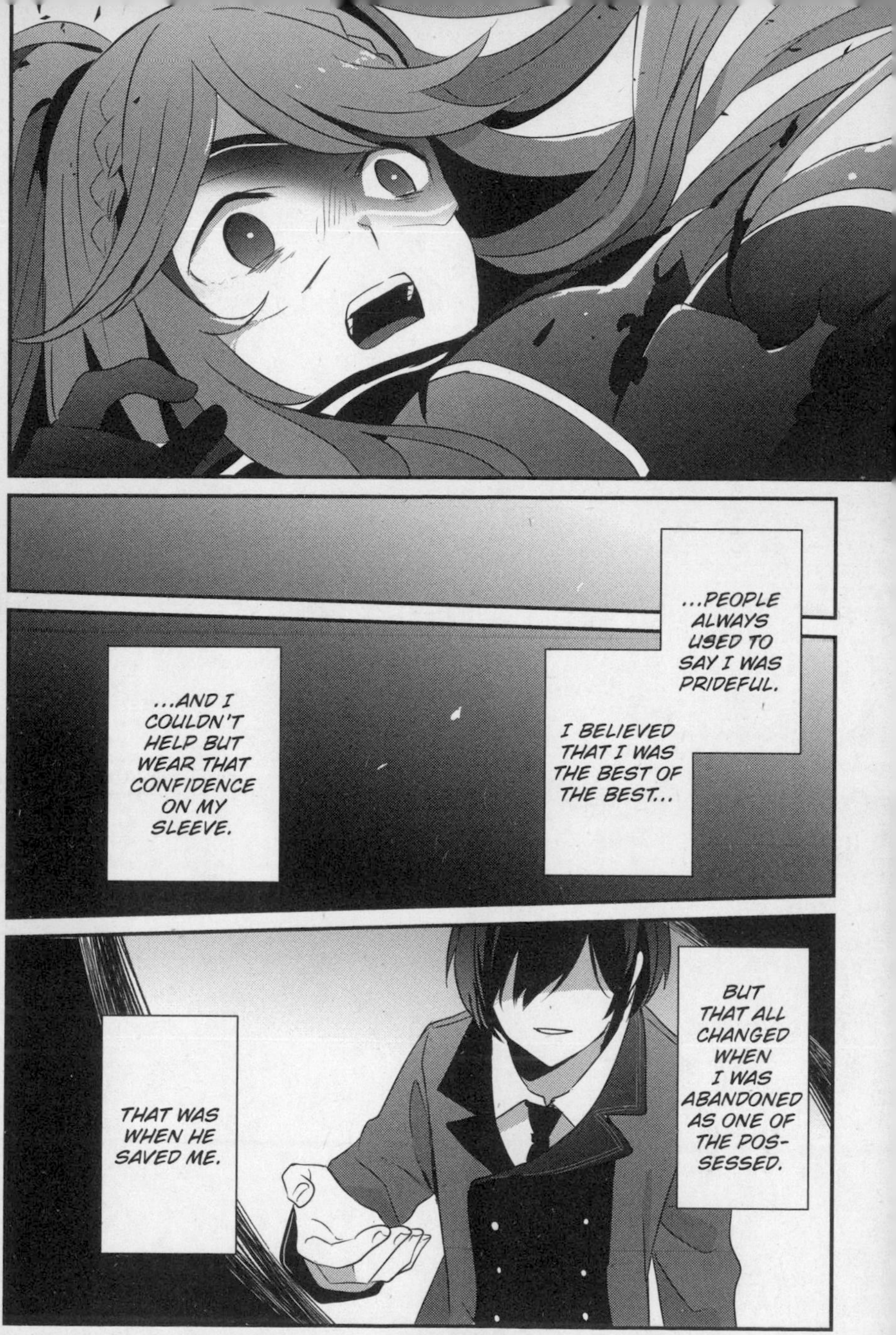
...PEOPLE ALWAYS USED TO SAY I WAS PRIDEFUL.
I BELIEVED THAT I WAS THE BEST OF THE BEST...
...AND I COULDN'T HELP BUT WEAR THAT CONFIDENCE ON MY SLEEVE.
BUT THAT ALL CHANGED WHEN I WAS ABANDONED AS ONE OF THE POS-SESSED.
THAT WAS WHEN HE SAVED ME.

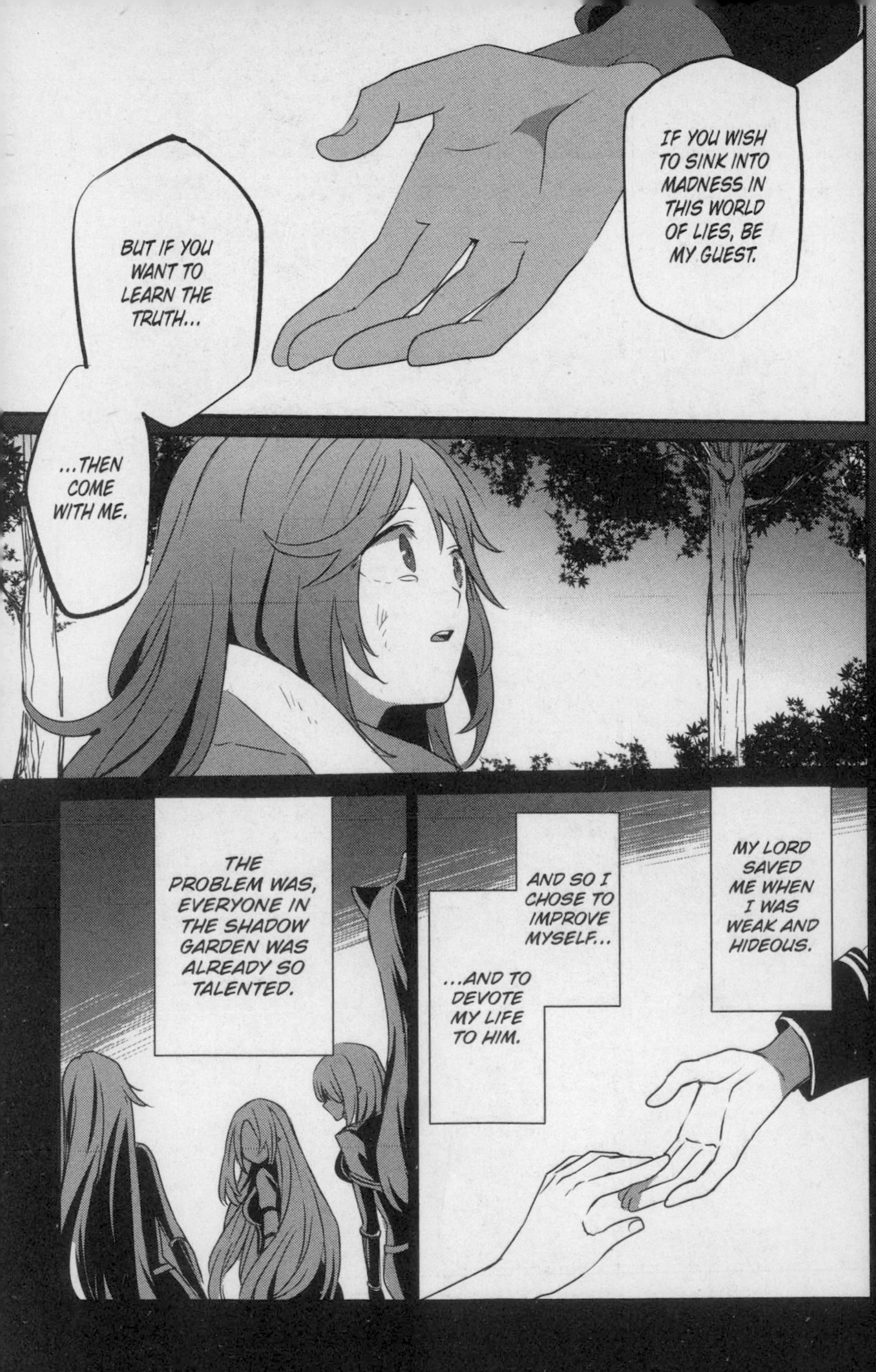
IF YOU WISH TO SINK INTO MADNESS IN THIS WORLD OF LIES, BE MY GUEST.
BUT IF YOU WANT TO LEARN THE TRUTH...
...THEN COME WITH ME.
MY LORD SAVED ME WHEN I WAS WEAK AND HIDEOUS.
AND SO I CHOSE TO IMPROVE MYSELF...
...AND TO DEVOTE MY LIFE TO HIM.
THE PROBLEM WAS, EVERYONE IN THE SHADOW GARDEN WAS ALREADY SO TALENTED.

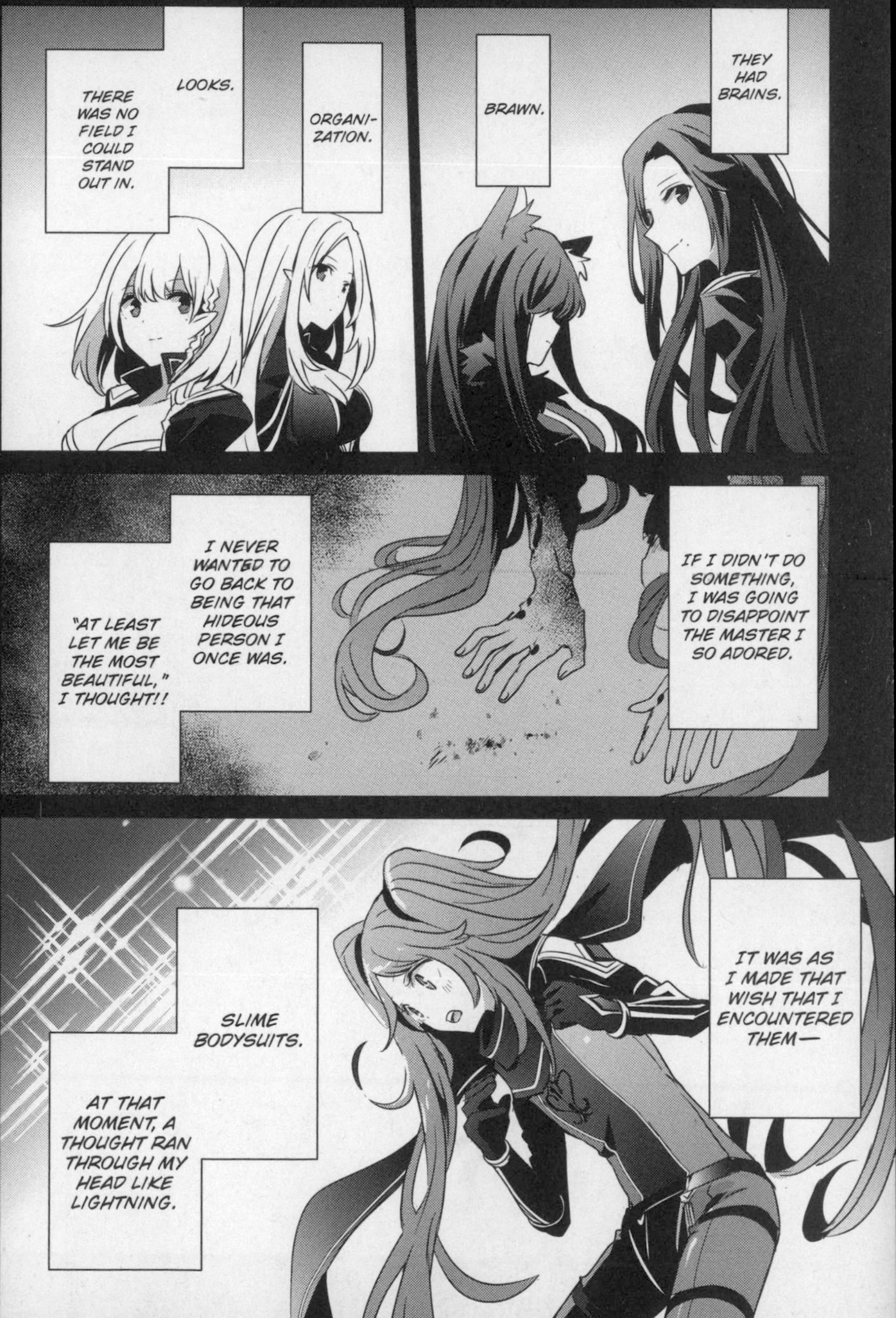
THEY HAD BRAINS.
BRAWN.
ORGANI-ZATION.
LOOKS.
THERE WAS NO FIELD I COULD STAND OUT IN.
IF I DIDN'T DO SOMETHING, I WAS GOING TO DISAPPOINT THE MASTER I SO ADORED.
I NEVER WANTED TO GO BACK TO BEING THAT HIDEOUS PERSON I ONCE WAS.
"AT LEAST LET ME BE THE MOST BEAUTIFUL," I THOUGHT!!
IT WAS AS I MADE THAT WISH THAT I ENCOUNTERED THEM—
SLIME BODYSUITS.
AT THAT MOMENT, A THOUGHT RAN THROUGH MY HEAD LIKE LIGHTNING.

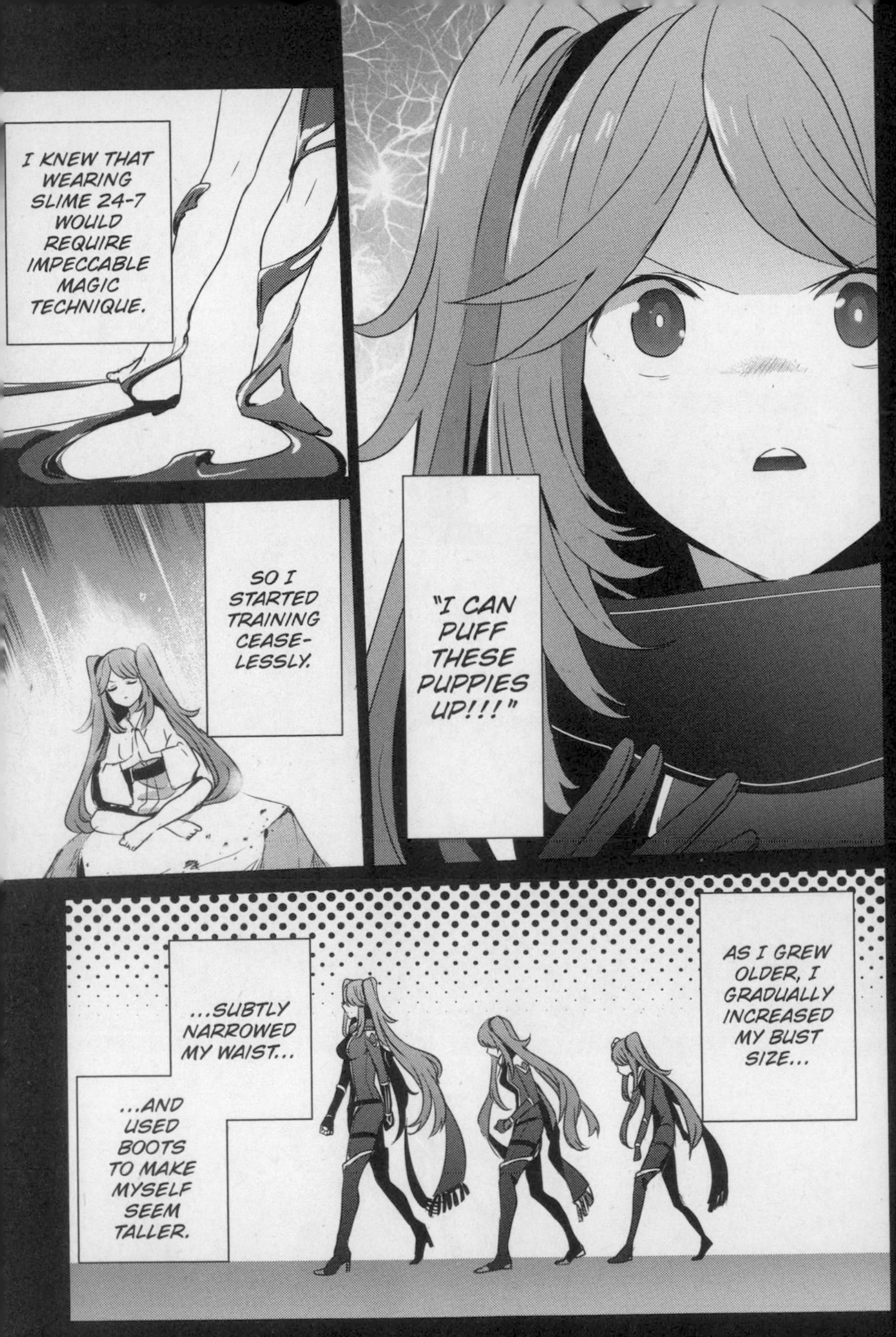
"I CAN PUFF THESE PUPPIES UP!!!"
I KNEW THAT WEARING SLIME 24-7 WOULD REQUIRE IMPECCABLE MAGIC TECHNIQUE.
SO I STARTED TRAINING CEASE-LESSLY.
AS I GREW OLDER, I GRADUALLY INCREASED MY BUST SIZE...
...SUBTLY NARROWED MY WAIST...
...AND USED BOOTS TO MAKE MYSELF SEEM TALLER.

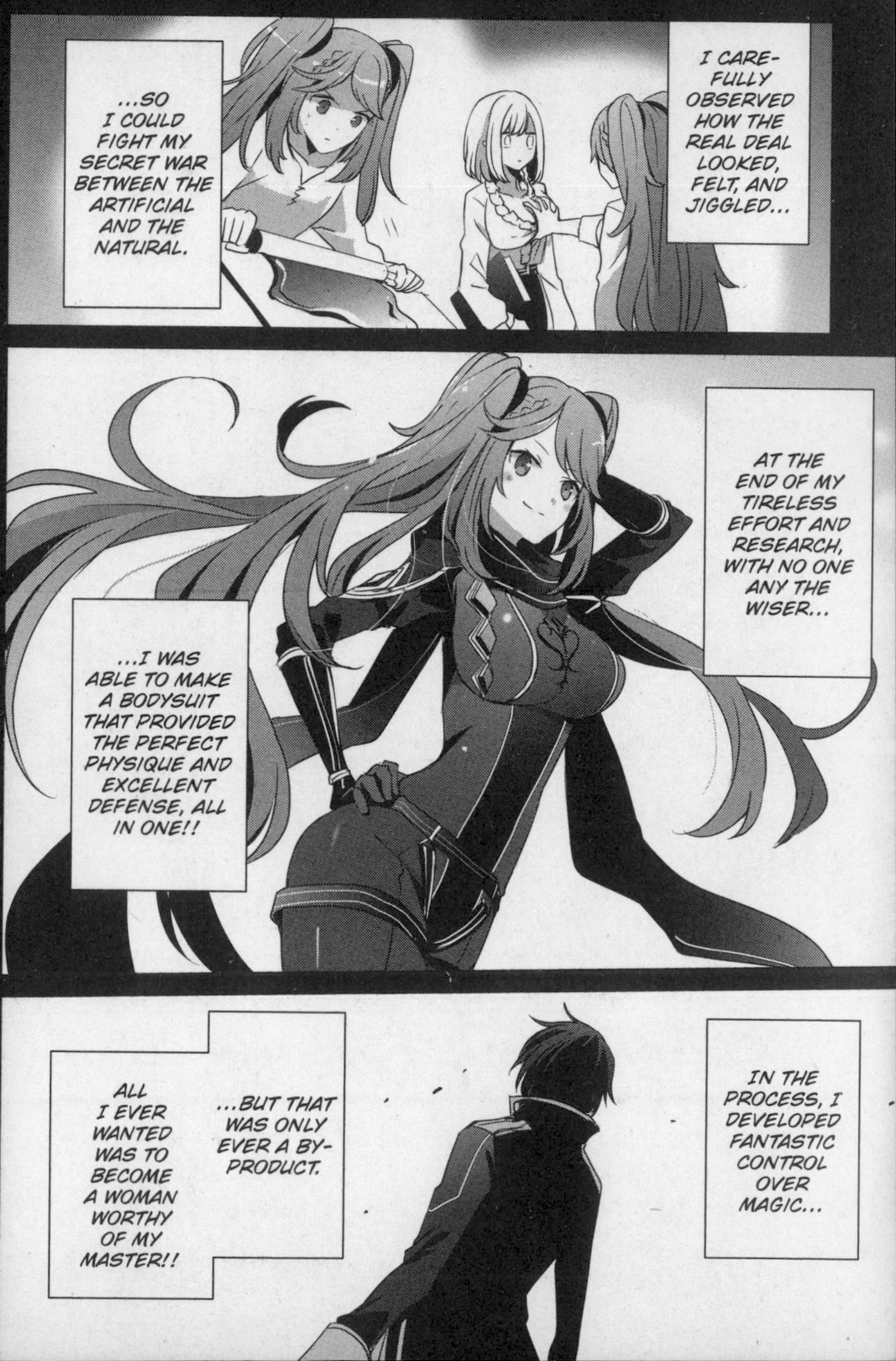
I CAREFULLY OBSERVED HOW THE REAL DEAL LOOKED, FELT, AND JIGGLED...
...SO I COULD FIGHT MY SECRET WAR BETWEEN THE ARTIFICIAL AND THE NATURAL.
AT THE END OF MY TIRELESS EFFORT AND RESEARCH, WITH NO ONE ANY THE WISER...
...I WAS ABLE TO MAKE A BODYSUIT THAT PROVIDED THE PERFECT PHYSIQUE AND EXCELLENT DEFENSE, ALL IN ONE!!
IN THE PROCESS, I DEVELOPED FANTASTIC CONTROL OVER MAGIC...
...BUT THAT WAS ONLY EVER A BY-PRODUCT.
ALL I EVER WANTED WAS TO BECOME A WOMAN WORTHY OF MY MASTER!!

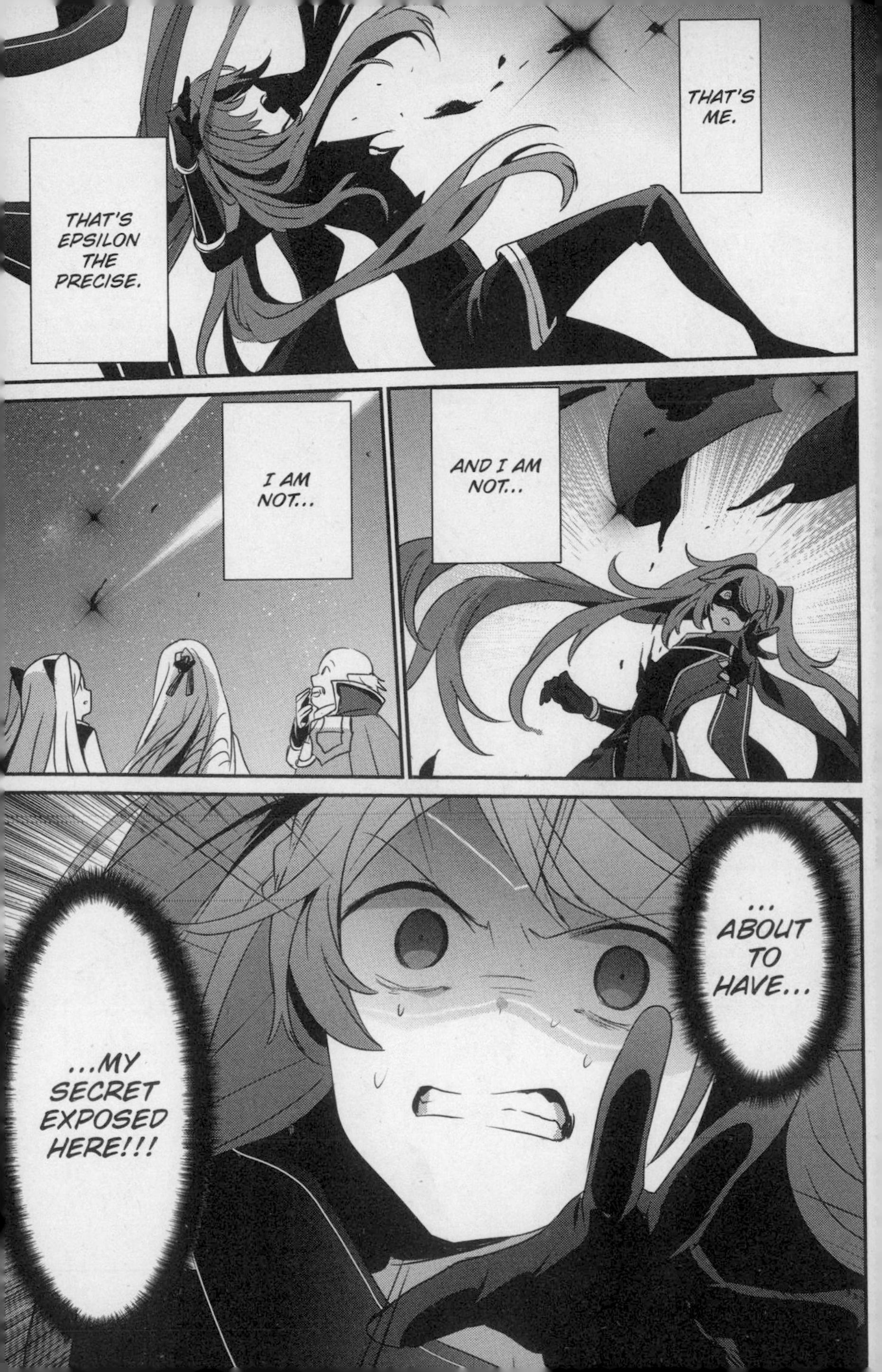
THAT'S ME.
THAT'S EPSILON THE PRECISE.
AND I AM NOT...
I AM NOT...
...ABOUT TO HAVE...
...MY SECRET EXPOSED HERE!!!

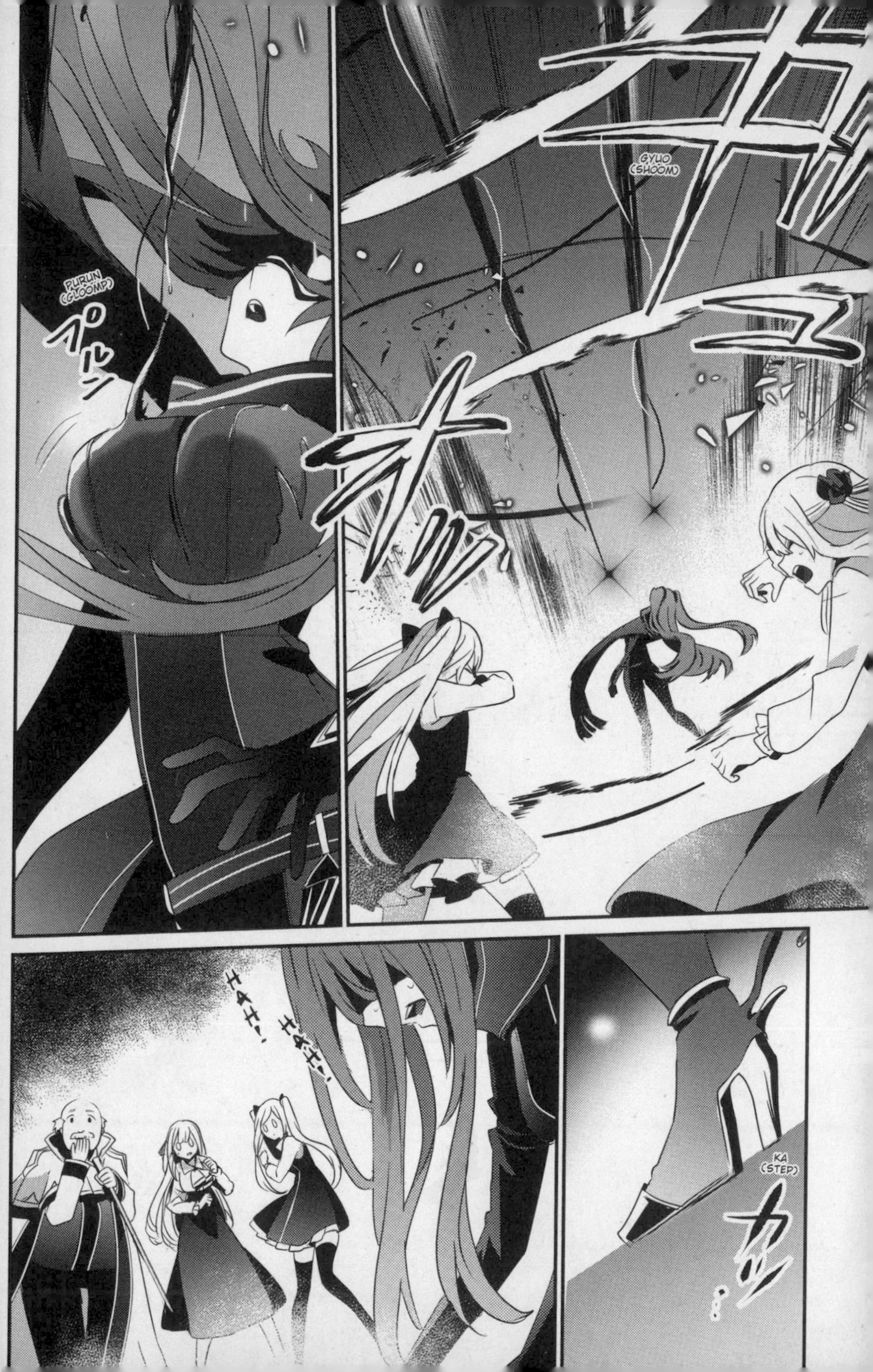
GYUO
(SHOOM)
PURUN
(GLOOMP)
KA
(STEP)
HAH!
HAH!

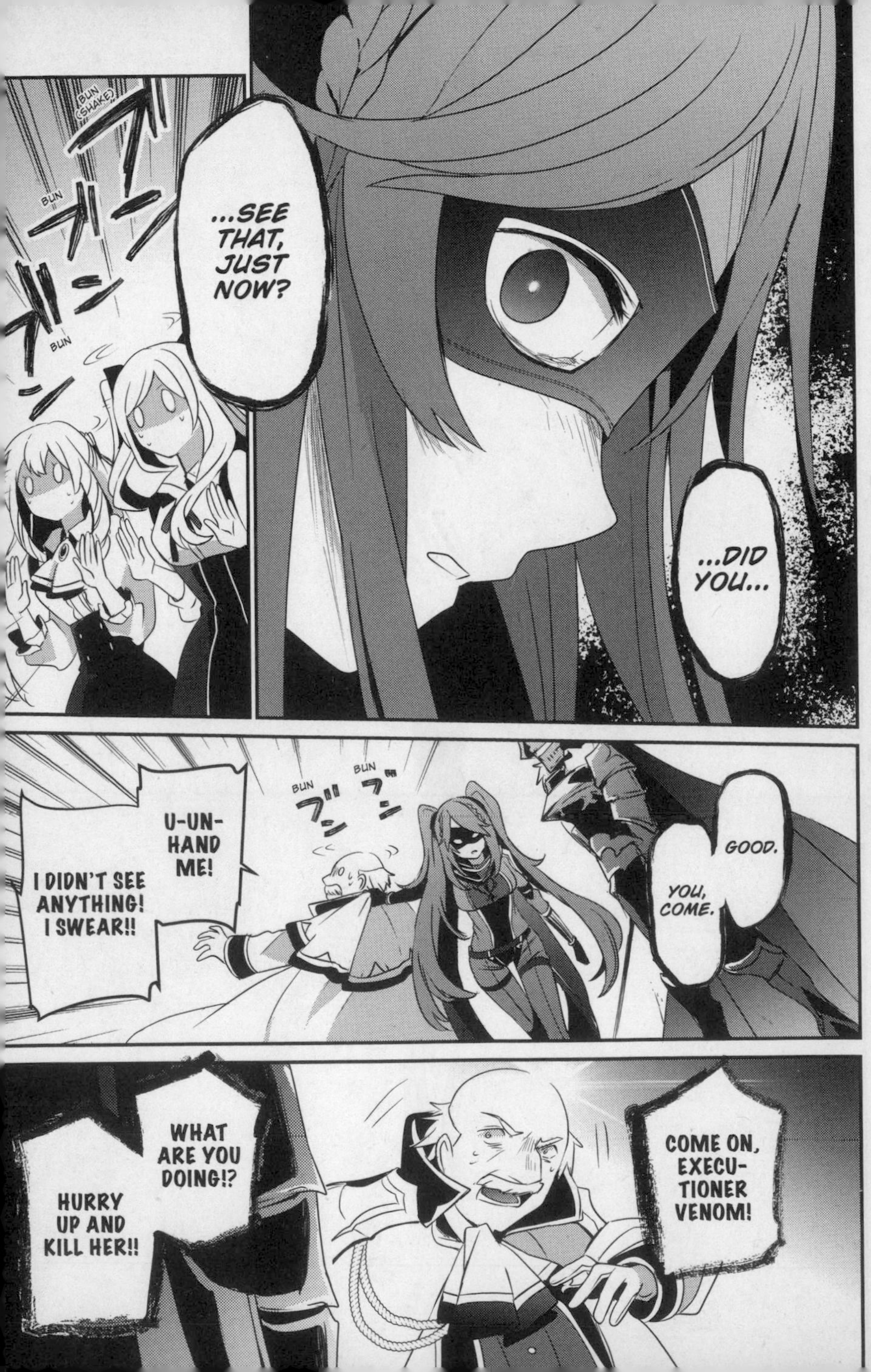
...DID YOU...
...SEE THAT, JUST NOW?
BUN (SHAKE)
BUN
BUN
GOOD.
YOU, COME.
BUN
BUN
U-UN-HAND ME!
I DIDN'T SEE ANYTHING! I SWEAR!!
COME ON, EXECU-TIONER VENOM!
WHAT ARE YOU DOING!?
HURRY UP AND KILL HER!!

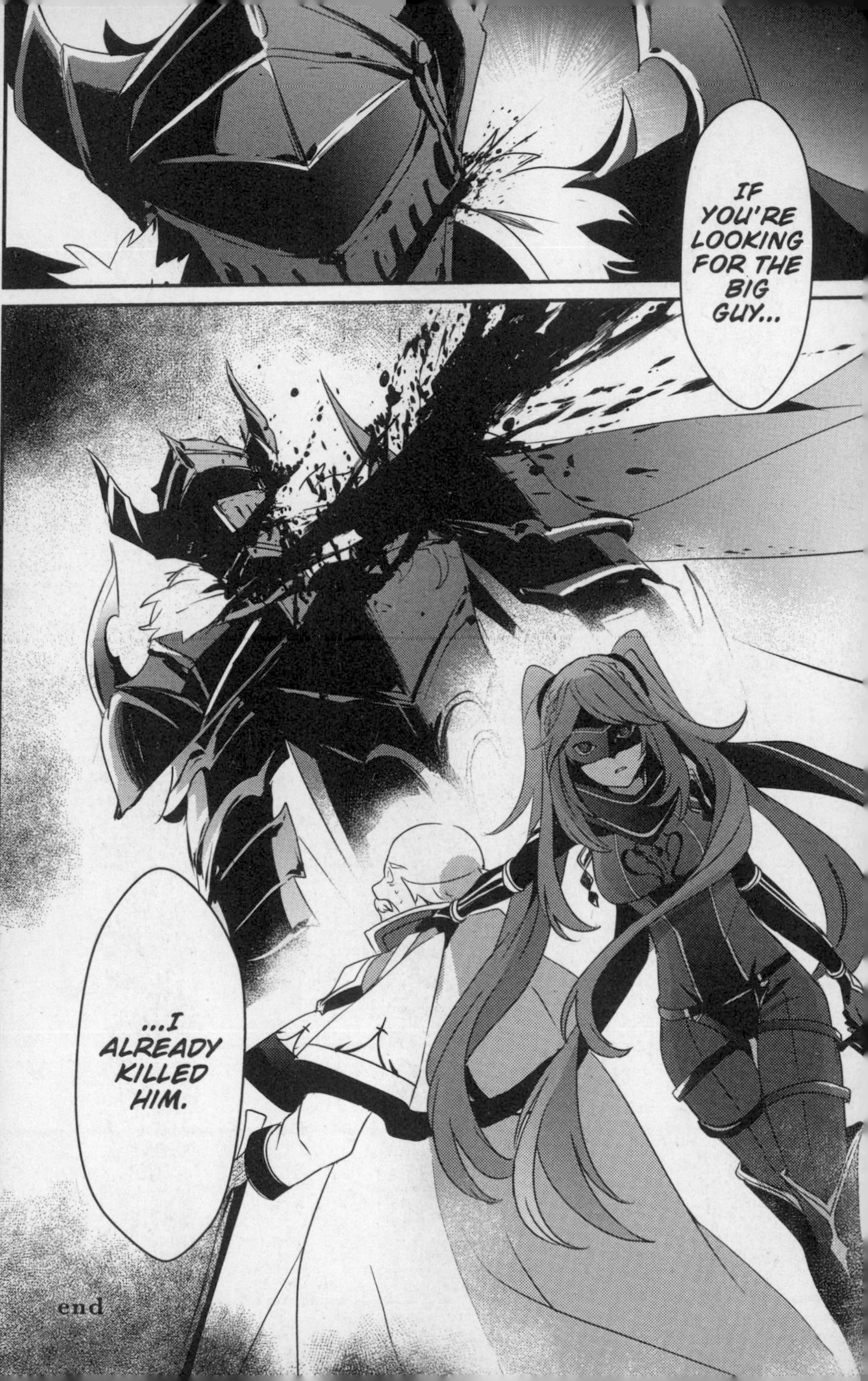
IF YOU'RE LOOKING FOR THE BIG GUY...
...I ALREADY KILLED HIM.
end

To be continued in *The Eminence in Shadow*, Vol. 5

Art
Anri Sakano
Original Story
Daisuke Aizawa
Character Design
Touzai

The Eminence in Shadow 4

LETTERING: Phil Christie

TRANSLATION: Nathaniel Hiroshi Thrasher

KAGE NO JITSURYOKUSHA
NI NARITAKUTE! Volume 4
©Anri Sakano 2020
©Daisuke Aizawa 2020
©Touzai 2020
First published in Japan in 2020 by
KADOKAWA CORPORATION, Tokyo.
English translation rights arranged
with KADOKAWA CORPORATION, Tokyo
through Tuttle-Mori Agency, Inc., Tokyo.

English translation © 2022 by
Yen Press, LLC

Yen Press
150 West 30th Street
19th Floor
New York, NY 10001

Visit us at yenpress.com
facebook.com/yenpress
twitter.com/yenpress
yenpress.tumblr.com
instagram.com/yenpress

First Yen Press Edition: June 2022
Edited by Yen Press Editorial:
Thomas McAlister
Designed by Yen Press Design:
Wendy Chan

Yen Press is an imprint of
Yen Press, LLC.
The Yen Press name and logo are
trademarks of Yen Press, LLC.

The publisher is not responsible for websites (or their content) that are not owned by the publisher.

Library of Congress Control Number:
2021935892

ISBNs: 978-1-9753-3876-3 (paperback)
       978-1-9753-3877-0 (ebook)

10 9 8 7 6 5 4 3 2 1

LSC-C

Printed in the United States of America